LEVEL FOUR

SCOPE ENGLISH ANTHOLOGY

Teaching Guide

SCHOLASTIC BOOK SERVICES®

New York Toronto London Sydney Auckland Tokyo

LITERATURE CONSULTANT

Theodore Hipple, Ph.D.
Professor, English Education
The University of Florida
Gainesville, Florida

CURRICULUM CONSULTANTS

Barbara Coulter
Director of Language Education
Detroit Public Schools
Detroit, Michigan

Nora Forester
Reading Coordinator
North Side School District
San Antonio, Texas

William Horst
Secondary Section Committee
National Council of Teachers of English

Barbara Krysiak, Ed.D.
Principal
North Hampton Elementary School
North Hampton, New Hampshire

Nancy McHugh
Teacher
Grant High School
Van Nuys, California

READING CONSULTANT

Virginia B. Modla, Ph.D.
Reading Curriculum Associate
School District of Cheltenham Township
Elkins Park, Pennsylvania

STAFF

Project Editor: Lewis Gardner
Level Four Editor: Lynda Steinberg
Editorial Production Director:
  Nancy DeWolfe

Design & Art Production:
  Kirchoff/Wohlberg, Inc.

Cover Design & Photograph:
  Jack George Tauss

ISBN 0-590-31434-3

12 11 10 9 8 7 6 5 4 3 2 1   8   4 5 6 7 8/8

LEVEL FOUR
Contents

Introduction

About the SCOPE ENGLISH Program

SCOPE ENGLISH is a basal language arts program designed primarily to meet the curriculum needs of students in grades 7–12 who are reading below grade level. At each of the six levels, which correspond to grades 7–12, there is a SCOPE ENGLISH Anthology and a SCOPE ENGLISH Grammar & Composition text. Both are supported by Teaching Guides and print-master Tests. In addition, there is a Workbook for each Grammar & Composition text to provide practice in the grammar and writing skills taught in the lessons.

The Anthology and Grammar & Composition materials may be used independently or jointly as a complete curriculum. If you choose to combine them, you might divide the week between the Grammar & Composition text and the Anthology. (See Lesson Plan, page 8.) In either case, you will find that the SCOPE ENGLISH Anthologies and Grammar & Composition texts do not duplicate topics but provide a complementary program at comparable levels of achievement.

SCOPE ENGLISH is a varied program. Its aims are (1) to help students develop and master essential skills in reading, writing, thinking, and speaking; (2) to interest students in literary works and in ways of analyzing and interpreting literature; (3) to help students develop an appreciation of fine literature; (4) to teach grammatical concepts and writing techniques that meet basic curriculum requirements and will prove valuable to students in their daily lives; and (5) to afford students a high level of success and satisfaction in language arts skills. Above all, SCOPE ENGLISH provides a basic English curriculum that students will find helpful and interesting.

Features of the SCOPE ENGLISH Anthology

1. **Stimulating, high-interest literature.** Students will enjoy reading stories, plays, poems, and nonfiction selections as they practice reading longer selections by important authors.
2. **Consistent instructional format.** The questions throughout each section focus on one literature skill. Each selection is followed by comprehension questions, discussion topics, a lesson in understanding literature, and a writing exercise. At the end of each section, a Section Review includes lessons in Vocabulary and Reading, a Quiz, and Composition topics.
3. **Cohesive sections.** Sections are organized appropriately for each grade level: Levels One, Two, and Three by author or theme; Level Four by genre and themes with examples of the genre; Level Five by themes and authors in a chronological study of American literature; and Level Six by themes in world literature.
4. **Extensive attention to writing and composition.** A writing activity follows each prose selection and composition topics are contained in each Section Review. Completing these exercises stimulates students' creativity and applies their knowledge of literary analysis.
5. **Vocabulary and reading lessons for each section.** These activities develop students' proficiency in English.

4

6. **Comprehension questions for each selection.** These questions aid students' reading comprehension and help insure their success.

7. **Frequent review.** There is a Quiz for each section—questions on Reading Comprehension and on Understanding Literature encourage students to back up their answers with information from the selection.

8. **Readable selections.** Vocabulary is appropriate for students reading below grade level.

9. **Glossary.** This section contains words students will find useful in their writing and in other subject areas.

10. **Easy-to-use handbook of literary terms.**

11. **Exciting, colorful art and appealing section-opening pages.**

Features of the Anthology Teaching Guide

1. **Easy-to-follow lesson plans for every selection.**

2. **Overview of each section.** The section outline lists titles and skills lessons with Anthology and Teaching Guide page numbers for quick reference. The Section Focus introduces selections, concepts, and skills covered in this section of the Anthology.

3. **Synopsis.** The Synopsis summarizes each selection.

4. **Complete lessons for teaching vocabulary.** Vocabulary words, teaching strategies, and a Quick Quiz are presented for each prose selection and some poetry selections.

5. **Consistent format for teaching each selection.** Synopsis summarizes the selection. Preparation provides background and context. Setting the Purpose involves students in the reading. Suggestions are given for directing the reading of each selection.

6. **Attention to reading comprehension and topics for discussion.** Questions from the Anthology are reprinted in the Teaching Guide, followed by the answers, complete with specific page references (when appropriate).

7. **Objectives.** Learning objectives are clearly stated for every Understanding Literature, Vocabulary, and Reading lesson.

8. **Complete lesson plans for teaching Understanding Literature, Vocabulary, and Reading.** The lesson plans include objectives, preparation activities, and questions from the Anthology with complete answers and specific page references (when appropriate).

9. **Attention to Writing and Composition.** For every topic there is an introductory lesson with suggestions for getting started. There are also complete lesson plans for end-of-section writing assignments in Levels Five and Six.

10. **Section Review Quiz.** Questions from the Anthology are reprinted. They are followed by the answers, complete with specific page references (when appropriate).

11. **Enrichment activities for every section.** The Teaching Guide suggests ways to develop and sustain students' interest in the literature, authors, or theme of each section.

12. **Authors.** Information about authors' lives and their other work is provided.

Features of the Print-Master Tests

Thirty-six complete two-page tests. There is a test for every major selection. Each test includes twenty questions covering reading and understanding, literary skills, vocabulary, and overall comprehension.

Teaching Overview

Teaching Vocabulary. The Vocabulary portion of each Teaching Guide presents words unfamiliar to students at this level of reading ability. The words are presented in order of their appearance in each selection, within groups of (1) unfamiliar words, (2) proper nouns, and (3) phrases and foreign-language words. Lessons for selections of two or more parts contain individual vocabulary lists corresponding to each part. The lists are followed by suggested activities and topics for discussion that focus on specific vocabulary words.

The teaching strategy for vocabulary may vary. You may wish to follow any or all of these guidelines:

1. Read aloud each word and its definition.

2. Have volunteers use each word in context.

OR

1. Write each word, its part of speech, and its definition on the board.

2. Read each word and its definition.

3. Have volunteers use each word in context.

4. Have students look up words in the Glossary at the back of the Anthology.

5. Have students examine word structure. Ask them to provide other forms of a vocabulary word. For example, have them expand the word *imitate* to *imitation* and use both words in context. Have students find words with prefixes and suffixes and determine the base word. Ask students to syllabicate vocabulary words then check with the dictionary for accuracy.

6. Have students examine word meanings. Discuss words with multiple meanings such as *lap:* "Sit in my *lap.*/Swim six *laps* around the pool." Discuss words that function as different parts of speech such as *reporting:* "I was *reporting* the news./ *Reporting* is an exciting career." Finally, have students check the dictionary to find synonyms, antonyms, and homonyms for the vocabulary words.

Note: The Glossary at the back of the Anthology contains words that students can incorporate into their vocabularies and their writing. Point out that the words in the vocabulary lists and in the Glossary are not found only in the reading selections but are functional and applicable to other subject areas. (Dictionary entries were derived from *The American Heritage School Dictionary.*)

7. Provide extension activities using the vocabulary words. Try games such as Hangman or a class spelling or vocabulary bee. Ask students to create their own puzzles such as word searches, acrostics, or crossword puzzles. Students may wish to try their puzzles on their classmates.

At the end of each vocabulary section, a Quick Quiz is provided to measure students' facility with vocabulary words. This test may be administered immediately after teaching the words or at the end of a section, using a few or all of the Quick Quiz items.

Teaching Reading Comprehension and For Discussion. The Reading Comprehension and For Discussion portion of the lesson contains questions to check students' overall understanding of each selection and may cover the following skill areas: recalling facts, sequencing facts, making inferences, and drawing conclusions. Discussion questions lead students to interpret the content of each selection. While students' answers and/or interpretations will vary, the Teaching Guide does provide alternative answers upon which to focus general discussion. Individual poetry selections do not have Reading Comprehension and For Discussion questions, but major groupings of poems do have the questions after the final poem.

There are four suggested strategies for teaching Reading Comprehension and For Discussion:

1. Have volunteers read the questions aloud and provide answers for each one. Encourage class discussion, particularly with the interpretive discussion questions. Ask students to support their answers with facts from the selection.

2. Have students write their answers on a separate sheet of paper. Review students' responses aloud by asking for volunteers to read their answers. Ask students to support their answers with facts from the selection.

3. Have students write their answers on a separate sheet of paper. Collect the students' work, or have classmates trade papers for correction.

4. Assign the questions as homework, and collect the students' work or review the answers aloud.

Administering the Quiz. In the Quiz at the end of each section, five Reading Comprehension questions and five Understanding Literature questions are provided to test the following: students' understanding of the selections, their understanding of the reading skill covered in the section, and their understanding of the literature skill covered in the section.

The Quiz is designed as an *open-book* test, providing an opportunity for students to locate answers in the selections. Since this skill is often required on standardized tests, students gain proficiency in quickly tracking important information.

Students also are often asked to support their answers with references to the reading material. Their responses may take the form of a discussion of an incident or a direct quotation from the text. All answers should be complete sentences.

The Quiz may be administered orally or as a written examination. It may be administered before or after the composition activity.

Lesson Plan

	Anthology	Grammar & Composition
Week 1	Section 1 Introduction "The Green Door" Print-Master Test 1 "Blue Eyes Far Away" Print-Master Test 2	Print-Master Test 1 (Grammar Pre-Test) Print-Master Test 2 (Composition Pre-Test)
Week 2	"Gentleman of Río en Medio" Print-Master Test 3 "Marigolds" Print-Master Test 4	Unit One: Lessons One and Two Workbook Practices One and Two
Week 3	"The Enemy" Print-Master Test 5 Section Review	Unit One: Lessons Three–Five Workbook Practices Three–Five
Week 4	Section 2 Introduction "The Sneeze" Print-Master Test 6	Unit One: Lessons Six–Nine Workbook Practices Six–Nine Print-Master Test 3
Week 5	"I Remember Mama" Print-Master Test 7 "Sudden Death" Print-Master Test 8	Unit Two Workbook Practice Ten Print-Master Test 4
Week 6	Section Review	Unit Three: Lessons One–Four Workbook Practices Eleven–Fifteen
Week 7	Section 3 Introduction "Leiningen Versus the Ants" Print-Master Test 9	Unit Three: Lessons Five–Seven Workbook Practices Sixteen–Twenty Print-Master Test 5
Week 8	"Flight Into Danger" Print-Master Test 10 "Mind Over Water" Print-Master Test 11	Unit Four: Lessons One and Two
Week 9	"In the Shadow of a Rainbow" Print-Master Test 12 Section Review	Unit Four: Lessons Three and Four Workbook Practice Twenty-one Print-Master Test 6
Week 10	Section 4 Introduction "The Haunted Chess Set" "The Adventure of The Copper Beeches" Print-Master Test 14	Unit Five: Lessons One and Two Workbook Practices Twenty-two and Twenty-three

Lesson Plan   (continued)

	Anthology	Grammar & Composition
Week 11	"The Third Level" Print-Master Test 15 Section Review	Unit Five: Lessons Three and Four Workbook Practices Twenty-four– Twenty-nine Print-Master Test 7
Week 12	Section 5 Introduction Narrative Poems	Unit Six Workbook Practice Thirty Print-Master Test 8
Week 13	Lyric Poems	Unit Seven: Lessons One and Two Workbook Practices Thirty-one and Thirty-two
Week 14	Message Poems	Unit Seven: Lessons Three–Five Workbook Practices Thirty-three– Thirty-six Print-Master Test 9
Week 15	Found Poems and Concrete Poems Section Review	Unit Eight Workbook Practice Thirty-seven Print-Master Test 10
Week 16	Section 6 Introduction "Very Special Shoes" Print-Master Test 16 "Letter to a Black Boy" Print-Master Test 17	Unit Nine: Lesson One Workbook Practice Thirty-eight
Week 17	"Celebration" "The Troublemaker" Print-Master Test 18 "Since You Left"	Unit Nine: Lessons Two and Three Workbook Practices Thirty-nine– Forty-three Print-Master Test 11
Week 18	"Road" "Long Walk to Forever" Print-Master Test 19 "If You Hear That a Thousand People Love You"	Unit Ten Workbook Practice Forty-four Print-Master Test 12
Week 19	Section Review Section 7 Introduction	Unit Eleven: Lessons One–Three Workbook Practices Forty-five– Forty-seven

Lesson Plan (continued)

	Anthology	Grammar & Composition
Week 20	"The Story of Little Sure-Shot" Print-Master Test 20 "The Electrical Wizard" Print-Master Test 21	Unit Eleven: Lessons Four and Five Workbook Practices Forty-Eight– Fifty Print-Master Test 13
Week 21	"Clemente—A Bittersweet Story" Print-Master Test 22 "400 Mulvaney Street" Print-Master Test 23	Unit Twelve Workbook Practice Fifty-one Print-Master Test 14
Week 22	"Knoxville, Tennessee" Section Review	Unit Thirteen Workbook Practices Fifty-two– Fifty-five Print-Master Test 15
Week 23	Section 8 Introduction "Central Park" "Steelworker: Mike Lefevre" Print-Master Test 24	Unit Fourteen: Lessons One and Two
Week 24	"The Acorn People" Print-Master Test 25 "Dolphins" Print-Master Test 26	Unit Fourteen: Lessons Three and Four Workbook Practice Fifty-six Print-Master Test 16
Week 25	"Emotion Twists Issues—Stick to the Facts" Print-Master Test 27 "Guns: A Serious Problem" Print-Master Test 28	Unit Fifteen Workbook Practices Fifty-seven– Sixty-two Print-Master Test 17
Week 26	Section Review	Unit Sixteen: Lessons One and Two
Week 27	Section 9 Introduction "Fresh Air Will Kill You" "And They Lived Happily Ever After for a While"	Unit Sixteen: Lesson Three Workbook Practice Sixty-three Print-Master Test 18
Week 28	"The Cow Who Liked to Kick" Print-Master Test 29 "Who's on First?"	Unit Seventeen: Lessons One–Four Workbook Practices Sixty-four– Sixty-seven

Lesson Plan (continued)

	Anthology	Grammer & Composition
Week 29	"How Beautiful With Mud" Print-Master Test 30 Section Review	Unit Seventeen: Lessons Five and Six Workbook Practices Sixty-eight and Sixty-nine
Week 30	Section 10 Introduction "By Any Other Name" Print-Master Test 31	Unit Seventeen: Lessons Seven and Eight Workbook Practices Seventy– Seventy-three Print-Master Test 19
Week 31	"The Rocking Horse" Print-Master Test 32 "A Trip for Mrs. Taylor" Print-Master Test 33	Unit Eighteen Workbook Practice Seventy-four Print Master Test 20
Week 32	"Dirge Without Music" Section Review	Unit Nineteen: Lessons One and Two Workbook Practice Seventy-five
Week 33	Section 11 Introduction Biography: John Steinbeck *The Pearl*—Chapters 1 and 2 Print-Master Test 34	Unit Nineteen: Lessons Three–Seven Workbook Practices Seventy-six and Seventy-seven
Week 34	*The Pearl*—Chapters 3 and 4 Print-Master Test 35	Unit Nineteen: Lessons Eight–Ten Workbook Practices Seventy-eight– Eighty Print-Master Test 21
Week 35	*The Pearl*—Chapters 5 and 6 Print-Master Test 36	Unit Twenty Workbook Practice Eighty-one Print-Master Test 22
Week 36	Section Review	Print-Master Test 23 (Grammar Post-Test) Print-Master Test 24 (Composition Post-Test)

Scope and Sequence of Skills in Level Four

	Literature Skill	Vocabulary Skill	Reading Skill	Composition and Writing
Section 1	Plot Purpose of events Plot and time order Setting Details Characterization Character motivation	Synonyms and Antonyms	Main Idea and Details	Summary of a plot Persuasive paragraph/argument Description Letter Continuation of a story or play Short story Diary/journal entry
Section 2	Setting Stage directions Characterization Through action Through dialogue	Synonyms and Antonyms in Context	Sequence	Continuation of a story or play Description Dialogue Letter News report Monologue
Section 3	Conflict Conflict and resolution Types of conflict Inner conflict Conflict, climax, and resolution	Experience Clues	Cause and Effect	Resolution News report Monologue Description From a different point of view Explanation

Scope and Sequence of Skills in Level Four (continued)

	Literature Skill	Vocabulary Skill	Reading Skill	Composition and Writing
Section 4	**Plot** Suspense and plot **Setting** Mood and setting **Tone and mood** Mood in a mystery	Multiple Meanings	Drawing Conclusions	Explanation About setting and mood Dialogue Continuation of a story or play Letter Character's point of view
Section 5	**Imagery** Symbols in a poem Images, similes, and metaphors **Tone and Mood** Symbols and mood in a poem	Denotation and Connotation	Figurative Language	Poem Similes and metaphors
Section 6	**Theme** Theme and symbols Theme and main idea Theme and characterization Theme and plot	Denotation and Connotation	Making Inferences	Summary of a plot Letter Continuation of a story or play Explanation Short story
Section 7	**Point of View** First person and third person Point of view and character Motivation Changing points of view First person	Word Parts	Recognizing Significant Details	From a different point of view First-person narrative Biography

13

Scope and Sequence of Skills in Level Four (continued)

	Literature Skill	Vocabulary Skill	Reading Skill	Composition and Writing
Section 8	**Tone and Mood** Understanding tone Changes in tone Serious, formal tone Argumentative tone Emotional vs. factual tone	Technical Terms	Separating Facts and Opinions	Description Person's point of view About a change in attitude Nonfiction Diary/journal entry Persuasive paragraph/argument Evaluation
Section 9	**Tone and Mood** Exaggeration Puns **Irony** Satire and irony Ironic situations	Idioms	Author's Purpose	Explanation About exaggeration Puns Advertisement Short story Limerick Description
Section 10	**Characterization** Character motivation	Shades of Meaning	Critical Reading	Letter Continuation of a story or play Diary/journal entry Description Evaluation Comparing/contrasting
Section 11	**Plot** Plot and subplots in a novel **Characterization** Techniques of characterization **Theme** Theme in a novel	Using Context Clues	Cloze Exercise	Description Prediction Character's point of view Continuation of a story or play Dialogue Short story

Section 1
Short Stories

Section Focus

The Introduction to Section 1 explains the essential elements of the short story—setting, plot, characters, and point of view. There are five short stories in this section.

Have students read and discuss each part of the Introduction on pp. 16–17 before they read the first story. This will familiarize them with the genre of the short story and its essential elements. You may want to use the following procedure.

Have students read the first two paragraphs, which briefly present the history of the short story. Discuss what might have happened to stories passed orally from one generation or village to the next.

Discuss the paragraph on *setting*, which mentions the setting for each of the stories in the section and explains that the setting influences the way the characters look, act, and feel.

Have students read and discuss the paragraphs about *plot*, which explain chronological order and the use of *flashbacks*. These paragraphs also introduce the terms *suspense* and *plot twist*.

Ask students to read the paragraph about *characters* and point out that a good writer portrays characters in a believable manner. This paragraph introduces the term *motivation*.

After students read the section on *points of view*, review the terms *narrator*, *first-person point of view*, *third-person point of view*, and *bias*. When the students have finished reading and discussing the Introduction, go on to the first short story.

The Green Door by O. Henry *(p. 18)*

Synopsis

Rudolf Steiner, a true adventurer, sells pianos by day and goes looking for the unexpected in the evenings. One evening he walks by a man handing out cards in front of a dentist's office. The man hands him a card which says only "The Green Door." Similar cards on the ground contain an ad for the dentist. But when Rudolf gets a second card, it also says "The Green Door." Never one to pass up a chance for adventure, he goes into the building, walks up the stairs, and comes to a green door. A frail young woman answers the door, then faints. Revived and appearing to Rudolf to be the reward for all his adventures, she tells him she has not eaten in three days. Rudolf goes out for groceries and returns to hear about her life of poverty and loneliness. He says he will be back the next day to see how she is. When she asks how he came to knock on her door, he does not tell her the truth. Instead, he says that one of the piano tuners lives in the building and he went to her door by mistake. When Rudolf leaves the building, he notices that all the doors are green. He then asks the man downstairs why he had given him the cards. The man replies that Rudolf is probably too late for the first act, and points to a theater with a sign for the play *The Green Door*. He explains that the theater manager had asked him to hand out cards for the play along with the ads for the dentist.

Preparation

Ask students if any of them have ever had a "lucky accident." Discuss very briefly any personal accounts of unexpected good fortune or lucky coincidences.

Ask students what they think it means to be an "adventurer." Have them think about what they might do to find adventure. Tell them that "The Green Door" involves a man who looks for adventure whenever he can.

Vocabulary

adventurer (*n.*) — a person who seeks adventure, risk, or danger
ignore (*v.*) — pay no attention to
paused (*v.*) — stopped briefly

Activities

A. See p. 6, Teaching Vocabulary.
B. Ask students what kinds of adventure they like. Discuss the qualities that adventure has—risk, danger, or the unknown.
C. The meaning of the words *ignore* and *paused* can each be acted out if you wish. Let students volunteer to play the roles.

Quick Quiz

1. adventurer: *a. someone who seeks adventure*   b. the winner of a prize
   c. a person looking for contentment or happiness
2. ignore: a. stupid move   b. study very hard   *c. pay no mind to*
3. paused: a. hated   *b. stopped briefly*   c. gave a reason

Setting the Purpose

Ask students what they think a story entitled "The Green Door" might be about. Have them read the story to find out what sort of adventure lies behind the green door.

The Selection

This story is very short, and it can be read in one sitting by most students.

Have one student read the brief headnote on p. 18 in the Anthology. Then have the class read the first page of the story silently. Before letting them turn the page, ask students to guess what they think Rudolf will find behind the door.

When students finish the story, have them discuss whether the ending surprised them. Then have them complete Reading Comprehension on pp. 20–21 in the Anthology.

Follow-Up

See p. 7, Teaching Reading Comprehension and For Discussion.

Reading Comprehension

1. Rudolf Steiner thought that interesting adventures   *c. could happen anywhere.* (Page 18, col. 1: "The most interesting thing in life, he thought, might lie just around the next corner.")
2. Rudolf went back to get a second card because he   *c. wanted to find out if the first card had been a mistake.*
3. For Rudolf, the cards were   *b. an invitation to adventure.* (Page 18, col. 2: "Rudolf could not ignore this chance for adventure.")
4. Rudolf found out that the cards were really   *a. ads for a new play* (page 20, col. 2).
5. Rudolf knocked at the young woman's door because   *a. it was the first green door he saw.* (Although he told the girl he was looking for a piano tuner, the card and his adventurous spirit led him to knock on the first green door he saw.)
6. Finding the young woman behind the green door was   *a. due to chance.* (It was simply an accident.)

For Discussion

1. Why did Rudolf decide that the girl should never know why he had actually knocked at her door? Do you think he should have told her the truth? *Accept answers the students can support.*
2. Rudolf went out every night in search of adventure. Do you think he was foolish or brave to do this? Would you have looked for the green door? Why or why not? *Answers will vary.*

Understanding Literature: Plot

Objective: Students will match events in the plot of a story with the purpose or purposes the author had for presenting them.

Preparation

Explain that the *plot* consists of the events that happen in the story in the order in which the author presents them. It is the sequence of events. In a good story, each event has a reason for being included. Discuss the different purposes for which an author might include an event in the plot of a story. Among the purposes are: (a) to provide background information; (b) to show what a character is like; (c) to develop or complicate a problem; (d) to lead up to other events.

Have students read and discuss the lesson on Plot on p. 21 in the Anthology. This lesson lists the purposes of plot events as stated above. Then have students complete the exercise, which asks them to identify the purpose(s) for each of five events from "The Green Door."

Questions and Answers

1. Rudolf went for a walk.   *a. to provide background information*
2. Rudolf thought a card given to him was a chance for adventure.   *b. to show what a character is like*
3. Rudolf found a pale young woman behind the green door.   *c. to develop or complicate a problem*
4. Rudolf discovered that all the doors on the floor were green.   *c. to develop or complicate a problem*
5. The man told Rudolf that the cards were really advertisements.   *b. to show what a character is like* (Rudolf took the words on the card as if they were more than an advertisement.) or   *d. to lead up to other events*

Writing

Think of someone or something else Rudolf might have found behind the green door. Write a paragraph describing the plot of a completely different adventure for Rudolf.

Before having students complete the writing assignment on p. 21 in the Anthology, discuss possible responses. Encourage the students to be imaginative and to create a plot by listing new events in sequence.

Blue Eyes Far Away   by Mackinlay Kantor   *(p. 22)*

Synopsis

Esther Lee's neighbors climb the steep road to her mountain home to tell Esther that her husband has been badly hurt in an automobile accident. They tell her that the police have the other driver, and a conviction will be sought. Esther knows then that her husband is dead. The other driver has a record of previous accidents and a reputation for carelessness, but he can easily afford a good defense lawyer and he does not worry about the case. Mrs. Lee's case is handled by the state prosecutor. She visits him the night before the trial. As the state's last witness, she appears to pose no threat to the defense. But when the prosecutor asks if she saw the accident, to everyone's surprise she says she did. She describes it in detail even though she was at home, three miles from the scene. The defense objects and the judge warns Esther about lying under oath. She explains that every night, she watched for her husband to come home, just as she did when he was a fisherman. Then she shows the court the telescope she used to watch for him.

Preparation

Ask students to imagine how people feel when someone close to them is injured in an accident caused by another person's recklessness. Ask how they think the person who caused the accident should be treated.

Explain that the next story deals with an accident and the efforts to obtain justice.

Vocabulary

convict (*v.*) — find to be guilty
reputation (*n.*) — what others think about a person
manslaughter (*n.*) — crime of killing a person
prosecutor (*n.*) — person who argues against the defendant in a court case

Activities

A. See p. 6, Teaching Vocabulary.
B. Ask students what the words have in common. (*They deal with crime or a criminal court case.*) Ask if they can think of any other special words that might be used in a story about a trial.

Quick Quiz

1. convict: a. persuade to be true   *b. find to be guilty*   c. arrest on the spot
2. reputation: *a. what others think about someone*   b. establishing the truth   c. disregard for someone's feelings
3. manslaughter: a. leaving someone near death   b. a terrible accident   *c. the crime of killing a person*

4. prosecutor: a. friend of the defendant's *b. one who argues against the defendant in court* c. person with criminal connections

Setting the Purpose

Tell students that they are about to read the story of an accident and the following court case. The court case is routine—until the last witness appears.

The Selection

This is a very short story that can be read in one sitting. Have a student volunteer to read the headnote on p. 22 in the Anthology. Then have the class read the first page of the story. Before going on, ask students if they think the young driver's lawyers are right about his case.

Have students complete the story. Ask them if the ending was a surprise. Have them look back and find clues to the ending that they might have missed during the first reading. Then have them complete Reading Comprehension on p. 25 in the Anthology.

Follow-Up

See p. 7, Teaching Reading Comprehension and For Discussion.

Reading Comprehension

1. Esther's neighbors thought it would be hard to *c. tell the woman about the accident.* (Page 22, col. 1: "They found their job easier than they had expected.")
2. Archie wasn't worried at the trial because *b. he thought there were no witnesses to the accident.* (Page 23, col. 1: "He watched, comfortably. . . .")
3. Archie grinned while Esther was telling her story because *a. he thought no one would believe Esther.* (Page 24, col. 1: "They couldn't pull anything like that and get away with it.")
4. The black bag helped people believe Esther by *c. explaining how she saw the accident.* (Page 24, col. 2: Esther kept her telescope in the bag.)

For Discussion

1. What kind of person was Esther Lee? Why did she wait until just before the trial to speak to the prosecutor? *Esther Lee was a devoted wife. She also seemed to be a very unassuming and private person.*
2. What kind of person was Archie Stolt? What did his actions in the courtroom reveal about him? *He was careless, irresponsible, and overconfident.*

Understanding Literature: Plot and Time Order

Objective: Students will list plot events in the order in which they were told in the story and in the order in which they actually occurred.

Preparation

Discuss *plot* and *time order.* Tell students that the order of events in a story might not be the order in which they actually happened. There is usually a good reason for an author to do this.

Have students read and discuss the Plot and Time Order lesson on p. 25 in the Anthology. Then have them complete the exercise, numbering the events in the order in which the author told readers about them (on the left) and in the order in which they actually occurred (on the right).

Questions and Answers

(1)	a.	Esther's neighbors climbed the hill to tell her about the crash.	(5)
(7)	b.	Esther Lee saw the car crash.	(4)
(2)	c.	Joseph Lee was in an accident.	(3)
(6)	d.	Mrs. Lee watched for her husband.	(2)
(5)	e.	Mrs. Lee appeared in court.	(7)
(4)	f.	Mrs. Lee called on the prosecutor.	(6)
(3)	g.	Archie Stolt was involved in several car accidents.	(1)

Writing

Before a court case goes to the jury, a lawyer sums up what he or she thinks to be the best possible case for the client. Write a paragraph telling what you think Archie's lawyer would have said before Esther Lee told her story. Then write another paragraph telling what Archie's lawyer might have said after Esther told her story.

Before having students complete the writing assignment on p. 25, discuss possible responses. Some students will find it easier to write the paragraphs if they list the points they intend to make before writing them in complete sentences.

Gentleman of Río en Medio

by Juan A. A. Sedillo   *(p. 26)*

Synopsis

Don Anselmo's people have lived in Río en Medio for hundreds of years. Now, Don Anselmo is selling some land, but the negotiations go very slowly. In a meeting carried out with great formality, he agrees to sell the land for the price he has asked—$1,200. He is told that the surveyor has found that there is nearly twice as much land as originally thought, because it extends to the other side of the river. The Americans who are buying the property want to be fair and offer an additional amount. But the old man refuses, because he has given his word and is honorable. He signs the deed on the original terms.

The new tenants move in and make some improvements. But one day they complain that the village children are overrunning the property and playing under the apple trees. They refuse to leave. When Don Anselmo is summoned to deal with the problem, he explains that this is to be expected. He only sold the land. The children own the trees. Every time a child was born in Río en Medio he planted a tree for that child. He says that the trees are not his to sell.

The Americans then buy the trees, one by one, from the descendants of Don Anselmo.

Preparation

Ask students to think about some traditions and customs that seem never to change. Then ask them to think of some things in life that can't be bought or sold. Tell them that "Gentleman of Río en Medio," the story they are about to read, is about an elderly man who is set in his own, very honorable ways. Tell them that this poses an interesting problem which they will read about.

Vocabulary

*__negotiation__ (*n.*) — bargaining; discussion to agree on something
__tilled__ (*v.*) — plowed and planted the soil
__orchard__ (*n.*) — place with group of fruit trees
*__gnarled__ (*adj.*) — twisted and knotted (as an old tree would be)
*__innumerable__ (*adj.*) — too many to count
__surveyor__ (*n.*) — person who measures land and identifies the boundaries
__adobe__ (*adj.*) — sun-dried clay bricks
*__broached__ (*v.*) — mentioned or suggested for the first time
*__descendants__ (*n.*) — offspring; family members following an ancestor
__individually__ (*adv.*) — one by one

*Glossary word

Activities

A. See p. 6, Teaching Vocabulary.
B. Have students identify and discuss the words on the list that might relate to the land.
C. Ask students to find the two words which refer to people.

Quick Quiz

1. negotiation: a. business expert *b. bargaining* c. place to stop
2. tilled: a. came later b. brewed a drink *c. plowed the soil*
3. orchard: a. large farm *b. place with fruit trees* c. enormous bird
4. gnarled: *a. twisted* b. angry c. noisy
5. innumerable a. easy to count *b. too many to count* c. exact number of
6. surveyor: a. someone who looks around *b. one who measures land* c. fine entertainer
7. adobe: a. attitude b. love *c. sun-dried brick*
8. broached: a. wore around the neck b. broke into pieces *c. mentioned for the first time*

9. descendants: a. older family members   *b. offspring*   c. people in a court case
10. individually: a. expertly   b. carefully   *c. one at a time*

Setting the Purpose

Ask students if any of them know what the words *Río en Medio* in the title of the story mean. Tell them that they mean "river in the middle," and that this is a clue to part of what happens in the story.

Ask students if they think it would be possible to sell a piece of land but still be able to use what grows on it. Then point out that this almost happens in the story they are about to read.

The Selection

"Río en Medio" is longer than the two previous stories, and you probably will want your students to read it in two or more parts.

Have a student read the headnote on p. 26 of the Anthology. Then have everyone read the beginning of the story silently and stop at the line on p. 27, col. 1 that reads "The money is here for you." Before going on, have them comment on how they think Don Anselmo feels about being offered more money. Then have them read on to find out.

Have students read all but the last paragraph. Ask them to suggest possible solutions to the problem before completing the story. If you wish, discuss the resolution briefly before having students complete Reading Comprehension on p. 29 in the Anthology.

Follow-Up

See p. 7, Teaching Reading Comprehension and For Discussion.

Reading Comprehension

1. Don Anselmo refused to take more money for his land because he   *a. had agreed on a price and wanted to keep his word.* (Page 27, col. 2: "I have agreed to sell my house and land for $1,200, and that is the price.")
2. The buyers of the land were bothered by   *c. children playing under the trees.* (Page 28, col. 1: The children were overrunning their property. They played under the trees and built little fences.)
3. Don Anselmo wouldn't tell the children to leave because   *b. the trees belonged to the children.* (Page 28, col. 2: He had planted a tree for the birth of each of his descendants and insisted that the trees belonged to the children.)
4. The new owners decided to buy the trees from Don Anselmo's descendants because the   *b. owners respected Don Anselmo's feelings.* (Page 28, col. 2: The children did not own the trees legally, even though Don Anselmo believed that they did. The new owners, however, had great respect for the old man and they were willing to spend time and money to work things out.)

For Discussion

According to the title, Don Anselmo was a "gentleman." In what ways did he live up

23

to that title? In what ways did the buyers live up to being called "good people"? *Don Anselmo kept his word and sold the property for the amount agreed upon even after it was found that the property was larger than he had thought. This is the major evidence that he was a gentleman. Many other details—his manner, his dress, his way of dealing with the children—also earned him this title. The buyers showed kindness and respect by buying the trees individually from his descendants.*

Understanding Literature: Setting

Objective: Students will identify statements about the setting as true or false.

Preparation

Discuss the *setting* in a work of literature by pointing out that a story must have a time and a place and that knowing about the setting helps the reader to understand the events. The setting also influences the way the characters behave.

Have students read and discuss the lesson on Setting on p. 29 in the Anthology. Then have them complete the exercise that follows.

Questions and Answers

1. The old man's family had lived in Río en Medio for many years.   *True*
2. Río en Medio was a wealthy area.   *False*
3. The people in the area had a close relationship with each other.   *True*
4. Change occurred slowly in Río en Medio.   *True*
5. People near Río en Medio lived in a very modern way.   *False*
6. The new owners understood the traditions before they moved in.   *False*
7. Respect was valued in Río en Medio.   *True*
8. Law was more important than tradition in this area.   *False*

Writing

Think about a place you know or have read about. Make a list of some of the ways people live or act in that place. Then develop your list into a short description of the place.

Students can discuss their responses to the writing assignment before beginning their lists. Two or more students may wish to work together to describe the same place. After they have created a list together, each can write a descriptive paragraph.

Marigolds   by Eugenia Collier   *(p. 30)*

Synopsis

The story begins with Lizabeth's memories of her childhood during the Great Depression—of the shantytown with dirt roads and grassless yards, the dust, and Miss Lottie's marigolds, which still haunt her many years later.

The children of the town are becoming bored with summer and they look for ways to entertain themselves. They like to annoy Miss Lottie, a woman once tall and strong, but now bent over with age and cares. Miss Lottie's son, John Burke, who is known as "queer-headed," sits all day rocking in his private dream world. He is also a favorite target for torment.

Miss Lottie has a marigold garden that presents an unusual contrast to the bleakness all around her. The marigolds are her pride and joy. One day, the children throw pebbles at the flowers until Miss Lottie drives them away. That night, Lizabeth can't sleep. The marigolds won't leave her mind. She gets up in the middle of the night and talks her brother into accompanying her to Miss Lottie's, where she destroys the entire patch of marigolds. With this destructive act, Lizabeth loses the innocence of childhood. Miss Lottie never plants any marigolds again, and Lizabeth's recollections of her deed remain with her.

Preparation

Ask students to consider whether it's possible for something beautiful to thrive in poor and ugly surroundings. Tell them that "Marigolds," the story they are about to read, tells what happened when someone tried to hold onto a small bit of beauty.

Vocabulary

*shantytown (n.) — town of poor, crudely built cabins or shacks
marigolds (n.) — a kind of bright yellow or orange flower
restlessness (n.) — uneasiness; constant motion
commanded (v.) — ordered
flinched (v.) — drew back from something unpleasant
*innocence (n.) — childlike simplicity; freedom from guilt or blame

*Glossary word

Activities

A. See p. 6, Teaching Vocabulary.
B. Ask students if they have ever seen *marigolds*. If not, describe them. Ask if the students think you would be likely to find *marigolds* growing in a *shantytown*. Why, or why not?
C. Ask if any of the students have ever had the feeling of *restlessness*. How does a restless person feel?

Quick Quiz

1. shantytown: a. small apartments *b. group of cabins and shacks* c. village by the sea
2. marigolds: a. inexpensive jewelry b. plants that don't flower *c. yellow flowers*
3. restlessness: *a. uneasiness* b. sleepiness c. unpleasantness
4. commanded: *a. ordered* b. disagreed c. gathered
5. flinched: a. threw it out *b. drew away from* c. hugged very hard
6. innocence: a. type of understanding *b. childlike simplicity* c. considerable harm

Setting the Purpose

Ask why a story set during the Depression in a poor shantytown might have the title "Marigolds." Point out that the marigolds play an important part in this story about a woman who, years later, still recalls her childhood and the only flowers that grew in her hometown.

The Selection

You may want to have students read this selection in several parts.

Have students read to the end of the first paragraph on p. 33, which ends with the line "Yeh, look at 'er." Before going on, have students briefly discuss what has happened and predict what the children will do next at Miss Lottie's.

Have students read the next part of the story to the middle of the first column on p. 35, "I only remember a feeling of great confusion and fear." Ask them to discuss how Lizabeth feels at this point, and to predict what will happen.

Have students read to the end of the story to find out what happens. Then have them complete Reading Comprehension on p. 37 in the Anthology.

Follow-Up

See p. 7, Teaching Reading Comprehension and For Discussion.

Reading Comprehension

1. The time in which "Marigolds" is set is   *a. during the Depression in the 1930's.* (Page 30, col. 2: "While I was growing up, the Depression gripped the country.")
2. The children weren't aware of how poor they really were because   *c. they knew little about the outside world* (page 30, col. 2).
3. The children in the story caused trouble because they   *a. were bored and had nothing else to do.*
4. The children picked on Miss Lottie and her marigolds because   *c. the woman and the flowers seemed out of place in the neighborhood.* (Page 33, col. 1: "They got in the way of the perfect ugliness of the place.")
5. When Lizabeth heard her father cry, she felt   *b. confused and afraid.* (Page 35, col. 1: "I do not now remember my thoughts. I only remember a feeling of great confusion and fear.")
6. In this story, "The world had lost its boundary lines," means   *b. Lizabeth was confused* (page 35, col. 1).
7. Lizabeth pulled out the marigolds because she   *a. wanted to destroy something beautiful.* (Page 35, col. 2: Lizabeth felt fearful and confused. She did not hate Miss Lottie. Students may infer that in feeling hopeless and crazy, she also felt destructive.)
8. The night she destroyed the marigolds, Lizabeth   *c. began to understand other people's feelings.* (Page 36, col. 2: "In that moment I looked beyond myself and into the depths of another person. This was the beginning of having feeling for another person.")

9. Lizbeth's life today is *b. very different from what it was at the time of the story.* (Page 37, col. 1: "The years have taken me worlds away from that time and place.")

For Discussion

1. What was Lizbeth's childhood like? What do you think were the main things that influenced the way she acted? *The childhood years described in the story were filled with poverty and restlessness.* (Page 33, col. 2: "Perhaps we had some small notion of what we were and how little chance we had of being anything else. Otherwise, why would we have wanted to destroy things so much?")
2. In this story, the marigolds are more than flowers in someone's garden. They have special meanings. What did the marigolds mean to Miss Lottie? Why do you think she never replanted the flowers after the children destroyed them? *The marigolds were a bit of beauty and joy in a bleak, harsh world. Miss Lottie probably felt too hurt and defeated to replant them.*

Understanding Literature: Characterization

Objective: Students will match quotations from the story with characters and explain what each quotation reveals about the character.

Preparation

Explain that understanding the characters is an important part of understanding an entire story. An author has several different techniques that can be used to reveal character. Discuss them with the class. These techniques include the following:
  a. physical appearance (telling what the character looks like)
  b. words and actions (telling what the character says and does)
  c. thoughts and feelings (telling what's going on inside the character)
  d. affect on others (telling how the character influences others in the story)
"Marigolds" is a story in which a study of the characters is very important. Through its characters, the story reveals much about human nature and growing up.
  After you have discussed techniques of *characterization* with the students, have them read and complete the exercise on p. 38 in the Anthology.

Questions and Answers

1. "He never talked when he could yell." *Lizbeth's brother Joey* (page 31).
2. "He sat rocking day in and day out in a mindless way." *John Burke* (page 31).
3. "The child in me sulked and said it was all in fun. The woman in me flinched at the thought of the mean attack that I had led." *Lizbeth* (page 34).
4. " 'What must a man do, tell me that?' " *Lizbeth's father* (page 34).

For each item in the above exercise, accept any statements that correctly tell what the quotation reveals about each character.

Writing

Many years later, Lizbeth still felt ashamed at having destroyed Miss Lottie's marigolds. Pretend you are Lizabeth. Write a letter to Miss Lottie in which you explain why you ruined her marigolds and apologize for your actions.

Before having students complete the writing assignment on p. 38, discuss ways to begin the letter. Some students will find it easier to list the points they are going to make before writing them in the form of a letter.

The Enemy   by Pearl S. Buck   *(p. 39)*

Synopsis

Dr. Sadao Hoki, a prominent Japanese physician and scientist, trained for his profession in America, where he met his Japanese wife, Hana. He returned to Japan to practice his profession and raise his family.

As the story begins, Japan and America are at war. The doctor and his wife see a person tossed onto the beach by a wave. They go to the injured man, who turns out to be an escaped American prisoner of war. The doctor's professional instincts take over, and despite the fact that the man is an enemy sailor, he and Hana take him into their house and treat his wound.

The doctor performs life-saving surgery on the gunshot wound, and the young man begins to recover. But Sadao and Hana face the problem of what to do with this enemy in their house. After a week, when the doctor is called to the palace to help the elderly, ailing General, he tells the General about the wounded American. The General says he will send his men to get rid of the prisoner. But the General is more concerned with his own ailments, and does nothing.

When the young man is well, the doctor puts him on a boat with supplies and directs him to a small offshore island to wait for rescue by a passing fishing boat. He gives him a light with which to signal if necessary.

When there is no signal, the doctor assumes that the prisoner has safely left the island. Then he thinks about Americans and prejudice, and wonders why he was unable to kill the young man.

Preparation

Tell students this story takes place during World War II, in Japan. Point out that the United States and Japan were at war.

Ask whether they think a doctor's first loyalty would be to his profession or to his country. Then tell them that the story they are about to read deals with this issue.

Vocabulary

responsibility (*n.*) — duty; something that should be done
casual (*adj.*) — easy; relaxed; by chance
courteously (*adv.*) — politely
***resistance** (*n.*) — a force that opposes another force

*sulfur (n.) — a yellow chemical used in making matches, explosives, and some medicines
liberation (n.) — the act of becoming free
precise (adj.) — exact
condemned (v.) — found guilty; sentenced to punishment
traitor (n.) — one who turns against his country

*Glossary word

Activities

A. See p. 6, Teaching Vocabulary.
B. Ask students what kind of story might use the words on this list. Have them guess what some of the elements of the setting might be.
C. Have students give examples of things that would be *casual,* and things that should be *precise.*
D. Have students identify the words on the list which relate to political or social issues.

Quick Quiz

1. responsibility: a. act of caring   *b. duty*   c. price
2. casual: *a. relaxed*   b. at a very low price   c. very interesting
3. courteously: a. royally   b. impolite   *c. politely*
4. resistance: *a. opposing force*   b. staying power   c. personal helper
5. sulfur: a. small plant   *b. yellow chemical*   c. fizzy drink
6. liberation: *a. freedom*   b. book storage   c. excitement
7. precise: a. torn apart   b. valuable   *c. exact*
8. condemned: a. enjoyed   *b. found guilty*   c. opened up
9. traitor: a. person who buys and sells   b. a loyal patriot   *c. someone who turns against the country*

Setting the Purpose

Remind students that the United States and Japan were at war during the time of this story. Ask what they think would happen when an American and a Japanese met individually, by accident, during wartime. Would the situation be different if one of them were a physician and the other were wounded? Have students read the story to find out what happened in such a situation.

The Selection

This story is best read in several parts.

Have one student volunteer read the brief headnote on p. 39 in the Anthology aloud. Let the students briefly discuss their personal answers to the question posed at the end of the headnote before beginning to read the story. Then have them read to p. 42, col. 2, stopping after the line, "Is this anything but a man? And a wounded, helpless man!"

Have students read the story to p. 43, col. 2: " 'Okay,' he whispered, his mouth a bitter line." Before going on, have students discuss what they think the doctor will do with the young man. What do they think he *should* do?

Have students read the story to p. 46, col. 1, where the doctor tells his wife, "Somehow I must get rid of him." Why is Hana so anxious to see the young man gone? Have students discuss the answer to this question and speculate on what they think the doctor will do now.

Have students read the story to p. 49, col. 1, in which the doctor decides that the young man must go because ". . . simply, it was not worth the strain." Ask them how they think the doctor is going to get rid of the young man. Then have them finish reading the story to find out.

Then have students complete Reading Comprehension on p. 51 in the Anthology.

Follow-Up

See p. 7, Teaching Reading Comprehension and For Discussion.

Reading Comprehension

1. Sadao had once studied medicine in *b. the United States* (page 39, col. 1).
2. At first, Sadao and Hana thought the man in the water *a. might be a fisherman.* (Page 39, col. 2: "A fisherman, perhaps . . . washed from his boat.")
3. Sadao worked to stop the man's bleeding because *c. his instincts as a doctor immediately took over* (page 40, col. 1).
4. The doctor was unable to kill the man because *a. he felt doctors must always try to save lives.*

For Discussion

1. How did Sadao feel about Americans? Why? Why did he save the sailor anyway? *Like all loyal Japanese, Sadao considered America as his enemy because the two countries were at war. He saved the American's life because his instincts as a doctor were stronger than his political feelings.*
2. How did Hana feel about having an enemy in the house? Why do you think she supported her husband? *Having the enemy there made her very uncomfortable. Accept explanations that the student can support with details from the story.*

Understanding Literature: Character Motivation

Objective: Students will identify the motivation for a character's action.

Preparation

Explain that *motivation* is a term used for the reasons characters speak and act as they do. In understanding a story, it's important to understand the motivation of the characters. Characters usually act in keeping with their personalities, and in a well-written story a character is believable.

Have students read and discuss the lesson on Character Motivation on p. 51 in the Anthology. Then have them complete the exercise.

Questions and Answers

1. No matter how she felt about having the sailor in her house, Hana always *c. supported her husband.*
2. Sadao's actions were most strongly influenced by his *b. values as a physician.*
3. Whenever he appeared in the story, the General *a. seemed concerned only with himself.*
4. The servants left because they *b. disapproved of helping an enemy.*

Writing

Write one or more paragraphs describing what you think happens after the story ends. Be sure the characters' actions fit their personalities.

Before students complete the writing assignment on p. 51, discuss some of the things that might have happened after the story ended. Discuss how the various characters would have acted.

Section Review

Vocabulary: Synonyms and Antonyms

Objective: Students will match words in context with synonyms and antonyms.

Preparation

Make sure that the students know the definition of *synonyms* and *antonyms* and can provide examples of each.

Have them read and discuss the brief lesson on Synonyms and Antonyms on p. 52 in the Anthology. Then have them complete the exercise.

Questions and Answers

1. "Rudolf could not *ignore* this chance for adventure."   *pass up, respond to*
2. "That curve of the road had been *deserted* at the time of the accident. . . . "   *empty, crowded*
3. " 'He tells us that your land *extends* across the river and that you own almost twice as much as you thought.' "   *spreads, stops*
4. "And so, when we saw the *tumble-down* shack, we had to stop and gather our courage."   *crumbling, well-built*
5. " 'Nobody lives on it [the island] because in storms it is *submerged*.' "   *underwater, exposed*

Reading: Main Ideas and Details

Objective: Students will identify the main idea statements and the supporting details.

Preparation

Make sure that students understand the difference between the *main ideas* and *details*. Explain that the main idea is the central, or most important, thought of a paragraph or a selection and that the details support or tell about the main idea.

Have students read and discuss the brief lesson on Main Ideas and Details on p. 52 in the Anthology. Then have them complete the exercise.

Questions and Answers

Group A
Main Idea: Rudolf was a true adventurer.
Details: In the evening, Rudolf went out walking. Rudolf knocked at the green door. He went back and got another card. He asked what the card meant.

Group B
Main Idea: What Don Anselmo had was lots of time.
Details: It took months of negotiations to come to an understanding. There was a great deal of conversation. Finally, everyone got down to business. He removed his hat and gloves, slowly and carefully.

Quiz

See p. 7, Administering the Quiz.

Reading Comprehension

1. What did the card that said "The Green Door" really mean? *The card that said "The Green Door" really meant that a play named "The Green Door" had just opened. At first, Rudolf Steiner didn't go where it suggested because he didn't know what it meant.*
2. In "Blue Eyes Far Away," what was Esther Lee doing when her husband died? Why was this important to what happened later? *When her husband died, Esther Lee was watching through her telescope for him to come home. This became important later when she testified as an eyewitness at the trial of the man who hit his car and killed him.*
3. In "Gentleman of Río en Medio," what problem did the new owners of the land face? How did they solve it? *The new owners of Río en Medio faced the problem of children in the apple trees. They bought each tree from the child who owned it.*
4. What were Lizabeth's memories of her home town in "Marigolds"? *Lizabeth's earliest memories include the dust and Miss Lottie's marigolds.*
5. In "The Enemy," why was the sailor lucky that a doctor found him? *The young man who washed up on the beach in "The Enemy" was an American sailor. He was lucky that a doctor found him because he got medical attention. Any other person would have treated him like a prisoner of war, and turned him in.*

Understanding Literature

6. In "The Green Door," what kind of person was Rudolf? Why was knocking on

the door typical of him? *Rudolf Steiner was adventurous. Going up the stairs and knocking on the green door fit in with his personality because he had no idea what he might find there. He was looking for adventure.*

7. How did Mrs. Lee feel about her husband in "Blue Eyes Far Away"? *Esther Lee cared very much for her husband.*

8. What happened in "Gentleman of Río en Medio" after the land was sold? *After the land was sold, the new owners replastered the house, pruned the trees, patched the fence, and moved in. Their apple trees were overrun with the children of the village. Don Anselmo explained that he had given each child a tree, and that the trees belonged to the children. The new owners bought the trees from the children, one by one.*

9. What is the setting of "Marigolds"? Why is the story's time important? *The setting of "Marigolds" was a poor town during the Great Depression. It was a shantytown, with dirt roads and grassless yards. Knowing the setting helps explain the extreme poverty and the condition which led the characters to behave as they did.*

10. How did earlier events in Sadao's life affect his feelings toward the American sailor in "The Enemy"? *Sadao studied in America, and returned to Japan as a famous scientist and doctor. He had met his Japanese wife in America. It was his training as a doctor that most influenced the way he felt about the American sailor. Even though the man was his enemy in the war, Sadao's instincts as a doctor required him to give medical aid.*

Composition

1. Suppose that Rudolf Steiner, the adventurer in "The Green Door," landed alone in a strange, unexplored place. Write a series of events that might make up the plot of a new short story about Rudolf. Then develop your events into a short story.

   Remind students that a short story must have a setting, characters, and a plot. They already know what Rudolf is like. The next task is to describe a setting and, perhaps, other characters. This can all be done in a discussion. Then have students list plot events that would occur in the setting and with the characters they have described. The events should be listed in the order in which they occur.

   More able students can go on to develop their list into a story. For some students, making the list is sufficient.

2. "Blue Eyes Far Away" was the title of a story you read in this section. The title might also be a good one for a love story or a mystery story. List a series of events that might make up the plot of a new story called "Blue Eyes Far Away." Then develop the events into a short story.

   As in the first composition, students can begin this writing assignment with a discussion. Have them decide whether they are going to do a mystery story or a love story, and then think about setting and characters. After the students have decided on the elements of setting and characters, have them list the events of the plot.

   More able students can continue with the assignment and develop the events into a story. For some students, the list will be sufficient.

3. The writer of "Gentleman of Río en Medio" presented a very clear description of the old man. Think of someone you know who does things in a slow or unusual way. Write a paragraph describing that person.

   This composition assignment is a good choice for less able students because they can describe a person they know. Have them discuss the person they choose before starting to write. Many students will find it helpful to list the things thay are going to mention before putting them in sentence and paragraph form.

4. In "Marigolds," Lizabeth learned an important lesson from something she did. Think of a lesson you learned from something you once did. Write one or two paragraphs in which you describe what you did and what you learned.

   Point out that this assignment can be written in the first person. Have students pretend that they are telling the story to a friend as if it just happened. The first paragraph can be about whatever the student did. The second paragraph can be about the lesson the student learned.

5. Choose one day during the time the young sailor was at the doctor's house in "The Enemy." Write a diary entry as if it were written by the sailor. Write another entry for Hana, and one for Sadao. How do their two versions of events on the same day differ?

   Discuss this writing assignment and remind students that a diary entry is written in the first person. (Some of them may keep diaries of their own.) Have the students pretend for a few moments to be each of the characters whose diary entries they are to write. Discuss briefly how the reactions of each of these characters to the same event would vary.

   Some students will find it easier to list what they are going to include in each diary entry before putting it in sentence form.

Enrichment

1. The short story genre is well suited to the needs of reluctant readers. Encourage your students to find other short stories by the authors in this section that interest them. Their short stories can be found in collections of their works.

2. Students who found "The Enemy" interesting might enjoy doing further research on the World War II events in the Pacific. Your school librarian can direct you to appropriate sources.

Authors

Pearl S. Buck. Born in West Virginia in 1892 into a missionary family, Pearl S. Buck spent most of her early life in China, and in fact learned to speak Chinese before English. After being educated in the United States, she returned to China as a missionary and university teacher. Her first book, *The Good Earth,* was published in 1931 and was followed by *A House Divided* (1935), *All Men are Brothers,* which was translated from the Chinese (1933), and *The Mother* (1934). She was awarded the Nobel Prize for Literature in 1938. In the United States, after World War II, she founded the Pearl S. Buck foundation for Asian refugee children, and continued in this work until her death in 1973.

Eugenia Collier. Eugenia Collier was born on April 6, 1928 in Baltimore, Maryland, where she continues to reside. Starting in 1950, she was a caseworker for five years for the Baltimore Department of Public Welfare. She then began teaching at various Baltimore colleges. In 1970 she became a professor of English at the Community College of Baltimore. Collier writes poetry, stories, and articles; her work has been included in many anthologies and has appeared in various journals and The New York Times. Collier is very conscious of her black heritage, and much of her writing and other professional activity is inspired by it. In 1969 the Negro Digest awarded her the Gwendolyn Brooks Award for Fiction for the story "Marigolds." Collier has contributed to books on black poetry and poets. Her more recent projects include critical histories of black writing of the 1960's and black American criticism.

Mackinlay Kantor. Mackinlay Kantor was born on February 4, 1904 in Webster City, Iowa. He was educated at schools in Iowa and Illinois, where from 1921 to 1931 he also worked as a newspaper reporter and columnist. He moved to Hollywood and wrote scenarios for several movie producers. Kantor served as a correspondent with the U.S. Air Force during World War II and the Korean War. From 1948 to 1950 he was a member of the New York City Police; his experiences as a policeman helped him write the novel *Signal Thirty-two*. Kantor is known primarily as a novelist, although he wrote short stories, ballads, nonfiction pieces, and children's books as well. In 1935 he won the O. Henry Award for his story "Silent Grow the Guns," and his novel *Andersonville* brought him a Pulitzer Prize in 1956. He was also a recipient of the Medal of Freedom. A number of Kantor's novels were made into movies, including *Glory for Me,* which became *The Best Years of Our Lives.* Kantor was also a fellow of The Society of American Historians. He died in 1977.

William Sydney Porter (O. Henry). William Sydney Porter was born in North Carolina in 1862. After minimal schooling, he worked at a succession of jobs before being convicted of embezzlement. After three years in jail, he began his own humorous newspaper, *The Rolling Stone* (1894–95). Despite its short life, this paper helped him to enter the world of journalism. He regularly contributed to newspaper columns and began to write the magazine stories for which he is famous. His first book of stories, *Cabbages and Kings,* was published in 1902, and among his many other volumes are *The Four Million* (1906), *The Voice of the City* (1908), and *Strictly Business* (1910). Though his writing covered a variety of locations, he is best remembered for his stories of life in New York. He died in 1910, leaving much work to be published posthumously.

Juan A. A. Sedillo. A descendant of Spanish colonists, Juan A. A. Sedillo was born in New Mexico in 1902. He was a lawyer and judge, and held a number of public offices. He wrote articles for New Mexico newspapers, and he also wrote stories. He currently lives in Mexico.

Section 2
Drama

Section Focus

Section 2, which deals with the genre of drama, contains three plays. The Introduction discusses the history of drama, and points out the differences between drama and other genres. Drama is meant to be seen and heard, and should be read with this in mind. A short story tells the reader about the characters and their actions. In a play, the characters reveal themselves through words and actions.

Have students read and discuss the Introduction on pp. 56–57 before starting the first play in this section.

Activities that follow individual selections focus on understanding stage directions, characterization and actions, and characterization and dialogue.

The Sneeze

by Neil Simon, based on a story by Anton Chekhov *(p. 58)*

Synopsis

Ivan Ilyitch Cherdyakov is a civil servant, a clerk in the Ministry of Parks, who loves the theater. He tries to be important and buys two of the best seats for an opening night performance, even though he can't afford it. He is clearly out of place. Cherdyakov's boss, General Brassilhov (the Minister of Public Parks), and his wife have the seats directly in front of Cherdyakov.

Trying to be impressive, Cherdyakov leans over and introduces himself to the General. He introduces his wife. He then introduces himself and his wife to the General's wife. He becomes a pest. They go back to watching the play. All of a sudden Cherdyakov sneezes on the back of the General's bald head. His embarrassed apologies go on and on. He can't let the matter rest.

Cherdyakov can't forget the incident. He waits all of the next day to see the General in order to apologize again. The General does not even recognize him, and says it was nothing.

But Cherdyakov is totally consumed by his guilt and embarrassment. He can't put the sneeze out of his mind. He again goes to the General and apologizes. This time, the General calls him an idiot and throws him out. He asks Cherdyakov for his name, which comes out again like a sneeze. The poor civil servant goes home, lies down on the sofa, and dies.

Preparation

Ask students if they know anyone who works hard to pretend to be more than he or she really is. Tell them that in the play they are preparing to read, a man tries to act important, with most dreadful results.

Vocabulary

grandeur *(n.)* — beauty and richness
flustered *(adj.)* — nervous or excited
*__infamous__ *(adj.)* — shamefully bad
*__literally__ *(adv.)* — true to fact; really
petition *(n.)* — formal request
gibber *(n.)* — foolish speech; chatter (usually called *gibberish*)
deliberately *(adv.)* — on purpose
humiliated — made to lose self-respect
*__exiled__ *(v.)* — sent out of the country
*__vital__ *(adj.)* — essential to life

*Glossary word

Activities

A. See p. 6, Teaching Vocabulary.
B. Ask students to give an example of *gibberish*. Ask them if someone who talked in this way *(gibbered)* might feel *humiliation*.
C. See how many of the words on the list a student can use in the same sentence.

Quick Quiz

1. grandeur: a. better   b. poor condition   *c. rich and beautiful*
2. flustered: a. ran from one place to another   *b. nervous or excited*   c. made a serious mistake
3. infamous: a. very well known   *b. shamefully bad*   c. quite interesting
4. literally: a. along with many others   b. uncomfortable   *c. really, or true to fact*
5. petition: a. room divider   *b. formal request*   c. strong belief
6. gibber: a. small salted fish   *b. chatter*   c. lunch snack
7. deliberately: a. accidentally   b. quite rapidly   *c. on purpose*
8. humiliated: *a. made to lose self-respect*   b. additional price   c. staying in one's place
9. exiled: a. rewritten   b. designed to be helpful   *c. sent out of the country*
10. vital: *a. absolutely necessary*   b. not necessary   c. sometimes needed

Setting the Purpose

Ask students what they think might happen when a civil service clerk meets the top boss of the organization in a theater. Should the man introduce himself? Have them read "The Sneeze" to find a humorous answer.

The Selection

"The Sneeze," like all plays, is best read aloud. Students can volunteer for the following parts: writer, the play's narrator; Ivan Ilyitch Cherdyakov, a Russian clerk; his wife, Madame Cherdyakov; General Mikhail Brassilhov, Minister of Public Parks and Cherdyakov's boss; Madam Brassilhov, the General's wife. Give students an opportunity to read and prepare the parts silently before asking them to read lines aloud in front of others. Have students do the best they can with the pronunciation of the Russian names, but don't belabor them.

Before students read the first part of the play, explain that the writer acts as a narrator while taking part in the action. As the play goes on, his comments help the reader or audience to understand what's happening. Have the students read up to the sneeze on p. 59.

Before having them continue, ask students what they think of Cherdyakov's behavior so far. Before the sneeze, what did Cherdyakov think of himself? Before the sneeze, what did the General and his wife think of the clerk behind them? Have students identify words and phrases in the text that are clues to these feelings. Then have them read to find out what happens after the sneeze. Have them stop at the line in which the General and his wife leave—p. 62, col. 1: *"(They are gone.)"*

Ask students what they think will happen next. Is Cherdyakov going to forget about the sneeze? Have them read to find out. Let them complete the play to learn the surprise ending, or if you wish, stop them briefly after Cherdyakov's wife says, "You were that reduced?" (p. 63, col. 2). Ask what they think Cherdyakov will do next. Then have the class finish the play.

When the students have finished the play, have them complete Reading Comprehension on p. 65 in the Anthology.

Follow-Up

See p. 7, Teaching Reading Comprehension and For Discussion.

Reading Comprehension

1. Cherdyakov purchased expensive tickets because   *b. he loved going to the theater* (page 58, col. 2).
2. When Cherdyakov sneezed on the General, he felt   *a. humiliated.*
3. Each time the General failed to recognize him, Cherdyakov felt   *c. even less important* (pages 62–64).
4. Cherdyakov caused his own death by   *c. making a small incident seem too important* (page 61, col. 1).

For Discussion

1. How did Cherdyakov's desire to be more important get him into trouble? Do you think he could have handled being important? Why or why not? *If he had never introduced himself to the General, the sneeze would not have been as important. He talked on and on and made no sense. Accept any reasonable interpretation of his behavior.*
2. At the end of the play, something "broke loose inside of Cherdyakov." What broke loose? How did this lead to his death? *Accept any responses that students can support and explain.*

Understanding Literature: Stage Directions

Objective: Students will interpret stage directions.

Preparation

Explain that *stage directions* give the reader important information about the play's setting, what the characters should look like, and what actions should take place on the stage.

Have students read and discuss the lesson on Stage Directions on p. 65 in the Anthology. Then have them complete the exercise.

Questions and Answers

1. *"He and his wife are dressed in their best, but are certainly no match for the grandeur around them."   characters—You learn that Cherdyakov and his wife are trying to be more important than they are. They are playing out of their league, so to speak.*

2. *"The General and his wife take their seats in the front row, the General directly in front of Cherdyakov."* setting and plot—The location of the General's seat is important to the action.
3. **General** *(turns, looks at Cherdyakov coldly)."* characters and plot—You learn about the General's attitude and also about what is going to happen next.
4. *"He starts to wipe the General's head. The General pushes his hand away."* characters and plot—These actions are part of the plot, and they tell a lot about the characters involved.
5. *"Cherdyakov takes off his coat. He sits on the sofa, head in hands."* plot and characters—This event is the resolution of the plot. It's the last bit of information you get about Cherdyakov.

Writing

Suppose Cherdyakov hadn't sneezed again. Plan a new ending. Write new dialogue and stage directions for your ending.

Discuss possible alternative endings to the play. Discuss what might have happened if Cherdyakov hadn't sneezed again. Remind students that stage directions for the new ending should describe the setting, the action, or the characters.

I Remember Mama

by John Van Druten, based on stories by Kathryn Forbes   *(p. 66)*

Synopsis

As the play opens, Mama, Papa, and their daughter Dagmar are in the kitchen. Their son Nels comes in with a letter for Katrin, the oldest child. It is a rejection slip from a magazine—one of many. Katrin wants to be a writer, but has not yet sold a story. She tells the family that she has changed her mind about going to college because she does not believe she will be successful as a writer.

A well-known novelist, Florence Dana Moorhead, is in town at that time. Unknown to Katrin, Mama takes a number of the manuscripts and waits for Moorhead in the lobby of her hotel. The writer says she has no time and that she doesn't read the unpublished material of others. Mama is extremely persuasive and talks Moorhead into reading the material in return for some of Mama's recipes.

Moorhead's advice for Katrin is to write about her own experience, rather than about what she has read in books. It works, and Katrin's first story, "I Remember Mama," which tells about her own family, brings a check for $500.

Preparation

Ask students if they have ever been discouraged about attaining a goal. Ask them if there's been anyone in the family or close circle of friends who has helped and encouraged them. Tell them that "I Remember Mama," the play they are about to read, begins with failure. As Mama begins to help her daughter, things begin to change.

Vocabulary

reveal (*v.*) — show or make known
***concerted** (*adj.*) — planned or carried out together
sincerity (*n.*) — honesty
***essential** (*adj.*) — absolutely necessary
***gastronomy** (*n.*) — the art or science of good eating
soufflé (*n.*) — light baked dish with beaten egg whites

*Glossary word

Activities

A. See p. 6, Teaching Vocabulary.
B. Ask students how the words *soufflé* and *gastronomy* might be related. Ask them if they have ever tried to make a soufflé.

Quick Quiz

1. reveal: a. keep to one's self   *b. show or make known*   c. cook a good dinner
2. concerted: a. very musical   *b. carried out together*   c. quite unpleasant
3. sincerity: *a. honesty*   b. phoniness   c. carelessness
4. essential: a. fair to middling   b. not needed   *c. absolutely necessary*
5. gastronomy: a. severe indigestion   *b. art of good eating*   c. study of the stars
6. soufflé: a. small waffle   b. hard-boiled egg dish   *c. baked dish made with egg whites*

Setting the Purpose

Tell students that Katrin, a major character in the play they are about to read, wants to be a writer. But she is not successful in getting her efforts published, and she is becoming very discouraged. Ask them what they would do if they wanted to accomplish something but kept failing at it. Have them read the play to find out what Katrin does.

The Selection

Begin by having students volunteer to read the different roles in the play. Or, if you wish, you can assign the parts. Let students read their parts silently before being called on to read them aloud. Assign one or more students to read the stage directions.

Have students read to the line in which Mama asks, "What is first edition?" Ask them what they think Mama is going to do next. Then have them continue.

Have students read to the line in which Mama agrees to write the recipe for Lutefisk. Ask them what they think Katrin is going to do when she finds out what her mother has done. Then have them go on.

Have students read to the end of the play to find out how Katrin's story is received when she follows Moorhead's advice. Ask why they think Katrin remembers Mama most of all.

When the students have finished reading the play, have them complete Reading Comprehension on p. 74 in the Anthology.

Follow-Up

See p. 7, Teaching Reading Comprehension and For Discussion.

Reading Comprehension

1. Katrin had wanted to go to college to   *c. learn to be a writer* (page 67, col. 2).
2. Katrin became depressed after   *b. receiving another rejection slip* (page 67, col. 1).
3. Mama got Miss Moorhead to read Katrin's stories by   *a. giving her recipes* (page 70).
4. Miss Moorhead advised Katrin to   *c. write about things she knew* (page 71, col. 2).
5. Katrin sold her first story because   *b. she followed Miss Moorhead's advice.*

For Discussion

Describe some of Mama's qualities. How did she make such a strong impression on her family? *Mama showed sensitivity and an understanding of what motivates others. She was also encouraging and determined. Accept other responses that students can explain and support with details from the play.*

Understanding Literature: Characterization and Actions

Objective: Students will make inferences about characters based on their actions.

Preparation

Explain that a character's actions tell a lot about the character. What a character does is often as important or even more important than what a character says.

Have students read and discuss the lesson on Characterization and Actions on p. 74 in the Anthology. Then have them complete the exercise.

Questions and Answers

1. She decided to appeal to Miss Moorhead's interest in gastronomy.   *d. clever: Mama knew that Moorhead would be so interested in recipes, she would read some of Katrin's stories.*
2. She kept telling Miss Moorhead about her recipes until the woman agreed to read Katrin's stories.   *b. determined: Mama was going to get help for Katrin no matter what she had to do.*
3. She suggested Katrin write about Papa.   *c. humble: She did not imagine that she was worthy of being the subject of a story.*
4. She listened carefully as Katrin explained her problems.   *a. understanding: Mama*

let Katrin talk although she disagreed with her. Then she went to see Moorhead because she knew Katrin really wanted to be a writer.

Writing

Miss Moorhead advised Katrin to write about things she knew. Could you write a story about someone you know? Write a paragraph explaining whom you would write about, some of the person's qualities, and some of the actions you would include in your story.

Have students choose the person they are going to write about. Then have them list the qualities they would mention and the actions they would include. Have them rewrite the list in sentences, and finally in a paragraph.

Sudden Death   by Tom Chehak & Joshua Brand   *(p. 75)*

Synopsis

Randy is a high school freshman with lots of talent in basketball. Coach Reeves thinks he has found a "coach's dream" and encourages the boy to go out for the team, but Randy's parents refuse to give permission. They want their boy, who is an excellent student, to study hard, get good grades, and go to college. They feel that a college education is more important than success in playing a sport. Reeves convinces them to let the boy try and promises that Randy will stop playing if his grades fall even one point.

During a practice session, Randy complains of being tired, and Reeves takes him out of the practice game and has him run laps to get into condition. Suddenly, Randy collapses. He is rushed to the hospital, where he dies of an aneurism.

Reeves feels guilty, although Randy had been examined by a doctor before being allowed to play. Some of the team members imply that the coach was at fault.

At the funeral, Randy's mother refuses to speak to Reeves. She blames him for her son's death. But Randy's father thanks the coach for giving the boy a team experience that made him happy. Finally, both parents accept the gift of Randy's uniform from the rest of the team.

Preparation

Ask students which they think is more important—working hard and getting good grades or being part of a team and getting along with others. Is it possible to find time for both? Tell them that the story they are preparing to read explores this question.

Vocabulary

talent (*n.*) — native ability; natural skill
delicate (*adj.*) — easily injured
appreciate (*v.*) — be grateful for

*aneurism (*n*.) — weak spot in a blood vessel
 responsible (*adj*.) — the cause of
*arteries (*n*.) — blood vessels that carry blood from the heart to the rest of the body

*Glossary word

Activities

A. See p. 6, Teaching Vocabulary.
B. Ask the students to use the words *arteries* and *aneurism* in the same sentence. Make sure that they understand these words, because they are crucial to the play.

Quick Quiz

1. talent: a. understanding   *b. natural skill*   c. upsetting experience
2. delicate: *a. not strong of body*   b. good for dessert   c. assign to someone else
3. appreciate: a. sell for a good price   b. cancel at the last minute   *c. be grateful for*
4. aneurism: a. great love for   b. interesting experience   *c. weak spot in blood vessel*
5. responsible: *a. the cause of*   b. not care about   c. bring one's friends along
6. arteries: a. dusty roads   *b. blood vessels*   c. oil paintings

Setting the Purpose

Have students read the title of the play: "Sudden Death." Ask if they know what the term "sudden death" means in sports. Tell them that this is not what the title refers to in this play. Then have them read the play to find out what it does mean.

The Selection

This play has 17 characters, and many speak only a few lines. It is an excellent opportunity for students to choose and play a role. Except for a few medical terms, most of the dialogue is easy to read. Have students read one scene at a time. This is a teleplay, and the scenes are indicated by stage directions that say "cut to. . . ." Have them read each scene silently before selecting parts and reading aloud.

When students have finished reading the play, have them complete Reading Comprehension on p. 86 in the Anthology.

Follow-Up

See p. 7, Teaching Reading Comprehension and For Discussion.

Reading Comprehension

1. Coach Reeves was excited about Randy joining the team because he   *c. thought Randy was talented.* (Page 75: Randy wasn't a great player yet, but the coach thought he could be.)
2. At first, Randy couldn't join the team because   *b. his parents objected.* (Page 75:

44

They wanted him to keep his grades up and go to college. His mother was afraid he might get hurt playing ball.)

3. Mr. Judd said, "We can't keep him in a glass cage forever." This means that *a. they couldn't keep protecting him* (page 79).

4. When Reeves said, "Is it going to kill you to run 10 laps?" he *c. was trying to get Randy to work harder* (page 80, col. 2).

5. The artery problem that led to Randy's aneurism started when he *b. was born.* (Page 81, col. 2: Basketball and running did not cause the weakness.)

6. After Randy's death, Coach Reeves felt *a. guilty.* (Page 81, col. 2: He felt responsible for getting Randy to play ball. He thought this had contributed to the illness.)

7. Mrs. Judd told Reeves she hoped Randy's death bothered him for the rest of his life because she *b. thought he was responsible for her son's death.* (Page 79, col. 1: She hadn't wanted him to play ball. The coach talked her into it.)

8. When Mr. Judd told Reeves that Randy's team experience was a "gift," Reeves felt *c. grateful* (page 86, col. 1).

9. Randy's death helped Reeves and the team members understand more about *b. what is important in life* (page 85).

For Discussion

1. Was Coach Reeves interested in Randy for selfish reasons? Why was he so pleased to have Randy on the team? *Students will have different opinions about Reeves's motivation. He did want Randy on the team to make it better; he did want to develop Randy into a "superstar"; he probably would have gotten personal fame when Randy became a great player. However, he did contribute to Randy's development. Randy's father says that he "never saw Randy happier" than when he made the team* (page 86).

2. Everyone wanted what was "best for Randy." How do you think Randy would have felt if he had not been allowed to play basketball? *Randy probably would have been unhappy. He was enthusiastic about being on the team* (pages 75–76) *and was happiest when he made the team* (page 86).

3. Several people try to convince Reeves that he shouldn't feel guilty about Randy's death. Do you think he should have felt guilty? Why or why no? *Answers will vary.*

Understanding Literature: Characterization and Dialogue

Objective: Students will make inferences about the characters based on dialogue.

Preparation

Explain that *dialogue* is what the characters say to each other in a play or story. Tell the students that it is possible to learn a great deal about a character from what he or she says.

Have the students read the lesson on Characterization and Dialogue on p. 87 in the Anthology. Then have them complete the exercise. Suggest that they read all the choices before beginning to make the matches.

Questions and Answers

1. **"Reeves:** But I'd love to create a good ballplayer out of Randy." *a. dedicated—Reeves is committed to developing his young players.*
2. **"Coolidge:** I had a cramp. I think I've got appendicitis." *c. fearful—Coolidge is afraid of any pain.*
3. **"Mrs. Judd:** We don't like your interfering. I must ask you to leave." *d. quick tempered—Mrs. Judd gave Reeves hardly any time to present his side of the matter.*
4. **"Mr. Judd:** I never saw Randy happier than when he made your team. I'm glad he had that experience." *b. comforting—Mr. Judd was able to ease Reeves's mind even though he was feeling great sorrow.*

Students should be able to find at least one other example for each character listed here.

Writing

Suppose Mrs. Judd came to Coach Reeves's office after Randy died. Write a dialogue between the two characters. Try to show Mrs. Judd's pain and anger and Reeves's sorrow and regret.

Discuss what Mrs. Judd is likely to have said to the coach, and what he might have replied. Have students discuss this before writing. Encourage them to write a strong opening line for Mrs. Judd as she walks into the coach's office.

Section Review

Vocabulary: Synonyms and Antonyms in Context

Objective: Students will use synonyms or antonyms in context to learn the meaning of an unfamiliar word.

Preparation

Make sure that the students know what synonyms and antonyms are. Explain how the context of a sentence can reveal the meaning of a particular word.

Have them read the lesson on Synonyms and Antonyms in Context on p. 88 in the Anthology. Then have them complete the exercise.

Questions and Answers

1. **"Cherdyakov:** All right? . . . It certainly is not all right! It's *unpardonable!*" *all right (antonym)*
2. **"Cherdyakov:** . . . Punish that which committed the crime, but *pardon* the innocent body behind it." *innocent (antonym)*

3. "**Madame Brassilhov:** I found it *utterly* charming."
   "**Writer:** I was completely charmed by it." *completely (synonym)*
4. "**Cherdyakov:** I was humiliated in such *subtle* fashion, it was almost unnotice-able." *unnoticeable (synonym)*

Reading: Sequence

Objective: Students will rearrange events in the correct sequence.

Preparation

Discuss sequence of events with the students. Make sure that they understand that the order of events is important in understanding a play or a story.

  Have students read the lesson on Sequence on p. 88 in the Anthology. Then have them complete the exercise that follows.

Questions and Answers

The correct sequence of events is:
9. Reeves told Randy that he had a lot to learn about basketball.
6. Randy told Reeves that his parents wouldn't let him join the team.
2. Mrs. Judd agreed to let Randy join the team.
3. Carver won a game, but Randy didn't get to play.
8. Randy screamed and held his head.
7. Willis told Reeves that he was not responsible for Randy's death.
1. Coolidge claimed to have a funny feeling in his head.
4. Mrs. Judd told Reeves that she hoped he would always feel responsible.
5. Reeves and Coolidge discussed the value of friendship.
10. Mrs. Judd accepted Randy's uniform.

Quiz

See p. 7, Administering the Quiz.

Reading Comprehension

1. Why did Cherdyakov introduce himself and his wife to General Brassilhov in "The Sneeze"? *Cherdyakov introduced himself and his wife to the General because he wanted to make a good impression and perhaps earn a promotion* (page 56).
2. How do you know the sneeze incident worried Cherdyakov more than it worried the General? *Cherdyakov could not forget the incident. But the General did not even remember meeting Cherdyakov* (pages 60–64).
3. In "I Remember Mama," how did Miss Moorhead's attitude toward Mama change? *At first, Miss Moorhead was upset at the intrusion and considered Mama an annoyance. She changed her attitude when she saw how much Mama really cared about Katrin. When Mama offered her the recipes she became friendly and helpful* (pages 69 and 70).

4. What was Miss Moorhead's advice to Katrin? How do you know the advice was good? *Miss Moorhead's advice to Katrin was to write about what she knew. The advice was good because it worked* (pages 71 and 73).

5. What caused Randy's death in the screenplay "Sudden Death"? When did this condition start? Why didn't the doctor stop Randy from playing? *Randy's death was caused by an aneurism. Randy was born with a weakness in the blood vessels. The doctor didn't stop Randy from playing because the aneurism wasn't something that could have been predicted.*

Understanding Literature

6. What kind of man was Cherdyakov? Find an action in "The Sneeze" to support your answer. *Cherdyakov was a man who tried to be more important than he was. He made a minor accident into a major disaster. He thinks Brassilhov will fire him* (page 62, col. 1), *and goes to see the General twice about the sneeze* (pages 62, 64).

7. How do you know that the General considered himself more important than Cherdyakov? Find dialogue from the play to support your answer. *On page 63, col. 1, the General says, ". . . don't bother me with this silly business again. . . ." Accept other answers that the student can support with dialogue from the play.)*

8. How does Mama speak in the play "I Remember Mama"? How does her dialogue demonstrate that she was not born in the United States? *She uses English words but not English grammar. Accept other answers that the student correctly supports with dialogue from the play.*

9. What is the setting at the beginning of "I Remember Mama"? How do you know the setting? *The setting at the beginning of "I Remember Mama" is a kitchen in 1910. The stage directions describe the setting* (page 66).

10. The action changed in "Sudden Death" much more often and quickly than in the other two plays in this section. How do the stage directions help you follow the changes in setting and plot? What special term is used in the stage directions of a TV screenplay? *The stage directions give the characters in a scene, the setting, and a general idea of the action that is taking place. When the scene changes, the teleplay directions say "Cut to. . . ."*

Composition

1. Imagine you are a close friend and co-worker of Cherdyakov. Write a short dialogue in which he describes the sneeze incident to you and you advise him what to do.

    Have each student pretend to be a friend of Cherdyakov. Discuss what kinds of advice each of these "friends" might be tempted to give the man who sneezed. Have students begin to write their dialogues with an opening sentence or two by Cherdyakov telling the friend what happened in the theater.

2. Write a letter from Katrin to Miss Moorhead. Thank her for her advice. Also explain why you chose Mama as the subject of your story.

    Before having students complete this writing assignment, discuss what Katrin would be likely to say to Miss Moorhead in a letter. Have the students include at least two reasons why Katrin chose Mama as the subject of her story.

3. Imagine that you work on the school newspaper at Carver High School. You are asked to write a story about Randy's death. Your story angle is the reaction of the Carver students. Include quotations from students and from Coach Reeves in your story.

   In preparation for this assignment, you might have students role play the students at Carver High School and participate in the interviews for this story. Choose a student volunteer to be the reporter. Interviews can be taped, or students can take notes. Suggest that students begin their stories with a quote that sums up the main point they are trying to make.

Enrichment

1. Have students produce and perform one or more scenes from the plays in this section. Students can volunteer for the different roles both onstage and behind the scenes.

2. Two or more students can work together to rewrite a scene from a short story into play form. This exercise highlights the basic differences between the genres of story and drama.

3. A *monologue* is a long speech or scene in a play in which only one character appears. The character often describes his or her inner thoughts. Write a monologue that Coach Reeves might speak as he shoots baskets alone after Randy's death.

   In preparation for this composition, have students imagine that they are Coach Reeves after Randy's death. Have them imagine what the coach would think or say to himself. Some students might find it helpful to say the words into a tape recorder before putting them on paper.

Authors

John Van Druten.   John Van Druten was born in London on June 1, 1901. He wrote over 25 plays, many of which he developed into books. Several of his plays were later produced as motion pictures, for example *I Am a Camera,* which became the stage musical and movie *Cabaret.* Van Druten is also known as the director of Rodgers and Hammerstein's *The King and I.* Although Van Druten is thought of mainly as a very skillful writer of domestic comedies or comedies of manners, he did explore other genres, such as psychological and religious drama. Many of his plays were very successful, and often won "Best Play of the Year" awards. His best known pieces include *Young Woodley, I Remember Mama,* and *The Distaff Side.* Van Druten died in 1957.

Neil Simon.   Born July 4, 1927, in New York City, Neil Simon became known as a comedy writer by working for such entertainers as Phil Silvers and Jackie Gleason in the 1950's. In 1963, he received Tony Award Nominations for the dialogue of the musical *Little Me* and for the play *Barefoot in the Park.* Among his works are *The Odd Couple* (1965), *Sweet Charity* (1966), and *Promises, Promises* (1968).

Section 3
Adventure

Section Focus

This section is built around the theme of adventure. One story, two nonfiction accounts, and a teleplay show how human beings test themselves in exciting and dangerous situations.

The Introduction on p. 92 tells students a little about the different types of adventures that have fascinated people, and sometimes frightened them, since the beginning of time. It discusses the popularity of adventure stories in general and goes on to explore the conflict that makes each of the selections exciting.

The activities following individual selections focus on understanding conflict and resolution, different types of conflict, inner conflict, and plot structure based on conflict, climax, and resolution.

Leiningen Versus the Ants

by Carl Stephenson   (p. 94)

Synopsis

Leiningen, a Brazilian plantation owner, is warned by a government official that the ants are on the way. A horde of ants, two miles by ten miles, is moving toward the plantation eating everything in its path. Leiningen refuses to abandon his land, and vows to fight the ants.

Water surrounds the plantation—a water-filled ditch on three sides, and the river on the fourth side. There is a dam at one end of the ditch that can be opened and closed. The army of ants approaches. Thousands of ants drown in the ditch, only to serve as bridges for others to cross. Ants take leaves and use them as rafts. Leiningen has his men alternately drain and flood the ditch to wash the ants away. But the man operating the dam runs away when the ants surround him. This allows the ants to cross the ditch.

The ants are greedy for flesh, and the men know that they will be devoured along with the animals if the ants win. So an inner ditch is flooded with gasoline, which is then ignited. Finally, Leiningen goes off to try to flood the whole plantation from the river. The ants get to him and tear at his flesh. But Leiningen succeeds in washing the ants away. He has won his battle.

Preparation

Explain that science fiction is imaginative literature based in *some* way on scientific knowledge. Science fiction takes the possible and the present a few extra steps into the maybe and the future. Tell students that the story they are preparing to read has been called science fiction. When they read it they will have a chance to compare science fiction with scientific knowledge.

Vocabulary

***plantation** (*n.*) — a farm or estate
***drought** (*n.*) — period of very dry weather
plague (*n.*) — highly catching, fatal disease
***sickle** (*n.*) — tool for cutting grain or grass
gruesome (*adj.*) — horrible and disgusting
throng (*n.*) — great number crowded together
sentries (*n.*) — guards
retreated (*v.*) — went back or withdrew

*Glossary word

Activities

A. See p. 6, Teaching Vocabulary.
B. Ask students what kind of a story they think would contain the words on this list.

C. Have the students locate two nouns on the list that name horrible things or situations (*drought* and *plague*). Have them find an adjective that would describe either of these two (*gruesome*).

Quick Quiz

1. plantation: *a. large farm or estate* b. yard for horses   c. vegetable garden
2. drought: a. battle   *b. very dry period*   c. type of wagon
3. plague: a. group of apple trees   b. uncomfortable feelings   *c. fatal and infectious disease*
4. sickle: a. rake for leaves   *b. tool to cut grass*   c. sour experience
5. gruesome: a. lovely to look at   b. more than one person   *c. horrible and disgusting*
6. throng: a. leather strap   b. not correct   *c. large crowd*
7. sentries: *a. guards*   b. gentlemen   c. places for food
8. retreated: a. begged to leave   *b. withdrew*   c. made quite happy

Setting the Purpose

Ask students what it would be like if the entire floor of the room were covered with insects. Tell them that the story they are about to read describes a battle with ants and that the ants in this story are almost beyond belief. Have them read to find out why.

The Selection

This selection, though long, is very exciting and likely to hold the interest of even the most reluctant readers. It breaks nicely into sections for discussion.

Have the students read the brief headnote. Ask them to imagine what a swarm of ants—ten miles long and two miles wide—would be like. Have them read to the end of the first paragraph on p. 95: "Let them come!" Ask students if they think Leiningen has made the right decision or if he is being foolish. Then have them continue.

Have students read to the end of the fourth paragraph on p. 98. Ask why they think Leiningen is able to sleep well. Is he going to win his battle with the ants?

Have the students read to the bottom of p. 100. Before they go on, ask what they think Leiningen's inspiration will be.

Have students finish the story to find out who wins the battle. Then have them complete Reading Comprehension on p. 103 in the Anthology.

Follow-Up

See p. 7, Teaching Reading Comprehension and For Discussion.

Reading Comprehension

1. Leiningen was determined not to leave his plantation because he was sure that *b. he could outsmart the ants.* (Page 94, col. 2: "He was sure that he was more than a match for the 'unbeatable' ants.")
2. Leiningen and his men dug a ditch around only three sides of the plantation

because   *c. the river formed the fourth side.* (Page 95, col. 1: "The fourth side faced the river.")

3. Thousands of ants drowned on purpose so that   *b. others might use them as a bridge* (page 96, col. 2).

4. Many of the ants began to gather green leaves to use them   *a. as rafts.* (Page 98, col. 2: "The rain of green was a rain of rafts.")

5. When Leiningen thought, "The odds against us are a thousand to one," he felt that   *c. the one chance was still worth trying.* (Page 97, col. 2: "But he still had his brain.")

6. Thinking about the dying stag helped save Leiningen's life because it made him   *a. keep moving.* (page 102, col. 1).

7. The "Note" at the end of the story tells you that what happened   *b. could not be true* (page 103).

For Discussion

1. Why were the ranch workers so loyal to Leiningen? What qualities made him a tough enemy for the ants? *The men trusted him and thought he was wise. His calmness inspired confidence, determination, and bravery, and his cleverness made him a tough enemy.*

2. Leiningen was sure the ants wouldn't get across the ditch—but he was wrong. In what ways did the ants show they were more clever than Leiningen thought they would be? *They used ants that had drowned as a bridge. They used leaves as rafts to cross the ditch.*

3. When it seemed that the ants couldn't get across the ditch, Leiningen felt almost sorry. Why was he disappointed? *The thrilling contest seemed too easy to win.*

4. Dr. Topoff of the American Museum of Natural History said this story is "great science fiction." What details were too fantastic to be true? *Details include: the number of ants and the area they covered; the way the ants devoured animals and human beings; and the way they planned strategy to beat Leiningen's defenses.*

Understanding Literature: Conflict and Resolution

Objective: Students will identify events as part of the conflict or the resolution in a story.

Preparation

Help students define *conflict* in literature as a struggle between opposing forces. Tell them that in most stories the main character is engaged in some kind of conflict with another person, a force of nature, or a problem of some kind. The way a conflict is worked out is called its *resolution*.

"Leiningen and the Ants" is a dramatic example of conflict and resolution. Have students read and discuss the lesson on Conflict and Resolution on p. 104 in the Anthology. Then have them complete the exercise.

Questions and Answers

1. Leiningen's men lopped off tree branches that hung over the water.   *conflict*

2. The ants began climbing over each other to cross the ditch. *conflict*
3. The ants used leaves as rafts. *conflict*
4. The entire plantation became flooded, and the ants were washed away. *resolution*
5. Leiningen woke up in his bed and learned that the ants were gone. *resolution*

Writing

Think about the following adventure story conflict: Two people are traveling on a raft down a river. As they approach some dangerous rapids, the raft begins to fall apart. How do you think the story will turn out? Write a paragraph in which you present the story's resolution.

Before students write the resolution, discuss the different possibilities. Some students will find it easier to list events before writing them in sentence and paragraph form.

Flight Into Danger   by Arthur Hailey   *(p. 105)*

Synopsis

This teleplay takes place on a flight from Winnipeg to Vancouver, Canada. Shortly after takeoff, dinner is served. The choices are meat or fish. A passenger becomes ill, and a doctor is located on board. He says the problem is serious and that the passenger requires hospitalization. The Captain says that fog will not permit a landing until they reach the coast, almost four hours later.

Soon other passengers become ill. The problem is identified as food poisoning. The fish served is the culprit. Both the Captain and the First Officer have eaten the fish and become ill. They cannot be revived. The doctor remembers that Spencer, the man sitting beside him, had flown fighter planes ten years earlier. Spencer did not eat the fish and is called on to bring the plane in.

He calls the tower in Vancouver for help. An experienced pilot is summoned to talk the plane down. He tells Spencer just what to do. The landing is bumpy, but successful. Spencer is a hero. He has done the impossible.

Preparation

Ask students if they think it's possible to do something under conditions of great danger that couldn't easily be done under normal circumstances. Tell them that the teleplay they are preparing to read is about one such situation.

Vocabulary

halibut *(n)* — type of fish
nausea *(n.)* — stomach sickness
retching *(v.)* — throwing up

***antidote** *(n.)* — medicine for cases of poisoning
***transmit** *(v.)* — send
***beacon** *(n.)* — signal light to guide or warn

food poisoning *(n.)* — illness caused by spoiled or tainted food

Mayday *(n.)* — a distress signal sent by radio from ships or planes

*Glossary word

Activities

A. See p. 6, Teaching Vocabulary.
B. Ask the students what kind of a story they think will contain the words in this list.
C. See how many words on the list the students can use in one sentence.

Quick Quiz

1. halibut: a. distress call   b. lots of fun   *c. type of fish*
2. nausea: a. ocean water   *b. stomach sickness*   c. reason for doing something
3. retching: *a. throwing up*   b. stretching out   c. painting
4. antidote: *a. medicine for poisoning*   b. kind of accident   c. seagoing vessel
5. transmit: a. televise   *b. send*   c. bus
6. beacon: a. breakfast food   b. sealed record   *c. guiding light*
7. food poisoning: a. unpleasant-tasting meal   *b. illness caused by spoiled food*   c. seasoning to improve a meal
8. Mayday: a. spring flower   b. woman's name   *c. distress call*

Setting the Purpose

Ask students what kinds of things can go wrong on an airplane. Then remind them of the words on the vocabulary list. Have them try to guess what is going to happen in the play. Then have them read the play to find out if they are right.

The Selection

This play is quite long and lends itself to being read in sections. Each act can be read as a unit. Have students volunteer to take the various roles and prepare to read the lines out loud.

Have students read to the bottom of <u>column 2 on p. 108</u>, which identifies the First Officer's illness with the fish he ate for dinner. Before going on, ask students what they think will happen next. See if they remember that the Captain had fish for dinner, too. Then have them continue to the end of Act One.

Have students read Act Two, which begins on p. 109. Ask if they think the emergency is going to become a disaster.

Have students read Act Three, which begins on p. 113. Stop briefly at the top of column 2 on p. 115, where Spencer says he will land even though he is told to keep flying. Ask students if they think he has made the correct decision. Then have them finish the play. When they have completed the play, have them complete Reading Comprehension on p. 118 in the Anthology.

Follow-Up

See p. 7, Teaching Reading Comprehension and For Discussion.

Reading Comprehension

1. People on the plane became sick after they   *b. ate fish for dinner* (page 108).
2. The Captain couldn't land the plane immediately after the first passenger became ill because   *a. there was heavy fog* (page 107, col. 2).
3. Spencer was nervous about flying the plane because he   *c. hadn't flown an airplane for 10 years* (page 111, col. 2).
4. The first thing Spencer did when he took over the plane was   *c. radio for help* (page 113, col. 1).
5. Spencer told Baird to make sure everyone was strapped in tight because   *b. people might be thrown and hurt in a bumpy landing.*
6. When he landed the plane, Spencer seemed to be   *b. in control of the situation.* (Pages 116–118: Spencer did what he thought he had to although the pilot guiding him had other ideas.)

For Discussion

1. In what ways did Taylor try to build Spencer's confidence? How did Taylor really feel about Spencer's chances of bringing in the plane safely? *He told him about himself. He told him that he didn't think there would be any trouble because DC-4's were easy to fly. He told him it was something you didn't forget how to do—like riding a bicycle. But Taylor really thought that Spencer's chances were slim.*
2. How did the author try to build up tension during the play? Was he successful? *Accept answers students can support with details from the play. Examples include the following: The passengers who get sick had fish, and we know that the Captain and First Officer had fish as well. The plane lurches for an unknown reason (the First Officer has become sick). The Captain becomes sick, and Spencer is the only one who can fly the plane. Spencer's experience is limited and his confidence level is low. Nobody at the airport believes Spencer can land the plane. When Spencer tries to land, he comes in too quickly and steeply. At the final moment, everything depends on Spencer.*
3. Why are airplane dramas often so dramatic and exciting? Why are movies and television shows about airplane adventures so popular? *Answers will vary. Perhaps the major reason for their excitement and popularity is that when an airplane crashes, there are usually no survivors. The element of high danger adds to the excitement.*

Extra Topic

Do you think something like this could really happen? Why or why not? *You might wish to reassure students that this would be extremely unlikely—almost impossible—on a commercial flight today since the crew is not served the same meal as the passengers.*

Understanding Literature: Types of Conflict

Objective: Students will identify the conflict in a situation.

Preparation

Discuss the following different types of *conflict* and have the students think of examples for each one: (1) person vs. person, (2) person vs. nature, (3) person vs. technology, (4) person vs. self. Explain that some stories may contain more than one type of conflict.

Have students read and discuss the lesson on Types of Conflict on p. 119 in the Anthology. Then have them complete the exercise.

Questions and Answers

1. A woman discovers that the brakes on the car she is driving down a hill do not work.   *person vs. technology*
2. The members of a climbing party encounter a blizzard as they try to reach the top of a mountain.   *person vs. nature*
3. A teenager gets a cramp in his leg during a marathon running race.   *person vs. self*
4. Two boys who dislike each other learn that they are going to be on the same basketball team.   *person vs. person*
5. A soldier must travel through 10 miles of enemy territory in order to reach his regiment.   *person vs. self, person vs. person*
6. A teenager's boyfriend asks her to help him by cheating on an exam.   *person vs. self*

Writing

Imagine that you are a passenger on Flight 714 being interviewed by a TV news reporter after the plane has landed. Write the dialogue of the interview in which you describe your feelings to the reporter.

Discuss what it might have been like to be a passenger on the plane. Then have students think of questions a news reporter would ask. After students have discussed the content of an interview, have them write questions they might ask if they were reporting. Then have them write the answers.

Mind Over Water   by Diana Nyad   *(p. 120)*

Synopsis

Diana Nyad swam around Manhattan Island in 1974, breaking the record set nearly 50 years earlier by a man. She tells about her sport—marathon swimming—in this selection.

Marathon swimming is a sport of endurance, not strength. It requires hours of practice every day for years. In Nyad's first marathon she finished ahead of Judith De Nijs, the world's best woman marathon swimmer at the time.

Marathon swimmers experience anxiety before a race because they don't know what the water will be like. To Nyad, 80 percent of success is mental guts. There is also great loneliness involved. It's important to get through the low points and not to quit. The toughest problem is cold water, which is even more difficult to handle than fatigue, seasickness, or pain. Coming out of the water at the end of a race makes it all worthwhile.

Preparation

Ask students if they know what a marathon is. Tell them that the selection they are preparing to read is about a particular type of marathon sport. It requires a very special type of person.

Vocabulary

sacrifice (*n.*) — the giving up of something of value in return for something else
***marathon** (*n.*) — long contest to test a person's endurance
conditioned (*adj.*) — well trained and fit
***anxiety** (*n.*) — nervousness

*Glossary word

Activities

A. See p. 6, Teaching Vocabulary.
B. Have students give examples of *sacrifice*.
C. Have them suggest different events that might be considered to be *marathons*.
D. See how many of the words a student can use in the same sentence.

Quick Quiz

1. sacrifice: a. being willing to help another *b. giving up something of value* c. building a large fire
2. marathon: a. baseball game b. event in a swimming pool *c. contest of endurance*
3. conditioned: *a. well trained and fit* b. extremely cool c. content and lazy
4. anxiety: a. entertainment b. will to win *c. nervousness*

Setting the Purpose

Tell students that Diana Nyad set a record for swimming around Manhattan Island. How did she manage to become a great marathon swimmer? Why does she do it? (Mention that her last name, Nyad, rhymes with *naiad*, which is a water nymph.) Have them read the selection to find out.

The Selection

This selection is very short and can easily be read in one session. After reading, have students complete Reading Comprehension on p. 124 in the Anthology.

Follow-Up

See p. 7, Teaching Reading Comprehension and For Discussion.

Reading Comprehension

1. Marathon swimming burns more calories than other sports because   *a. all parts of a person's body are involved* (page 120).
2. Before a race, marathon swimmers are usually   *c. tense* (page 121, col. 1).
3. Diana Nyad believes that 80 percent of the success in a long-distance race is due to *b. the power of the mind* (page 121, col. 2).
4. The hardest problem Diana Nyad has to overcome is   *b. cold water.* (Page 123, col. 1: "I can handle tiredness, pain, and huge waves. The hardest part is cold water.")

For Discussion

1. What can people learn about themselves in contests of great physical stress and endurance? *Answers will vary. People can learn that the limits of their abilities are much higher than they thought. They can learn that they can do things they never thought they could do.*
2. What does Diana Nyad mean by "mental guts"? How can this help people succeed in sports and in life? *Students can infer that mental guts involves courage and a positive attitude. "I have to dig down deep" suggests inner strength.*

Understanding Literature: Person vs. Self Conflict

Objective: Students will write a resolution for the inner conflict described in each paragraph.

Preparation

Review the following different types of conflict: person vs. person, person vs. nature, person vs. technology, person vs. self. Have students read and discuss the lesson on Person vs. Conflict on p. 124 in the Anthology. Then have them complete the exercise.

Questions and Answers

1. Larry has accidentally seen the answers to an upcoming history test. He is not sure whether he should take the test anyway or tell his teacher. *Answers will vary. Example: Larry tells his teacher that he saw the answers. The teacher commends Larry for his honesty, and makes up a special test for Larry to take.*
2. Joan is an excellent diver who is also afraid of heights. More than anything else, she wants to be able to dive from the high board in the state meet. *Answers will*

vary. Example: Joan practices diving from a higher and higher board until she conquers her fear and dives from the high board.

3. Hector has always been shy and unsure of himself. A new girl has moved into the neighborhood. She seems to like him, but Hector is afraid to get to know her. *Answers will vary. Example: Hector writes the new girl a letter welcoming her to the neighborhood. She calls Hector back, thanks him for welcoming her, and says she would like to meet him since his letter was so friendly. They arrange to get together after school.*

Writing

A *monologue* is a speech in which a character reveals his or her inner thoughts to an audience. Imagine you are swimming a marathon race. Write three short monologues in which you describe your thoughts at the beginning, middle, and end of the race.

Discuss the writing assignment before students begin. Have them list the major point they are going to make in each monologue.

In the Shadow of a Rainbow

by Robert Franklin Leslie   *(p. 125)*

Synopsis

Gregory Tah-Kloma, a young Indian, has an interesting story to tell. He is looking for gold when a man, Eugene Charley, asks him if he has seen Nahani, a she-wolf who leads a pack. There is a reward for her because she and her pack are killers. Greg, a loner in the wilderness, sees Nahani and over many days and weeks makes friends with her. When it turns cold the wolves go to their winter quarters.

There is a bounty for Nahani and many try to catch her. Trapper Dan and his men greedily go after the wolf. Greg rents a cabin from Trapper Dan, but does not trust him. Eugene Charley is also after Nahani. A young Indian warns Greg that Trapper Dan will kill Charley and claim the wolf for his own if Charley gets her first. Charley is killed. Trapper Dan wants people to believe that Greg has done it.

The next summer Greg finds Nahani and her band again. In October, hunters find Greg. They tell him that Trapper Dan has died. He was bitten by a wolf he claimed was Nahani. He died of rabies. The hunters agree not to kill Nahani. At the end of October it snows, and she leads her pack away into the Yukon.

Preparation

Ask students if they think it is possible for a human being to have a special kind of communication with a wild animal. Tell them that the account they are preparing to read is about such a case.

Vocabulary

forepaws (*n.*) — front feet

wilderness (*n.*) — place where people don't normally live (such as deep forest)
*__legend__ (*n.*) — story handed down from one person to another
rumors (*n.*) — stories of doubtful truth; gossip or hearsay
binoculars (*n.*) — small telescopes fitted to both eyes for seeing things far away
snarled (*v.*) — growled and showed teeth

*Glossary word

Activities

A. See p. 6, Teaching Vocabulary.
B. Ask students what kind of a story they think would contain the words on this list. Where would it be likely to take place?
C. Ask students how a *legend* differs from *rumors*.

Quick Quiz

1. forepaws: a. stop very quickly *b. front feet* c. rear toes
2. wilderness: a. lakes and mountains *b. place where people don't live* c. nice place for vacation
3. legend: *a. story passed on from one person to another* b. beginning of a forest fire c. home for animals and plants
4. rumors: *a. gossip or hearsay* b. true stories c. people who rent cabins
5. binoculars: *a. two-eyed telescope* b. fuel for campfires c. wild forest animal
6. snarled: a. was extremely hungry b. smiled and laughed *c. growled and showed teeth*

Setting the Purpose

Tell students that Gregory Tah-Kloma is a person some would describe as a loner. He is not much of a loner, however, when it comes to being with a wolf pack. Have them read this unusual account about a man in the wilderness.

The Selection

"In the Shadow of a Rainbow" is quite long and should be read in several parts. Have a volunteer read the brief headnote aloud. Then have the class read silently to the line on p. 127, col. 2 that says, "It was time for him to go home." Ask students what they think Greg will do. Will he return to the wilderness?

Have students read to the paragraph on p. 130 that ends ". . . planning a day-by-day trip from June to September." Ask what they think Greg is going to do now. Will he ever find Nahani again?

Have students finish the story. Ask if they think Nahani is gone for good this time. Then have them complete Reading Comprehension on p. 134 in the Anthology.

Follow-Up

See p. 7, Teaching Reading Comprehension and For Discussion.

Reading Comprehension

1. Trapper Dan and Eugene Charley tried to capture Nahani because they *c. wanted a reward* (pages 125, col. 1 and 128, col. 2).
2. At first, Greg walked on all fours because he *b. didn't want to scare away the wolves* (page 125).
3. Greg decided to rent a cabin during the winter because he *b. wanted to warn Nahani about the other hunters* (page 128, col. 2).
4. Greg searched for Nahani because *a. he wanted to continue their friendship.*
5. Nahani showed her friendship for Greg by *b. walking on the beach with him* (page 131, col. 2).
6. When Nahani headed for the Yukon, Greg knew that *c. he might never see her again* (page 134, col. 1).
7. The story of Gregory Tah-Kloma and Nahani *b. really happened* (page 125).

For Discussion

1. What kind of person was Gregory Tah-Kloma? How did he show he was sensitive to animals and understood how they acted? *Accept a description of Greg that the students can support with details from the story. If he had not been sensitive to animals and had not understood them, he would never have been able to make friends with Nahani.*
2. How did most of the people in the account feel about Nahani and the other wolves? Why did they feel this way? *Most of the people saw the wolves as enemies or as prizes to be hunted. Accept any explanation that students can support with details from the story.*
3. How did the relationship between Greg and Nahani grow? How did she finally show that she had accepted Greg as a member of her pack? *It grew slowly as Nahani learned to trust Greg. She finally accepted Greg by letting the rest of the pack approach him.*
4. What did Greg's people mean when they said that "friends have walked in the shadow of a rainbow"? Why did Greg tell Nahani, "We did walk in the shadow of a rainbow"? *A strong friendship is very special, and Greg's friendship with Nahani was certainly special. Answers will vary.*

Understanding Literature: Climax

Objective: Students will identify events in the plot as part of the conflict, climax, or resolution.

Preparation

Review *conflict* with the students. Tell them that the high point of the conflict is often referred to as the *climax,* or turning point. After the climax, the conflict is resolved.

Have students read and discuss the lesson on Climax on p. 135 in the Anthology. Then have them complete the exercise.

Questions and Answers

1. Nahani led the pack to the Yukon.

2. Greg found Nahani again.
3. Nahani and the other wolves walked with Greg along the beach.
4. Greg gained the wolves' trust and began walking upright around them.

The correct diagram is:

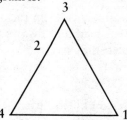

Writing

What would have happened if Trapper Dan had caught Nahani when Greg was there? Would he have killed the wolf? Would Greg have stopped him? Write a paragraph in which you present a different climax and resolution.

Discuss each question before students begin to write. Some students may find it helpful to list the events they are going to include.

Section Review

Vocabulary: Experience Clues

Objective: Students will infer the meaning of a word from context.

Preparation

Review context clues with the students. Point out that their own experiences can provide clues to the meaning of an unfamiliar word.

Have students read and discuss the lesson on p. 136 in the Anthology. Then have them complete the exercise. Answers will vary. Accept definitions and explanations that make sense.

Questions and Answers

1. "A few [ants], bigger than the rest, carried stings that *injected* a burning poison." *Injected — shot into through a sharp needle.*
2. "Screaming with pain, the man danced and *twirled." Twirled — spun around frantically.*
3. "... the jaws of the swarming Brazilian army ant are just not equipped to tear flesh — much less *pare* a person down to a pile of bones in six minutes." *Pare — cut down in size.*
4. "I'm pretty *rusty* now. But I used to fly fighters in the Air Force." *Rusty — out of practice.*

Reading: Cause and Effect

Objective: Students will identify the cause and effect pattern in passages.

Preparation

Discuss *cause and effect* with the students. Help them to identify clue words that signal cause and effect. Have them read and discuss the lesson on p. 136 in the Anthology. Then have them complete the exercise.

Questions and Answers

1. " 'Many of the Indians believe you killed Eugene Charley. That's why Dan left you a rifle at the cabin. He figured you hated Charley enough to kill him.' " *Cause: Dan left Greg a rifle. Many of the Indians thought Greg killed Eugene Charley. Clue words: That's why.*
2. "My heartbeat is 47 or 48 when I am at rest; this is compared to the normal 72 for other people. A conditioned athlete usually has a heartbeat of 60 plus. This is all due to swimming hour after hour, year after year." *Cause: Diana Nyad swims hour after hour, year after year. Effect: Her heartbeat is 47 or 48. Clue words: This is all due to.*

Quiz

See p. 7, Administering the Quiz.

Reading Comprehension

1. In "Leiningen Versus the Ants," what defenses did Leiningen set up against the attack by the ants? In what ways did his defenses succeed? In what ways did they fail? *Leiningen prepared ditches on three sides of the plantation in which water could be controlled by a dam. He also used gasoline set on fire. But the ditches did not completely succeed. The ants used bodies of dead comrades as bridges. They used leaves as rafts. The machinery to open and close the dam failed. Finally the dam was used to flood the entire plantation in a successful defense.*
2. In "Flight Into Danger," what events led to Spencer's successful landing of Flight 714? *Spencer had not eaten the fish. He was willing to try to land the plane when he had no choice. He managed to make the radio work and contact help. He listened to the pilot in the tower and brought the plane down.*
3. In what ways did Spencer show that he was in charge of the situation? *Spencer showed he was in charge of the situation by telling the tower that he was coming in even though they said to wait. He knew that the sick passengers couldn't last long, and he brought the plane in safely.*
4. What are some of the problems that marathon swimmers such as Diana Nyad have to overcome? *Among the problems are fatigue, cold water, rough water, seasickness, and loneliness.*
5. What qualities did Gregory Tah-Kloma have that led to his being accepted by the wolves? *Gregory Tah-Kloma was quiet, sensitive, patient, and did not frighten the wolves. He was also willing to work hard and did not give up his goal.*

Understanding Literature

6. "Leiningen Versus the Ants" is an example of a person vs. nature conflict. What human qualities did Leiningen bring to the conflict? What natural qualities did the ants bring? *The human qualities Leiningen brought to the conflict include intellect, pride, and stubbornness. The ants were willing to sacrifice some of their number to achieve their objective. They kept going on without regard to what might happen. They also consumed everything in their path.*

7. What event marks the climax of Leiningen's conflict with the ants? How is the story finally resolved? *The climax of Leiningen's conflict with the ants occurs when he manages to turn the wheel to dam the river and flood the plantation. The conflict is resolved when the ants are washed away.*

8. In what ways is "Flight Into Danger" an example of a person vs. self type of conflict? How is it resolved? *Spencer, in "Flight Into Danger," has to fight his own fear and hesitancy in order to fly the plane. When there is no other choice, he makes an effort and succeeds.*

9. What forces of nature does Diana Nyad have to battle when she swims marathon races? What forces within herself does she have to overcome? *The forces of nature include cold water, rough water, and creatures in the water. Forces within herself include nausea, loneliness, and fatigue.*

10. Describe Gregory's conflicts with nature and with other people in "In the Shadow of a Rainbow." How are these conflicts resolved? *Gregory must work very slowly and carefully to get the wolves to trust him. He rents a cabin in the wilderness and battles the elements. He comes into conflict with other people because he is a friend of Nahani. These conflicts are resolved when he is accepted by the wolves, and both Trapper Dan and Eugene Charley fail to get the reward for Nahani's skin.*

Composition

1. In "Leiningen Versus the Ants," only Leiningen's side is presented. Suppose the ants had a brave leader named Rothar. How would he or she describe what happened? The ants didn't attack the plantation out of meanness. They were searching for food. Write 3 or 4 paragraphs about the battle from Rothar's point of view.

   Discuss the events of "Leiningen Versus the Ants" from the point of view of the ants. Take one incident from the story and help the students to retell it from the ants' point of view. Use this as an example. Then have the students select four or five other incidents and retell them.

2. You are a newspaper reporter covering the landing of Flight 714. Write a story of what happened. Include quotations from people involved.

   If you wish, this assignment can be role played by the students before they write. Have one student volunteer to be the newspaper reporter. Have other students play the passengers on the plane. The mock interview can be tape recorded or students can take notes. Then have them write it as a news story.

3. In "Mind Over Water," Diana Nyad described marathon swimming and the feelings of swimmers. Choose an athlete you have read about. Write 2 or 3

paragraphs in which you describe the athlete and his or her feelings about competing in sports.

Each student who selects this writing topic should first identify an athlete about whom he or she will write. The selections and the sports involved can be described and discussed briefly with the class. Many students will find it easier to write the composition by first listing points to be made.

4. In "In the Shadow of a Rainbow," Greg showed his understanding of the way wolves act. Imagine you are Greg. Make a list of rules that might be called "How to Get Along with Wolves."

To help students get the information to complete this assignment, have them go back to the story and identify specific instances in which Greg handled the wolves well. As each item is located, it can be noted on a piece of paper and then rewritten as a rule. You might wish to do the first one with the students.

This is an excellent assignment for less able readers. It can be done independently or as a group activity.

Enrichment

1. The theme of this section is *adventure*. Have each student identify an activity or pursuit that would be a personal adventure. Students may choose something within the realm of possibility for them or engage in fantasy. Have each student find out as much as possible about the adventure he or she has chosen. Some obvious topics are space travel, skydiving, or mountain climbing. Your students will probably be able to come up with many more original ideas.

2. Have students identify and do research about people they consider to be adventurers. Marathon swimmer Diana Nyad is the example used in this section. Students will be able to find many additional examples in newspapers, magazines, and other media.

Authors

Arthur Hailey. Born April 5, 1920 in Luton, England, Arthur Hailey moved to Canada in 1947. He began writing novels in the late 1950's and found his first notable success with *The Final Diagnosis* (1959). Since then he has published a succession of enormously popular novels, of which *Hotel* (1965), *Airport* (1968), and *Wheels* (1971) are among the best known.

Robert Franklin Leslie. Robert Franklin Leslie was born on October 21, 1911, in Texas. Part Cherokee Indian, Leslie is a great lover of nature. Leslie writes and lectures on wilderness preservation. Most of his writing is nonfiction and based on his experiences as an outdoorsman and traveler. He has written several books for children and young adults, among them the award-winning *The Bears and I.* Leslie's other books include *Read the Wild Water: 780 Miles by Canoe Down the Green River* and *High Trails West.*

Diana Nyad. Diana Nyad is a champion marathon swimmer. She has traversed bodies of water all over the world, and written accounts of her experiences.

Section 4
Mysteries

Section Focus

Section 4 presents three mysteries—a story in which strange events result in the unjust accusation of an innocent person, a story about a famous detective (adapted as a play), and a story about a mysterious trip to another time and place.

The Introduction to this section describes the techniques mystery writers use to create suspense and let their readers find clues to solve the mystery, a little bit at a time. These techniques include the use of surprise, hidden clues, and mood.

Have students read and discuss the Introduction to this section before reading the first selection. "With a mystery, it is sometimes more exciting and intriguing not to know all of the answers." Ask the students if they agree, and why.

The activities after each selection focus on understanding how events in a mystery create suspense, mood in a mystery, and the relationship between mood and descriptions of the setting.

The Haunted Chess Set by Julia Remine Piggin *(p. 141)*

Synopsis

As the story begins, Angelica Ramos is dreaming. In her dream, someone is riding a horse along the boardwalk. She can hear the horse's hooves and the waves. A small object hits her cheek and awakens her. Angelica, a retired architect, has little difficulty figuring out what has happened. The sound of the waves are part of her life in her oceanfront apartment. The tapping sound was her neighbor's hammering as he hung a picture. The vibration of the thin wall caused objects on her bureau to move, and a perfume bottle fell and woke her up.

Angelica gets ready for a meeting with Emil Cooper, chairman of the committee for the town's new civic center. On the way, she meets her niece Iris, who has just started a summer job in Cooper's office. Iris tells her aunt that she has just been accused of trying to steal money from Cooper's cash box, and that she has been fired. She denies that she has been in the room where the box is kept.

Angelica confronts Cooper, who insists that he has proof that Iris is lying. He says that chess pieces on the board have been moved, and that Iris must have done it. They enter the room so he can show Angelica. The chess pieces have been moved again, and Cooper concludes that the set must be haunted. Angelica knows what has happened, and she knows her niece is innocent. She insists that Cooper type an apology immediately. The next time they look, the pieces have moved again. The typewriter and the chess table are on either side of the same wall. Whenever the typewriter is used, the vibrations cause the chess pieces to move.

Preparation

Ask students if they believe that a dream can predict the future. Do dreams sometimes come true? Tell them that the story they are preparing to read is a mystery that begins with a dream. In the dream is a clue to the solution of the mystery.

Vocabulary

vibration *(n.)* — quivering; shaking
*__architect__ *(n.)* — person who designs buildings or other structures
consultant *(n.)* — person who gives expert advice
*__medieval__ *(adj.)* — having to do with the Middle Ages
miniature *(adj.)* — very small; on a small scale
*__casualty__ *(n.)* — someone injured or killed in an accident or battle

*Glossary word

Activities

A. See p. 6, Teaching Vocabulary.
B. Have students identify the two words on the list which refer to jobs a person might do. *architect, consultant*
C. Have them find the word that tells what they should not become. *casualty*

Quick Quiz

1. vibration: a. sensation *b. quivering* c. bright color
2. architect: a. physician b. toll collector *c. building designer*
3. consultant: *a. person who gives advice* b. person who governs c. retired executive
4. medieval: a. extremely bad b. from very ancient times *c. from the Middle Ages*
5. miniature: a. breed of cat *b. on a small scale* c. time of day
6. casualty: a. nothing serious *b. someone hurt or killed* c. result of a theft

Setting the Purpose

Ask students if they believe that something can be haunted. What would they expect of a haunted house, for example? Tell them that the story they are about to read contains a chess set that appears to be haunted. Ask if they believe that could be so. Have them read the story to find out.

The Selection

This story is quite short, and it can easily be read by most students at one sitting. If you prefer, you can divide the text and stop for a brief discussion between the two parts.

Have the students read to the bottom of p. 142. Before they turn the page, ask them to guess what the explanation for the strange events might be. Have them continue the story to the end to find out if they were right.

After students have completed the story, have them complete Reading Comprehension on p. 145 in the Anthology.

Follow-Up

See p. 7, Teaching Reading Comprehension and For Discussion.

Reading Comprehension

1. Angelica's perfume fell off her bureau because of the *b. vibrations of someone's hammering* (page 141).
2. Angelica became involved in the mystery of the haunted chess set because she *a. wanted to help her niece* (page 143).
3. Mr. Cooper accused Iris of *c. going into his private study* (page 142, col. 2).
4. Mr. Cooper asked Angelica if she believed in ghosts because *b. no person could have gotten into the room* (page 143, col. 2).
5. The clue that reminded Angelica of her dream was *c. the knight in silver armor* (page 145, col. 2).
6. When Angelica said the answer just "struck" her, she meant *c. both of the above.*
7. Angelica demonstrated her ability to solve problems by the way she *b. weighed all the facts in the situation.*

For Discussion

1. How did Angelica Ramos know what had caused the chess pieces to move? *A wall*

vibrating from hammering had caused the perfume bottle to wake her from a dream. The chess pieces, too, were moved by a vibrating wall. The fact that Angelica was an architect might have helped her to figure it out.

2. How did Emil Cooper show that he was a person who jumped to conclusions? What mistakes in judgment did he make? *He accused Iris of trying to find money in his cash box and of being in his private study when he had told her never to go in there. The chess pieces had moved, and he jumped to the conclusion that "someone had been in there hunting for something." But there was no proof of this. He concluded that Iris was guilty because she was the only one who had been in the house. When she denied her guilt, he fired her anyway.*

3. Do you think Angelica Ramos is the kind of person who believes in ghosts? Why or why not? Are there usually logical explanations for things people blame on ghosts? *Answers will vary. Ramos probably does not believe in ghosts; she did not listen to Cooper when he claimed his chess set was haunted. Logical explanations can usually be found to explain unusual phenomena.*

Understanding Literature: Suspense and Plot

Objective: Students will explain how events in a mystery are related.

Preparation

Discuss how the author of a mystery story arranges the *plot* to build suspense. Explain that *suspense* is the feeling of tension that comes from not knowing exactly how things are going to turn out. Have students give examples of situations in which they have felt suspense. Then have them read and discuss the lesson on Suspense and Plot on p. 146 in the Anthology.

Questions and Answers

1. Angelica's dream and her neighbor's hammering. *Angelica's dream contained a horse galloping on the boardwalk. This sound corresponded to her neighbor's hammering (page 141).*

2. Angelica's dream and the movement of the pieces on the chessboard. *There was a moving horse in Angelica's dream. One of the chess pieces that moved was the knight on a horse (pages 141 and 145).*

3. The neighbor's hammering and Emil Cooper's typing. *The neighbor's hammering and Emil Cooper's typing both made the wall vibrate and move objects on the other side (pages 141 and 143).*

4. The fall of the perfume bottle and the movement of the pieces. *The name of the perfume that fell was "Silver Night" (page 141). There was a silver knight on the chess board (page 143).*

5. Angelica's thoughts about her date and about the chess pieces. *She was thinking about wearing a silvery dress to meet Robert, who would be wearing a uniform (page 142). The knight that moved had silver armor (page 143).*

Writing

Being an architect helped Angelica Ramos solve the mystery of the moving chess pieces. Write a paragraph in which you explain how Angelica's profession helped her find the solution to the mystery.

Discuss how Angelica's knowledge of building construction helped her to understand first why the perfume bottle moved, and then why the chess pieces did the same. Then have students write a paragraph telling how Angelica's profession helped her solve the mystery.

The Adventure of The Copper Beeches
adapted from a story by Sir Arthur Conan Doyle   *(p. 147)*

Synopsis

The play begins with Dr. Watson and Sherlock Holmes conversing about the unimportance of the case at hand. They are about to be visited by Violet Hunter, a young woman who seeks their advice about whether to take a position as a governess. The salary is more than twice what similar positions would pay, and the employer, Mr. Rucastle, insists that the young woman cut her red hair. Holmes warns her of danger and tells her not to take the job. Nevertheless, Violet does take the job because she needs money.

Strange things happen at The Copper Beeches, the estate where she becomes the governess for a six-year-old boy. The child is mean and cruel. And from time to time, she is ordered to wear a blue dress and sit by a window reading. There is a part of the house into which she is forbidden to go. She finds a coil of red hair much like her own in a locked drawer.

Violet asks Holmes and Watson for help. One night when the owners of the estate are out, she locks the housekeeper in the cellar, takes the keys, and explores the forbidden wing with her guests. Watson breaks down the door, but no one is in the room. An open skylight and ladder to the roof suggest that someone has just escaped. The Rucastles return, and Mr. Rucastle is attacked by his own guard dog.

Holmes deduces that Violet Hunter was hired to impersonate heiress Alice Rucastle, the daughter of Mr. Rucastle and his first wife. Alice was imprisoned to keep her away from her fiance who, if they married, would have access to her fortune. With the help of the housekeeper, Alice had been rescued by her fiance and the two eloped.

Preparation

Ask students if they have ever heard the expression "Things are seldom as they seem." Ask what they think this might mean. Then tell students that, as the Introduction to this section suggests, the mystery at the beginning of "The Adventure of The Copper Beeches" seems to be that *there is no mystery*. However, as the play goes on, the mystery unfolds.

Vocabulary

governess (*n.*) — woman who teaches and cares for children in a private home

* **capital** (*adj.*) — excellent; first-rate
* **apparel** (*n.*) — clothing
  duplicates (*n.*) — exact doubles or copies
* **resourceful** (*adj.*) — clever; able to deal skillfully with new problems

*Glossary word

Activities

A. See p. 6, Teaching Vocabulary.
B. Ask students which two words on the list would describe a good governess. *capital, resourceful*

Quick Quiz

1. governess: a. like a president   *b. teacher for children in a private home*   c. group that makes a country's laws
2. capital: *a. excellent or first-rate*   b. fairly large town   c. long, hooded garment
3. apparel: a. two or more   *b. clothing*   c. dessert
4. duplicates: a. type of trouble   b. complications   *c. exact doubles*
5. resourceful: *a. able to deal with new problems*   b. located near a large lake c. containing enough to eat

Setting the Purpose

Tell students that Violet Hunter, a young woman in need of a job, accepts employment as a governess even though the job has some strange requirements. Has she walked into a dangerous situation? Is there really a mystery involved with the job? Have students read "The Adventure of The Copper Beeches" to find out.

The Selection

Like all plays, this one is designed to be read aloud. Let each student volunteer to prepare a part. Divide the play into three or four sections so that everyone will have a chance to play a role.

Begin by having students read up to the line on p. 149, col. 2, where Holmes says, ". . . at any time, day or night, a telegram will bring me to help you." Before going on, discuss what students think might be going on at Miss Hunter's place of employment. Ask if they can think of any logical reason for the odd requests.

Have students read the next section of the play, to p. 152, col. 2, where Mrs. Toller says, "And don't say a word to the Rucastles, or it won't go well with you." Ask students, now that they have more details, if they have a better idea of what is going on.

Have students read the next section of the play in which Sherlock Holmes, Dr. Watson, and Miss Hunter explore the secret wing of The Copper Beeches. Stop on p. 155, col. 1, after the line where Holmes says, "Someone's coming. Have your pistol ready." Ask students whom they think is coming and why.

Have students finish reading the play to find the solution to the mystery. Ask if they think Rucastle got what he deserved. Then have them complete Reading Comprehension on p. 157.

Follow-Up

See p. 7, Teaching Reading Comprehension and For Discussion.

Reading Comprehension

1. Violet Hunter came to see Holmes and Watson   *a. for advice about taking a job* (pages 147–148).
2. While Violet sat in the drawing room, Mr. Rucastle   *c. told her funny stories* (page 150, col. 2).
3. Mr. Rucastle accused Mrs. Toller of drinking because she   *b. was about to spoil his plans* (page 151).
4. Mr. Rucastle didn't want Fowler to marry his daughter because he   *b. wanted to control her inheritance.* (Page 156, col. 1: "But when she became Mrs. Francis Fowler, her husband would be in charge of it. The greedy Rucastles couldn't allow that.")
5. When Holmes said, "Gold is the key," he meant   *a. money was the secret of the mystery* (page 156, col. 1)

For Discussion

Why did the Rucastles think Violet was a "perfect" choice to be governess? *She was a perfect choice because she was the same size as Alice Rucastle and she had the same color hair.*

Understanding Literature: Mood

Objective: Students will write questions about unexplained incidents in a mystery.

Preparation

Discuss *mood* and how it contributes to the effectiveness of a story. Mood is the emotion that a story makes a reader feel. Discuss the moods that would be suitable for a mystery story. Have the students offer examples.

Then have students read and discuss the lesson on Mood on p. 157 in the Anthology. Have them complete the exercise, which contains incidents from the mystery they have just read and asks them to write questions each incident suggests.

Questions and Answers

Following are suggested answers. Accept any wording and response that makes sense.

1. Violet was offered too much money to become the Rucastles' governess. *Why are they paying her so much? They didn't need her as a governess. They needed her to impersonate Alice Rucastle. Violet was worth a lot because she was the same size and had the same color hair as Alice.*
2. Mr. Rucastle told Violet funny stories, but Mrs. Rucastle just looked sadder and sadder. *Why did he find it necessary to entertain the woman he has hired? Why did Mrs. Rucastle look so sad? He wanted Violet to appear happy so that the man on the road would notice. Mrs. Rucastle may have looked sad because she felt guilty.*

3. Mr. Rucastle accused Mrs. Toller of being drunk. *Why did he do this? He had to keep the woman from revealing what was going on.*
4. A man was standing in the road looking in the window. *Who was the man? Why was he doing this? The man was Alice Rucastle's fiance. He was unwilling to give up his love for Alice.*
5. Mr. Rucastle angrily left the "empty" wing of the house. *What made him angry? Why didn't he want Violet to know what was going on there? He was concealing his daughter Alice in a locked room.*

Writing

Watson called Violet "resourceful." Make a list of some of the ways Violet demonstrated her resourcefulness in the play. Develop your list into a paragraph.

Discuss what Dr. Watson meant when he called Violet "resourceful." Students can develop their lists independently or as a class. Then have them rewrite the list into sentence and paragraph form.

The Third Level by Jack Finney *(p. 158)*

Synopsis

The narrator has found a third level in Grand Central Station, although most people are aware of only two levels. His psychiatrist tells him that he is unhappy, and that this is a "waking-dream." Charley admits to wanting to escape from modern-day pressures, but he still insists that he has found a third level. The third level takes people back into the nineteenth century. It is lit by open-flame gaslights, and everyone in the station is dressed in the fashions of the 1890's. The narrator attempts to buy two tickets to Galesburg, Illinois, but the clerk won't accept his modern money. He exchanges his money at a coin dealer's, but is unable to find the third level again.

Louise, the narrator's wife, is worried and tells Charley to stop looking for the third level. He agrees to stop, and goes back to his stamp collection for escape. In the meanwhile, his friend Sam disappears. Charley is sure that Sam is in Galesburg. In his grandfather's stamp collection he finds an envelope with a July 18, 1894 postmark. Inside is a letter from Sam telling him that he was right—there is a third level, and he and Louisa should keep looking until they find it. Who is this Sam, who has found the way to the past? Sam is Charley's psychiatrist!

Preparation

Ask students if they believe it is possible to travel into another dimension of time or space. Have them discuss which time in history (or in the future) they would enter if they could find a way. Tell them that the story they are preparing to read involves travel to another time.

Vocabulary

residents (*n.*) — people who live in a place
psychiatrist (*n.*) — doctor who treats mental and emotional problems
corridor (*n.*) — long hallway
*__flickering__ (*adj.*) — not strong or steady
*__spittoons__ (*n.*) — bowls to spit in

*Glossary word

Activities

A. See p. 6, Teaching Vocabulary.
B. Ask students to identify the two words on the list that refer to people. *residents, psychiatrist*
C. See if they can make up a sentence which uses all three of the other words (*corridor, flickering, spittoons*) in one sentence. The only rule is that the sentence must make some sense, and be grammatically correct.

Quick Quiz

1. residents: a. small house or apartment   *b. people who live in a place*   c. a group of unhappy people
2. psychiatrist: *a. doctor for the mind*   b. type of surgeon   c. furniture salesperson
3. corridor: a. entrance or exit   b. understanding   *c. long hallway*
4. flickering: *a. not strong or steady*   b. brilliantly lit   c. too warm to handle
5. spittoons: a. things like kites   *b. bowls to spit in*   c. oddly shaped trousers

Setting the Purpose

Tell students that part of the story they are about to read is set in Grand Central Station, a major railroad terminal in New York City. Tell them that Grand Central has two levels. Then have them read the title of the story. Ask what they think the title might mean. Then have them read the story to find out.

The Selection

"The Third Level" is a short piece that can be easily read in one session by most students. Also, students will want to continue reading to find out what happens. You can break briefly for discussion before having the students read the surprise ending.

Have a student volunteer read the headnote aloud. Then have the class read the story silently up to p. 161, col. 2: ". . . although I've tried often enough."

Before going on, have students comment on what has happened. Do they believe it? Ask what they think of Charley. What do they think will happen next? Then have them read the rest of the story to find out. After they have finished reading the story, have them complete Reading Comprehension on p. 162 in the Anthology.

Follow-Up

See p. 7, Teaching Reading Comprehension and For Discussion.

Reading Comprehension

1. When you buy a ticket on the third level of Grand Central Station, you can *b. escape to the past.* (Page 159, col. 2: ". . . I could buy tickets that would take Louisa and me anywhere in the United States — in the year 1894.")
2. Charley knew he had returned to the year 1894 because he *c. saw a newspaper's front page.* (Page 159, col. 2: "It was printed June 11, 1894.")
3. Another thing that showed Charley he was in the past when he found the third level was *b. the way people dressed* (page 159, col. 2).
4. Charley wanted to go back to Galesburg, Illinois, in 1894 because *c. it was a peaceful time and place* (page 161, col. 1).
5. Sam wouldn't have gone back to his old business in 1894 because *a. small towns like Galesburg didn't have psychiatrists then* (page 162, col. 1).

For Discussion

1. Why was Charley dissatisfied with modern life? What appealed to him about life in the past? *His psychiatrist friend thought fear, war, and worry made Charley want to escape. Life in the past seemed peaceful and simple.*
2. Why didn't Louisa want Charley to look for the third level at first? Why did she change her mind and start looking with him? *At first, Louisa worried about Charley's search, and probably thought there was something wrong with Charley. But Sam's letter changed her mind.*
3. What kind of life did Sam discover people lived in Galesburg in 1894? Did he like his life in the present or life in the past better? How do you know? *Sam discovered a life of good times. He liked it so much that he encouraged Charley and Louisa to keep looking for the third level.*
4. How did the discovery of the letter from Sam add to the mysteriousness of the story? *Charley's belief that there was a third level is explained at first by his desire to escape his worries. But there is the logical explanation for Sam's note!*

Understanding Literature: Mood and Setting

Objective: Students will choose the correct word to describe the mood in each passage.

Preparation

Explain that one of the ways an author creates a *mood* in a selection is by describing the *setting*. Have students think of different settings and the mood each one evokes. Point out that a story or play can have more than one setting, and that the mood may change.

Have the students read and discuss the lesson on Mood and Setting on p. 163 in the Anthology. Then have them complete the exercise.

Questions and Answers

1. "Sometimes I think Grand Central is growing like a tree, pushing out new corridors and staircases like roots. There's probably a long tunnel that nobody

knows about under the city right now, on its way to Times Square." *c. joking*

2. "The corridor I was in slanted downward. I thought that was wrong, but I kept on walking. All I could hear was the empty sound of my own footsteps. I didn't pass a soul." *a. eerie*
3. "Have you ever been there? It's a wonderful town still, with big old frame houses, huge lawns, and tremendous trees." *b. peaceful*

Writing

In what kind of setting would you expect the mood to be scary? Sad? Peaceful? Pick a setting and write a brief description of it in which you establish a scary, sad, or peaceful mood.

Discuss setting and its relationship to mood once more before having the students complete the writing assignment. After each student has selected a setting to describe, and decided on a mood to create, it might be helpful to have students list the details they are going to include before they put them into sentence and paragraph form.

Section Review

Vocabulary: Multiple Meanings

Objective: Students will use the context to choose the correct definition of a word.

Preparation

Make sure that students understand that some words have more than one meaning, and that the correct meaning can be figured out from the context.

Have students read and discuss the lesson on Multiple Meanings on p. 164 in the Anthology, and then have them complete the exercise. Accept any correct use of the alternate meaning in a complete sentence.

Questions and Answers

1. "Angelica's *bureau* had been pushed against her side of the same wall." *chest of drawers* (alternate meaning: *government department*)
2. "When she presented Iris's case, he jumped up and began to *storm* around the room." *rush around angrily* (alternate meaning: *rain heavily*)
3. " 'I should say so! *Capital!* I could not ask for anything better!' " *excellent* (alternate meaning: *money used in business*)
4. "You can buy old money at almost any coin dealer's, but you have to pay a *premium*." *additional amount above the usual* (alternate meaning: *something offered free*)

Reading: Drawing Conclusions

Objective: Students will draw conclusions based on facts in a passage.

Preparation

Discuss what it means to draw a conclusion. Point out that it is often important to be able to put details together to draw conclusions when reading or solving a mystery.

Have students read and discuss the lesson on Drawing Conclusions on p. 164 in the Anthology. Then have them complete the exercise that follows. Answers to the questions will vary. Accept any reasonable conclusions.

Questions and Answers

1. The child could barely lift the bowling ball. He started it rolling down the center of the alley, but it slowly began edging toward the side.

   How many pins did the ball probably knock down? *None.*

2. Helen is a cashier at a supermarket. One customer pays her with two $10 bills. Helen notices that both bills have the same serial number. She tells her boss to stop the customer.

   Why does Helen want the customer to be stopped? *The bills are counterfeit.*

3. A murder is committed during a heavy rainstorm. Muddy footprints on the carpet lead toward the body. A police officer says, "I want to know which people now in the house have been outside the building in the past hour."

   Why does the police officer want this information? *Anyone who had been outside in the storm would have muddy shoes, and could be a suspect.*

Quiz

See p. 7, Administering the Quiz.

Reading Comprehension

1. In "The Haunted Chess Set," why did Emil Cooper suspect that ghosts were haunting his chess set? What did the ghosts turn out to be? *The chess pieces moved although there were no people in the room. The ghosts turn out to be vibrations from typing in the next room.*

2. In "The Adventure of The Copper Beeches," why was Violet Hunter nervous about taking the job? Why did she decide to take it? *Violet Hunter was nervous because she was asked to do odd things, such as cut her hair. The salary was also unusually high. She took the job anyway because she needed money.*

3. How did Mr. Rucastle try to keep his daughter from marrying Francis Fowler? What was his motivation? *He lied to Francis Fowler and kept Alice locked in a room, hoping she would agree never to see Fowler again. He hired Violet to impersonate Alice. He wanted to control his daughter's inheritance.*

4. In "The Third Level," why did Charley do his searching at Grand Central Station? Why was he certain that the third level existed? *Charley searched for the third level at Grand Central Station because he wanted to buy a ticket to go back into the past. He was certain that the third level existed because of the letter from Sam.*

5. Why is it surprising that Sam Weiner turned out to be the person who found and

used the third level? *It is surprising because Sam was Charley's psychiatrist, who tried to persuade Charley that he had not seen the third level.*

Understanding Literature

6. At the beginning of "The Haunted Chess Set," Angelica's dream was interrupted when something small and hard hit her on the cheek. What mood does this incident create in the story? Why? *The incident establishes a mysterious mood because it creates suspense.*

7. How did Emil Cooper's excitability add to the mysterious mood of "The Haunted Chess Set"? *Cooper's excitability creates uncertainty. His quick moves and hasty conclusions are more confusing than correct.*

8. How did Violet Hunter feel when she discovered the coil of red hair in the locked drawer? How does this incident add to the suspense of "The Adventure of The Copper Beeches"? *Violet is confused and frightened. The reader wonders at the coincidence. The hair resembles her own* (page 152, col. 2).

9. Why is it important that Charley found the third level once but not a second time? How does this fact add to the suspense of "The Third Level"? *It makes you wonder whether he will find the third level again.*

10. What unanswered questions does the discovery of the letter from Sam bring to your mind? *How did Sam find the third level? Is there another explanation for the letter? Does the third level really exist? Answers will vary.*

Composition

1. Suppose Iris never received Emil Cooper's apology and went to his office to ask for her job back. Write a dialogue that might take place between the two characters.

    You can have students role play this situation before writing the dialogue. Have one student volunteer to be Iris, another to take the part of Emil Cooper. Or, if you wish, two students can do the assignment together.

    Some students will find it easier to write the dialogue if they list the points to be made before writing them in sentences.

2. Make up a dream that Dr. Watson might have had to help him solve the mystery at The Copper Beeches.

    Have the class discuss the clues that led to the solution of the Copper Beeches mystery. Then have students try to put these clues into a dream. To give students an idea of how a dream might be useful, refer them to the story about the haunted chess set, in which a dream gave clues to solving the mystery.

3. In "The Adventure of The Copper Beeches," Francis Fowler watched Violet Hunter and thought she was Alice Rucastle. Write a letter from Fowler to Alice in which he describes what he saw and how he felt.

    Discuss with students how Francis Fowler must have felt when he saw a woman he thought to be his loved one sitting by the window and ignoring him. Then have students write the letter from Francis to Alice. If you wish, you can help students begin this way: "Dear Alice: When I saw you wearing my favorite blue dress, my heart. . . ."

4. Imagine that you are Louisa in "The Third Level." Each weekend you and Charley search unsuccessfully for the third level. One Saturday you search alone and find it. What do you do? Do you go on alone or go back and get Charley? Choose one of these alternatives and write a new ending for the story.

   If several students are going to do this assignment, try to have both possible endings represented. Discuss the alternatives before students begin to write. You may wish to use this opening sentence to get students started: "The lights flickered and I realized that I had come upon the third level. 'What now?' I asked myself."

Enrichment

1. Students who enjoyed "The Adventure of The Copper Beeches" should be directed to additional Sherlock Holmes mysteries.
2. Additional works with a mystery theme available from Scholastic include: Mini-Mysteries, More Two-Minute Mysteries, Instant Mysteries, and Stories of Suspense. Consult Scholastic's Reader's Choice Catalogue for additional titles.
3. Students might enjoy researching the cases of people who have mysteriously disappeared. Suggest names such as Ambrose Bierce, Judge Crater, or Amelia Earhart. Some persons who disappear are crime victims. Have the students explore the possibility that these people may have entered another dimension.

Authors

Arthur Conan Doyle.   Arthur Conan Doyle was born in Edinburgh, Scotland on May 22, 1859. He was a practicing physician for many years before becoming a full-time writer. Doyle is famous as the creator of Sherlock Holmes. He wrote four novels and over 50 stories based on Holmes's adventures. The first story, "A Study in Scarlet," appeared in 1887. Doyle also wrote historical novels and scholarly works, upon which he would have preferred that his literary reputation be based. Later in life he became deeply interested in spiritualism and wrote mostly on that subject, producing just a few Sherlock Holmes stories to keep his fans satisfied. Doyle died in England in 1930.

Jack Finney.   Jack Finney was born in Milwaukee, Wisconsin, in 1911. He worked in an advertising agency in New York City. He has written short stories and novels, two of which—*Five Against the House* and *The Body Snatchers*—have been made into movies. Finney's stories are often very imaginative and unusual. Some of his short stories are collected in the book *The Third Level*, and he wrote *Time and Again,* which expands his concept of time travel to novel length. He now lives in California.

Section 5
Poetry

Section Focus

Section 5 explores the genre of poetry. The Introduction on p. 168 in the Anthology tells students that poetry began as song, and that it is still meant to be read aloud. The poems in this section are presented in four different categories—*narrative poems, lyric poems, message poems,* and *found and concrete poems.* Narrative poems tell a story. Lyric poems describe by using words to create images, or pictures. A message poem expresses the poet's ideas or opinion about a particular topic. In a found poem, the poet takes words and phrases found elsewhere and arranges them in a new way. In concrete poetry, the graphic appearance of the letters and words is an essential part of the poem.

Have students read and discuss the Introduction before reading the poems. Unlike the other sections, complete exercises do not appear after each selection. Reading Comprehension and For Discussion questions appear at the end of each subsection. Understanding Literature lessons (also after each subsection) focus on understanding symbols; images, similes, and metaphors; symbols and mood; and the meaning of graphic arrangement in concrete poems.

Narrative Poems

Before having students read the four poems in this section, remind them that a narrative poem tells a story. Like a short story or a play, a narrative poem may have characters, a setting, a plot, and a theme.

Don't Take Your Guns to Town

by Johnny Cash   *(p. 170)*

Preparation

Tell students that the poem they are about to read is a well-known country-and-western song.

Vocabulary

wanderlust (*n.*) — great desire to travel

The Selection

Have a volunteer read each stanza, with the rest of the class joining in for the two-line refrain at the end of each stanza.

A recording of "Don't Take Your Guns to Town" should be easy to find in your library or local record store. Students will enjoy listening to this popular record.

Follow-Up

Discuss the questions that accompany the poem.

You may wish to have students bring in additional records by Johnny Cash or other artists to compare them with this selection.

Questions and Answers

1. Why was it important to Billy Joe that he take his guns to town? *He thought this proved that he was a man.* (Line 7: "Your Billy Joe's a man.")
2. Why was his mother against his taking his guns to town? How did she see her son? Did she think he was a man yet? *She didn't think he was mature enough to take his guns to town.*
3. Why did Billy draw his gun? Do you think he had a good reason? *Billy Joe drew his gun because a cowpoke was laughing at him, and this filled him with rage. There was no reason to draw his gun. (Encourage the students to discuss this. Note that drink probably contributed to Billy Joe's poor judgment. The foolishness of his behavior should be obvious to the students, but using the poem to preach a lesson should be avoided.)*
4. Just as every story has a setting, this song has a setting. What are some of the details that help you to know the time and place? *Accept any answer that students can support with specific references to the selection. The poem did not take place in modern times, but most likely in the American West of the 1800's.*

Ghosts   by Sandra Gardner   *(p. 173)*

Preparation

Have students think about the title of the poem, "Ghosts." Ask what kind of a narrative might have such a title.

Vocabulary

widowed (*adj.*) — left alone by the death of a mate
scandals (*n.*) — disgraceful actions

The Selection

Have students read the poem silently in preparation for reading it aloud. Then students can volunteer to read it aloud. As the poem is being read, tell students to try to visualize just what is happening and how the scene looks.

Follow-Up

Discuss the questions that accompany the poem.

Questions and Answers

1. You never met the speaker's aunt, yet you can tell things about her from the poem. What kind of woman was she? *Accept any answer students can support with details from the poem. The woman obviously had strong family ties and had been a peacemaker in the family. She "... had bound them together, made them put aside/differences, made them become friends. ..."*
2. What is the mood or feeling in the first stanza (section)? What is the mood in the last stanza? How are they different from each other? *The mood of the first stanza is reflective and peaceful. It describes happy memories. The mood of the last stanza is lonely, bleak, and cold.*

Frankenstein   by Edward Field   *(p. 174)*

Preparation

Ask students if they have heard of Frankenstein. Tell them that Frankenstein was a monster created by Baron Frankenstein in the novel written by Mary Shelley in 1818. The poem they are about to read uses the character in the Frankenstein story to tell another story.

Vocabulary

dungeon (*n.*) — underground prison (as in a castle)
cadavers (*n.*) — dead bodies; corpses
cudgels (*n.*) — short, thick sticks used as weapons; clubs
recoils (*v.*) — draws back
***tentative** (*adj.*) — unsure
pursue (*v.*) — chase after

*Glossary word

The Selection

This poem contains some difficult words, and you might choose to begin by reading it aloud before having students read it on their own. You may wish to stop the reading before the final stanza, and ask students how they think the story will turn out. Then continue to the end, and discuss what the poet is saying about humanity.

Follow-Up

The action in this narrative poem easily lends itself to dramatization. Some students might enjoy acting it out while others read aloud.

Discuss the questions that accompany the poem.

Questions and Answers

1. The poem reveals two separate sides to the monster's personality. Which side did the townspeople see? Which side did the blind man uncover? *The townspeople saw the ugly appearance and heard the noises the monster made. They thought he was dangerous and evil because he was ugly. The blind man couldn't see the monster's ugly appearance, so he got to know another side of the monster—his tender heart.*

2. Why was the blind man good to the monster? What did he teach the monster? *The blind man was good to the monster because he had longed for a friend to share his lonely life. The blind man couldn't see the ugliness and so was not afraid. He taught the monster about kindness. He also taught the monster to eat and drink, smoke a cigar, enjoy music, and to enjoy sharing these simple pleasures of life.*

3. What had happened to the monster before he met the blind man? What will happen to him after he leaves the blind man? How do you know? *Before he met the blind man, the monster had been treated cruelly by his creator, the Baron, and by the villagers. The villagers chased him with firebrands, cudgels, and rakes. The mob will find him again and will chase him to the edge of a whirlpool, where he will fall to his death. You know this because the last stanza of the poem looks into the monster's future.*

Last Day at the Job

by Gretchen Cryer & Nancy Ford   *(p. 177)*

Preparation

Ask students what kind of a story they would expect in a narrative poem with the title "Last Day at the Job." Ask what they think the mood of the poem will be. Then have them read the poem to find out.

The Selection

This narrative poem lends itself to oral reading in parts. Have one student volunteer to be the woman who is leaving her job. Have another be the narrator, and have another speak for her friends and still another be the "fat-bellied boss."

Follow-Up

Discuss the questions that accompany the poem.

Questions and Answers

1. Who is the speaker in this narrative poem? How do you think she feels about the decision that has been made? *The speaker is the daughter of a woman who has been a bank teller for 20 years. (The poet refers to her as "Mom.") Accept any interpretation of her feelings that students can support with details from the poem.*
2. What is the overall mood of this poem? What images, or word pictures, in the poem help to create the mood? *The mood is one of reflection, anticipation, and release. Images that help to create the mood include: the narrator's mother working so long in one small place that she forgot about the sky; the activities the narrator's mother is planning to bring beauty and peace back into her life.*

Follow-Up

See p. 7, Teaching Reading Comprehension and For Discussion.

Reading Comprehension

1. Billy Joe's last words show that he   *a. knew his mother was right* (page 171).
2. In "Ghosts," the old men spent their Sunday mornings   *c. drinking coffee in the sewing room.* (Page 173: ". . . my father and my uncle, / . . . would sit together . . . over coffee . . . / . . . in the sunny room / that had been my aunt's sewing room.")
3. The Frankenstein monster did not harm the old man because the monster   *b. had a tender heart.* (Page 174: "for in spite of his awful looks he has a tender heart.")
4. When the mother in "Last Day at the Job" said, "I never got to sit," she meant that she   *b. never had time to pay attention to life* (page 177).

For Discussion

1. Compare the mood in each of the four narrative poems. How does each one of them make you feel? *Accept answers students can support with details from the poems. "Don't Take Your Guns to Town" should make the reader sad at the waste of Billy Joe's life. "Ghosts" should make the reader ponder what happens when a loved one dies. "Frankenstein" should make the reader angry about the monster's treatment, but glad that he found one friend. "Last Day at the Job" should make the reader glad for Mom and her triumph of leaving her job.*
2. How did the mother in "Last Day at the Job" feel about turning 62? How do you know? *She saw leaving her job as an opportunity to enjoy life more fully. The repetition of her plans shows that she strongly desires to carry them out.*

Extra Topics

1. Explain to students that a narrative poem tells a story. Ask if they think that a poem was a good choice for telling each of the stories in this section. Or, would a play or prose form have told the story better? Explain your answer. *Accept any answers students can support and explain. Answers will vary.*

2. Can you think of any stories that might be told in the form of a narrative poem? Why do you think a poem would be a good vehicle for these stories? *Answers will vary. Accept any answers students can support.*

Understanding Literature: Symbols

Objective: Students will match symbols with their meaning in each poem.

Preparation

Explain to students that *symbols* are objects or actions that stand for something else. (The term appears in the Handbook of Terms in Literature.) See if they can suggest examples of symbols from their own experience. Have them read and discuss the lesson on Symbols on p. 178 in the Anthology. Then have them complete the exercise.

Questions and Answers

1. Billy Joe's guns   *c. proof of manhood*
2. the sunny room in "Ghosts"   *e. warm memories*
3. the cold black night in "Ghosts"   *f. death*
4. the shared meal in "Frankenstein"   *a. friendship*
5. the chasing of the monster by the townspeople   *d. people's prejudices*
6. planting flowers in "Last Day at the Job"   *b. beginning all over again*

Writing

Choose one of the words or phrases below. Decide what it could symbolize. Write a short story or a short narrative poem in which you use the symbol to stand for an idea or feeling.

dawn	the ocean
sunlight	some coins
a broken swing	a lightning bolt

Discuss what each item on the list might symbolize. (Note that there need not be unanimity of opinion.) Then have each student choose one of the things on the list and identify what it will symbolize in the story or narrative poem they will write. Some students may find it easier to list events they will include in their poem or story before they write.

Lyric Poems

Explain that a lyric poem is a short poem that expresses the poet's personal thoughts or feelings about a topic. Originally, lyric poems were sung and accompanied by a lyre, a stringed instrument that was strummed much like a guitar.

Hector the Collector   by Shel Silverstein   *(p. 179)*

Preparation

Ask students what image the title of the poem brings to mind. Ask if they have ever collected anything.

Vocabulary

Gatlin' gun (*n.*) — early type of machine gun named for its inventor, J. Gatling

The Selection

Have students read the poem once silently and then aloud. It can be read chorally if you wish.

Follow-Up

Discuss the questions that accompany the poem.

Ask students if they have ever met anyone like "Hector the Collector." Ask if they think Hector's things are junk or treasures.

Questions and Answers

1. What happened when Hector let other people see his collection? Why do you think he decided to share his "treasure trunk"? *Other people thought his collection was junk. They didn't have the creative, imaginative spirit that Hector did. Hector decided to let people share his treasure trunk because he loved his things and was so excited about them. But they didn't understand.*
2. Read the poem aloud. Do the rhythm and rhymes make it sound a little like a children's song? In what ways? *Answers will vary. In addition to the regular rhymes and the singsong rhythm, the choice of words suggest childhood.*

Of Kings and Things   by Lillian Morrison   *(p. 181)*

Preparation

Ask students if they have ever played stickball. Tell them that this poem is about the "king" of that game in the speaker's neighborhood years ago.

Vocabulary

spaldeen (*n.*) — small, pink rubber ball
trajectory (*n.*) — the curved flight path of a rocket or a batted ball

*eluding (*v.*) — escaping from
constellation (*n.*) — group of stars

The Selection

Have students read the poem silently before reading it aloud. Then have a volunteer read it aloud to the class.

Follow-Up

The speaker remembers the king of stickball in the neighborhood. Ask students to consider what and whom they think they will remember years from now. Then discuss the questions that accompany the poem.

Questions and Answers

1. What kind of game is stickball? What do you learn about the game in the poem?
   Stickball is a game like baseball, but it is played on city streets. It uses a mop handle for a bat, and a pink rubber ball ("spaldeen"). The distance a ball is hit is measured by the number of sewers the batted ball passes while in the air.
2. How does the speaker feel about Joey? What images does she use to describe him?
   She remembers him with awe, admiration, and great respect. She describes him as a king ("invisible crown"), an angel or saint ("body-haloed / In the street-lamp night"), a star ("famous in another constellation"), and a god ("The god of stickball").
3. Babe Ruth was a great baseball player. Why was Joey "better than Babe Ruth"?
   Joey was better because the speaker could actually see him in person, whereas the speaker probably never saw Babe Ruth play.

Still   by Andrés Purificasion   *(p. 182)*

Preparation

Ask students what images the word *still* brings to mind. Many will suggest images involving peacefulness or the absence of movement. Make sure that they relate to the meaning of *still* as "up to now, even, or yet." (You may want students to look the word up in the dictionary to find several meanings.)

Vocabulary

revolutions (*n.*) — movements in a circular path or orbit
haunts (*v.*) — returns constantly to a person's mind, causing distress or longing

The Selection

Have students read the poem silently. Then have a student volunteer read it aloud. Ask students how the speaker feels about the "she" in the poem.

Follow-Up

Discuss the questions that accompany the poem.

Questions and Answers

1. Who is the "she" of the poem? *Accept any response that makes sense. The "she" must be someone the poet once knew and loved.*
2. "She" is not a ghost. What does the poet mean when he says, "And she still haunts me"? *What the poet means is that "she" keeps coming to mind, and that this upsets him, or makes him long for her.*

Medicine by Alice Walker *(p. 183)*

Preparation

Ask students to define the word *medicine (any drug used to relieve disease or pain).* Then extend the meaning beyond the preparations that come in containers from a pharmacy, and be sure students understand that medicine can include love, comfort, and care, as well.

Vocabulary

withered (*adj.*) — dried up; shriveled; having lost the freshness of youth

The Selection

Call attention to the shape of the poem. See if students can figure out what the shape might be.

   Have a student volunteer read the poem aloud. Or, you may read it first to the class.

Follow-Up

Discuss the questions that accompany the poem.

Questions and Answers

1. How is Grandma's long unbraided hair a kind of medicine for Grandpa? *Her presence is loving and supportive. She soothes Grandpa; and her hair gives him a sense of security.*
2. In what ways does the poem itself look like "long unbraided hair"? *It looks like the twisted locks when a braid is undone.*

Could Be   by Langston Hughes   *(p. 185)*

Preparation

Have students think about what sort of situations the expression *could be* suggests to them.

Vocabulary

pawned (*v.*) — gave something as security for a loan or a promise

The Selection

Have students read the poem silently. Then ask why they think the speaker mentions so many different streets and intersections. Ask what the speaker is feeling. Then have students volunteer to read the poem aloud with expression.

Follow-Up

Discuss the questions that accompany the poem.

Questions and Answers

1. What are some of the ways in which this poem is like a song? What effect do the rhymes and repetition have? *Answers will vary. The words are simple, and they build a single image, like a song. The rhythm is also like a song's rhythm. The rhymes and repetition help hold the poem together, and give the poem a sad mood.*
2. What does the speaker mean by saying, "When you pawned my watch / You pawned my heart"? *The watch is a symbol. When the person to whom the poem is addressed was willing to part with the watch for money, it was as if love was being abandoned, too.*

Butterfly   by Donald James Solomon (student)   *(p. 186)*

Preparation

Ask students what qualities a butterfly has, and if or how they might compare a butterfly to love.

Vocabulary

plucked (*v.*) — pulled off or out

The Selection

Tell the class that the poem they are about to read was written by a student. Have students read the poem silently and then have a volunteer read it aloud. You might wish to have them read the first three lines and stop for a brief discussion before they even look at the ending.

Follow-Up

Discuss the questions that accompany the poem. If you had the students compare love to a butterfly before reading the poem, ask if they have anything to add or change now that they have read the poem.

Questions and Answers

1. In this poem love is compared to a butterfly. What do the two have in common? *Answers include beauty, frailty, development, and the ability to take flight.*
2. What type of poem do you expect from reading the first three lines? But then what happens? Does the contrast make the ending seem even harsher? *The first three lines suggest a person's love for someone that is beautiful and tender. However, the loved one treats the lover cruelly. The contrast does make the ending seem harsher, because one person is hurting another.*

A Red, Red Rose by Robert Burns *(p. 187)*

Preparation

Tell students that the poem they are about to read is one of the most famous love poems ever written. To introduce the poem, ask a volunteer to read Question 1 at the bottom of the page.

Vocabulary

luve (*n.*) — love
bonie (*adj.*) — beautiful
a' (*adj.*) — all
gang (*v.*) — go
weel (*adv.*) — well

The Selection

To help students understand the pronunciation and meaning of the unfamiliar words in this selection, read the poem to the class. Then ask volunteers to read each stanza.

Follow-Up

Discuss the questions that accompany the poem.

Questions and Answers

1. Robert Burns lived in the 18th century in Scotland. He wrote in the Scottish dialect of that time. In this poem, *luve* means love; *bonie:* beautiful; *a':* all; *gang:* go; and *weel:* well. *Call students' attention to each of these words in the context of the poem. Have them identify any other examples of dialect they can find.*

2. In stanzas 1 and 2, to what does Robert Burns compare his love? *In the first stanza, the poet uses two similes. He compares his love to a red, red rose (suggesting richness, and great intensity)—and to a sweetly played melody. In the second stanza he compares the depth of his love to the fairness of the person he loves.*

3. In stanzas 3 and 4, Robert Burns declares that his love will last. How does he make this point? *He describes the lasting quality of his love by saying he will love his beloved until the seas go dry and the sun melts the rocks. The lasting quality of the love is further suggested by the references to "sands o' life," which—if there were an hourglass with capacity for a lifetime—would run very slowly and last a long time. The poet says that his love will last as long as he lives, and that he will return to her even if the distance is ten thousand miles (which, in the time before air travel, was a very long way).*

Starting at Dawn

by Sun Yün-feng (translated by Kenneth Rexroth & Ling Chung)   *(p. 188)*

Preparation

Tell students that the brief poem they are about to read packs vivid imagery into very few words. Have them concentrate on seeing, hearing, and feeling the scene the poet creates.

Vocabulary

waning (*adj.*) — becoming weaker or less bright; fading

The Selection

Have students read the poem silently. Then have a volunteer read it aloud. Tell students to close their eyes as they listen and to try to visualize the scene in their minds.

Follow-Up

Discuss the questions that accompany the poem.

Questions and Answers

1. In what season does this poem take place? What details tell you this? *The poem takes place in autumn. Details include frost and yellow leaves.*

2. What is the overall mood of the poem? Does it seem sad or cheerful? What are the phrases that create the mood? *Answers will vary. The mood is calm and relaxing. It is also expectant, because the new day represents a new start. Phrases that create the mood include "In the dawn," "As the sun rises," and the last three lines of the poem.*

Player Piano   by John Updike   *(p. 189)*

Preparation

Before students read the poem, make sure that they know what a player piano is. You might wish to have them read question 1 at the bottom of the page. It contains a brief description of a player piano.

Vocabulary

snicker (*n.*) — disrespectful laugh
melodies (*n.*) — tunes
abandon (*n.*) — complete giving over of oneself to feeling or impulse
*****caper** (v.) — leap or skip about in a lively way
dint (*n.*) — force or power

*Glossary word

The Selection

Have students read the poem silently. Tell them to concentrate on using the words to figure out what a player piano looks like, and what it sounds like.

Then read the poem aloud to students. Make the rhythm and tone of your reading suggest a player piano. Finally, have students volunteer to read the poem to the class.

Follow-Up

If you have any recordings of music played on a player piano (or a picture of one) you might wish to share this with the class. Then, discuss the questions that accompany the poem.

Questions and Answers

1. A player piano is a mechanical instrument. A paper roll with holes in it makes the keys move as if someone were playing the instrument. What lines describe how a player piano works? Which words and lines suggest the *sounds* a player piano makes? *Lines 1–8 describe how a player piano works. Lines 9 and 10 describe its sounds — "jumble of rumbles" and "light like the moon." Students should recognize that the whole poem sounds like the player piano's tune.*
2. Who is the speaker of this poem? What words or phrases make the piano seem almost human? *The piano is the speaker. Accept any evidence of the piano's humanity that can be supported with words or phrases from the poem. Answers include the use of the pronouns* I, me, mine; *the verb* pluck; *and the adjective* light-footed.
3. This poem rhymes. But not just at the end of the lines. "My paper can caper" is an example. What are some others? *Virtually every line contains a rhyme of some sort within it. Accept any correct examples students can find.*

The Earth's a Baked Apple

by Michael Colgrass   *(p. 190)*

Preparation

Ask if students have ever made baked apples. Have them describe the process.

Vocabulary

patience (*n.*) — willingness to wait, or to put up with difficulties

The Selection

Let students read the poem at least once silently. Then have a student volunteer read it aloud.

Follow-Up

Discuss the questions that accompany the poem.

Questions and Answers

1. Why does the speaker call the earth a "baked apple"? What mental pictures does this image make you see? *The speaker calls the earth a "baked apple" because it is round, beautiful, and can feed people. Students' mental images will vary.*
2. Why does the speaker suggest adding patience and letting the earth cool? Who are the 3½ billion to be served? *The speaker is saying we must not use up or destroy the earth. The 3½ billion are the people on the earth.*

Follow-Up

See p. 7, Teaching Reading Comprehension and For Discussion.

Reading Comprehension

1. Hector the Collector collected   *c. things no one else wanted* (page 179).
2. In "Of Kings and Things," Joey was a "king" of   *a. stickball* (page 181).
3. Two images of love that are used in the poems are   *b. a butterfly and a red rose* (pages 186 and 187).
4. In "The Earth's a Baked Apple," the poet suggests that people learn to   *b. be patient* (page 190).

For Discussion

1. Which poems in this group were the most fun to read? Why? *Answers will vary.*
2. Which of the poets wrote about love? What are some of the different opinions they expressed about love? *Love need not be mentioned directly. Hector the Collector loved his collection, although no one else saw it as he did. In "Medicine,"*

Grandma's love for Grandpa soothes his pain. In "Still," love is a haunting memory, and in "Could Be" it is a sad memory. "Butterfly" expresses the fragility of love, and "A Red, Red Rose" shows the deep joy of love.

3. Which image in these poems stands out most in your mind? Explain your answer. *Answers will vary.*

Understanding Literature: Images, Similes, and Metaphors

Objective: Students will identify similes and metaphors.

Preparation

Discuss the concept of imagery. (The three terms appear in the Handbook of Terms in Literature). Explain that a writer uses *images* to appeal to the reader's senses. Images make a reader see, hear, smell, feel, or taste in his or her mind what the writer describes.

Have students read the lesson on Images, Similes, and Metaphors on p. 192 in the Anthology. Then have them complete the exercise that follows.

Questions and Answers

1. "The memory is gray, like an October New York City day." *simile*
2. "O, my luve is like the melodie, / That's sweetly play'd in tune." *simile*
3. "The earth's a baked apple" *metaphor*
4. "At times I'm a jumble of rumbles" *metaphor*

Writing

Create your own images. Write similes for 1–3 and metaphors for 4–6.

1. a winter storm
2. a kitten's fur
3. a sunny day
4. happiness
5. fear
6. love

Have the class discuss different images for the items listed, or provide additional items before students begin to write. To get them started (and to clarify the difference between metaphor and simile), you might wish to write on the board: "A winter storm is like _____." "Happiness is _____."

Message Poems

Explain that a poet may sometimes use a poem to communicate a message or to influence readers on a particular issue or topic. Poems that do this are sometimes called message or persuasive poems.

As students read each of the poems in this section, they should pay careful attention to the message the poet is trying to communicate.

Thief by Tom Whitecloud *(p. 193)*

Preparation

Have students identify the poet as a Native American. Then ask them to think about the meaning of the poem's title.

Vocabulary

*__diplomats__ (*n.*) — those who deal tactfully and skillfully with others
__democrats__ (*n.*) — those who believe in democracy and social equality for all

*Glossary word

The Selection

Have students read the poem silently once, and then have a volunteer reader for each stanza.

Follow-Up

Discuss the questions that accompany the poem.

Questions and Answers

1. Who are the "we" of this poem? Who are the "you"? What happened between "we" and "you"? *The "we" are Native Americans who lived in North America long before European settlers came. The "you" are the white people who came to America and took over the land.*
2. According to the poem, how do Native Americans feel about nature and the land? What does the speaker mean by "You live on it; not with it"? *Land is extremely important to many Native Americans, whose lives are often intertwined with nature. They live with the land—that is, they are part of it. They live in harmony with it. The speaker feels that white persons live on the land but not as a part of nature.*

A Work of Artifice by Marge Piercy *(p. 195)*

Preparation

Ask students if they know what the expression "a work of art" means. Then read the title of this poem to them. Tell them that an artifice is a clever trick. It is unrelated to art, although the title is a play on words.

Explain that a bonsai tree is grown in a pot and is deliberately dwarfed by pruning, pinching of the roots, and wiring that makes it grow in a certain way.

Vocabulary

*artifice (*n.*) — clever trick
bonsai tree (*n.*) — tree grown in a pot and dwarfed by pruning and other techniques
pruned (*v.*) — trimmed a tree or a shrub
croons (*v.*) — sings in a soft, low voice

*Glossary word

The Selection

Have students read the poem silently. Then have a volunteer read it aloud to the class.

As the poem is being read, discuss each point the poet is making. Ask students to comment on whether or not they think a tree should be left to grow naturally. Ask what they think the tree could have become without the pruning.

Follow-Up

Discuss the questions that accompany the poem. Ask if students think the poet's comparison of the bonsai tree and women is a valid one.

Questions and Answers

1. What is a bonsai tree? What special care does it require? *A bonsai tree is planted in a pot, pruned and dwarfed by having its roots pinched. It grows less than a foot high. It is often wired to grow in a particular shape. Without continuous pruning and attention, it will grow like a normal tree.*
2. Why does the speaker feel women are like bonsai trees? According to the poet, what special care do women receive? Why? *The speaker says that women are trained to have certain characteristics, just as a bonsai tree. Women have their growth dwarfed early, by bound feet, lack of encouragement in using their minds, training their hair to look a certain way using curlers, or keeping their hands soft.*
3. What is the mood of the poem? Sad? Happy? Angry? Calm? How do you know? *Answers will vary. Encourage students to discuss reasons for their interpretations.*

Telephone Conversation by Susan Keady *(p. 196)*

Preparation

Ask students if there are things they would be willing to tell someone on the telephone that they might not say in person. Ask how talking with someone on the telephone differs from talking face to face. Tell them that the poem they are about to read contains a message from the poet about communication with another person.

Vocabulary

*anonymity (*n.*) — namelessness

confide (*v.*) — tell secrets to
awkward (*adj.*) — clumsy; troublesome or difficult
vulnerability (*n.*) — state of being easy to hurt

The Selection

The poem contains some words that are difficult to pronounce. It might be best for you to read it aloud once before students take a turn.

Follow-Up

Discuss the questions that accompany the poem. Ask students if they have ever personally experienced what the poet is describing. Ask what message they think the poet is trying to tell the readers about life.

Questions and Answers

1. How does a telephone help bring people together? How does it keep them apart at the same time? Why does the speaker call a phone "armor"? *A telephone can connect people, by voice, who are thousands of miles apart. However, the people involved cannot see each other's expressions, which often show real feelings. A telephone is armor because it protects people from the hurt or ridicule that they expect in a face-to-face conversation.*

2. Do you think there are some things that people should only tell each other face to face? Why or why not? *Opinions will vary.*

Where the Rainbow Ends by Richard Rive *(p. 197)*

Preparation

Ask students what they would expect to find at the end of a rainbow. Most will suggest a pot of gold. Explain that what Richard Rive sees at the end of the rainbow is a very special place. Have them read the poem to find out what this place is.

The Selection

First, have students read the poem silently. Then have a student volunteer read it aloud. The poem can be read chorally if you wish.

Follow-Up

Discuss the questions that accompany the poem. Ask students why they think the poet uses the image of the rainbow's end as a setting for his hopes.

Questions and Answers

1. The writer of this poem comes from South Africa where there is strict separation

between white and black people. How does the speaker feel about this separation? *The speaker feels that the separation is wrong and that it will someday be over. He realizes that it will be difficult for blacks and whites to work together, but he sees the value in the effort.*

2. Who is the speaker calling "brother"? *He is addressing the poem to whites, whom he refers to as "brother."*

3. Why is the song "sad"? According to the speaker, what could make the song a happier one? *The song is "sad" because blacks and whites in South Africa don't know how to work together. The song will be happier when they learn.*

Memo to the 21st Century

by Philip Appleman   *(p. 198)*

Preparation

Ask students to read the title of the poem. Make sure that they understand what a memo is. Ask what they would tell the people of the 21st century if they could prepare a message for them.

Vocabulary

marigolds (*n.*) — bright yellow flowers
phlox (*n.*) — tall plants with clusters of white or pink flowers
diesels (*n.*) — large machines (trucks or tractors) powered by diesel fuel

The Selection

Have students read the first stanza and try to picture just what it was like in Indiana as the poem tells about it. Discuss the scene before going on. Compare it to where the students live.

Then have students read the second stanza, which continues in the same vein. Have them read the last stanza and discuss how the image changes.

Follow-Up

Discuss the questions that accompany the poem. Ask students if they think the poem's message applies to places other than Indiana.

Questions and Answers

1. A *memo* is a note or reminder. What is the memo reminding the 21st century of? Did the poet really write the message for the people of the future, or for the people of today? *The memo is reminding the 21st century of what it used to be like when there still were fertile places for things to grow. But the poet's message is really for the people of today.*

2. Is the picture the poet paints of Indiana something that you are familiar with? Is it anything like where you live? *Answers will vary.*
3. Does the poet believe there is hope for the 21st century? Does he think it will ever again be the way it once was in Indiana? *The poet believes there is hope for the people of the 21st century. He is speaking to them, and if people hear him and search for the earth, they will find it.*

Do Not Go Gentle Into That Good Night

by Dylan Thomas   *(p. 200)*

Preparation

Tell students that this poem is the poet's message to someone very dear at a very special point in that person's life. Have them keep this in mind as they read the poem.

Vocabulary

rave (*v.*) — make a furious disturbance
frail (*adj.*) — weak; not strong
grieved (*v.*) — felt deep sadness
meteors (*n.*) — shooting stars

The Selection

Discuss the title of the poem and ask students what they think it means to "go gentle." Tell them that the expression "that good night" has a special meaning in this poem and that they will have to find out what the poet means by these words in order to understand the poem. Have a volunteer read each stanza aloud.

If you wish, you might call attention to the poem's form. It is a *villanelle*, which is a poem of fixed form made up of tercets (three-line stanzas) and a final quatrain. There are usually five tercets. The entire poem is based on two rhymes.

A villanelle is a comparatively easy form for student writing.

Follow-Up

Discuss the questions that accompany the poem. Ask students whether or not they agree with the poet's views on death.

Questions and Answers

1. What is "that good night" another name for? What does "rage against the dying light" mean? Does the poet think we should give in to death? *"That good night" means death. "Rage against the dying light" means to fight for life. The poet does not feel we should give in to death. He believes that death should be fought hard—raged against.*

2. To whom is the speaker addressing the poem? How do you think he feels about that person? *He is addressing his dying father and asking him to fight for life. He loves his father and does not want him to be resigned to death.*

Follow-Up

See p. 7, Teaching Reading Comprehension and For Discussion.

Reading Comprehension

1. In "Thief," the speaker says the white man has stolen the Native Americans' *c. land and future hopes.* (Page 193, lines 10, 16–17: "You took the land"; "Why did you steal the smiles / From our children?")
2. The speaker in "Where the Rainbow Ends" hopes to persuade people to *c. live together peacefully* (page 197).
3. In "Memo to the 21st Century," the speaker believes that someday there will be no *a. fertile soil.* (Page 198, lines 33–34: "Listen: / in Indiana once, things grew in it.")
4. A message of the poem by Dylan Thomas is that people should *b. fight against death* (page 200).

For Discussion

1. Why are the poets of "Thief" and "A Work of Artifice" angry? How are they being sarcastic in their poems? *These poets are angry because each is a member of a group that has been wronged by others. The author of "Thief" is a Native American; he is angry because his land and his children's future have been taken away. The author of "A Work of Artifice" is a woman; she is angry because women have been controlled and kept in their carefully arranged place. Accept examples of sarcasm that students can identify and explain. For example, "how lucky, little tree, / to have a pot to grow in."*
2. According to Susan Keady, why do many people confide things on the phone rather than in person? *The distance and the anonymity make it easier to confide and makes people feel less vulnerable.*

Understanding Literature: Symbols and Mood

Objective: Students will identify a mood with passages from poems.

Preparation

Have students read the lesson on Symbols and Mood on p. 201 in the Anthology. Discuss the poet's use of symbols to create mood. Have students supply examples of symbols in the poems they have read. Then have them complete the exercise.

Questions and Answers

1. "Why did you steal the smiles / From our children?" *guilty*
2. "The bonsai tree . . . / could have grown eighty feet tall. . . . But a gardener carefully pruned it." *sad*

3. "There's only music, brother, / And it's music we're going to sing / Where the rainbow ends." *happy*
4. "and I think of you, the billions of you, wrapped / in your twenty-first century concrete," *worried*
5. "Rage, rage against the dying of the light." *angry*

Writing

Think of an issue that you feel strongly about. Write a short poem to persuade others to feel the way you do about the issue. Think about a mood you would like to create. Try to use a symbol in your poem that will help to create the mood.

Have students discuss possible topics for the writing assignment. Encourage students to select issues that really matter to them. Then have each student identify a symbol that will communicate a message about that issue. Reassure students that a poem need not be long to have a message.

Found Poems and Concrete Poems

Make sure that students understand that *found poetry* is just what the name suggests. It is poetry that is found in words and phrases the poet happens to see.

Concrete poetry, on the other hand, involves arranging the words and lines so that they make a visual picture that is important to understanding the poem.

Right of Way by Marjorie Burns (p. 202)

Preparation

Ask what the expression "right of way" means. Then ask students where and when they last heard those words.

The Selection

Ask students to think about where the poet found the words she arranged to make this poem. Call their attention to the double line down the middle of the poem.

Follow-Up

Discuss the questions that accompany the poem.

Questions and Answers

1. A *found poem* is made up of lines or phrases the poet has found written or printed

somewhere. Where do you think the poet found the words for this poem? *The poet found these words on street signs.*

2. Why has the poet drawn two parallel lines down the middle of "Right of Way"? *The lines could represent the double line often found in the middle of a road. Or, they could represent the street itself.*

Food Processor by Marjorie Burns *(p. 204)*

Preparation

Ask students if they have ever seen or used a food processor. (Many will have seen one in ads, if not the real thing.) Ask what different things a food processor can do.

Vocabulary

mince *(v.)* — cut into very small pieces
puree *(v.)* — make into a soft mass

The Selection

Have students read the found poem silently. Then have a student volunteer read it aloud. Suggest that the student try to read the words in a rhythm that suggests the action of the appliance.

Follow-Up

Have students discuss the questions that accompany the poem.

Questions and Answers

1. Where do you think the poet found the words for this poem? *On the directions or packaging of a food processor, or on the controls for the machine.*
2. What effect does the repetition of words have in creating a mood? *The repetition suggests the mechanical action of a food processor.*

Urban Landscape by Spike St. Croix *(p. 205)*

Preparation

Remind students that a concrete poem makes its point in the shape and arrangement of the words. Then ask students what they think the words "urban landscape" mean.

The Selection

Have students look at the urban landscape in this concrete poem. Ask them what they see. Point out that the words are shaped to look like the objects they name.

Follow-Up

Discuss the questions that accompany the poem.

Questions and Answers

1. This poem presents a picture of a city. Is the single flower too important in the picture? Why do you think the poet made it appear so large and important in the picture? *Answers will vary. Accept any interpretations that students can support.*
2. What are some other details of the view of a city that could have been included? *Answers will vary.*

Tribute to Henry Ford—3

by Richard Kostelanetz   *(p. 206)*

Preparation

Before having students interpret the concrete poem "Tribute to Henry Ford—3," make sure that they know who Henry Ford was.

The Selection

Have students look at this concrete poem and pretend that they are up in an airplane looking down at something. Ask them to describe what they see.

Follow-Up

Have students discuss the questions that follow the poem.

Questions and Answers

1. What do the letters in this poem symbolize? Clue: Two of the early cars designed by Henry Ford were the Model T and the Model A. *The letters in this poem symbolize cars.*
2. Why are the letters arranged the way they are in the poem? What is the poet trying to show about American society from Henry Ford's time to our own time? *The letters are arranged in a cloverleaf traffic pattern in what appears to be bumper-to-bumper traffic. The poet is commenting on the strong influence the automobile has had on American society. Interpretations will vary.*

Follow-Up

See p. 7, Teaching Reading Comprehension and For Discussion.

Reading Comprehension

1. The poem "Food Processor" describes   *c. the different functions of a food processor* (page 204).
2. Marjorie Burns found the words she used in "Right of Way"   *b. on street signs* (page 202).
3. In "Tribute to Henry Ford—3," the poet describes   *b. the importance of cars today* (page 206).
4. In "Urban Landscape," the cloud over the flower means that   *b. it's hard to grow flowers in the city* (page 205).

For Discussion

1. Which of the visual and found poems did you enjoy the most? Why? *Answers will vary.*
2. Do you think that concrete and found poems are "true" poems? Do they present intense feelings the way other kinds of poems do? *Accept responses students can support.*

Understanding Literature: Physical Symbols

Objective: Students will interpret symbols in concrete poems.

Preparation

Have students read and discuss the brief lesson on Physical Symbols on p. 207. It reminds them that the shape and way the words are physically arranged on a page is an important part of found or concrete poetry.

Questions and Answers

1. Two of the poets use physical symbols related to   *b. highways* ("Right of Way," page 202; and "Tribute to Henry Ford—3," page 206).
2. The double line in "Right of Way" symbolizes how road signs   *c. control people* (page 202).
3. Richard Kostelanetz uses a cloverleaf pattern to symbolize   *a. the confusion of traffic on many roads today* (page 206).

Writing

Think of something from everyday life. Then create your own concrete poem. Arrange the words on the page to make a physical symbol. The shape of the poem should illustrate what you are saying in the poem.

Some students may wish to discuss briefly the topic or the arrangement they are going to use before beginning to construct a concrete poem.

Section Review

Vocabulary: Denotation and Connotation

Objective: Students will write the connotation of words used in the poems.

Preparation

Discuss *denotation* and *connotation*. (These terms appear in the Handbook of Terms in Literature.) Make sure students understand that the dictionary definition is the word's *denotation*. *Connotation* is the associated, extra meaning derived from the context or the feelings a reader has about the word.

Have students read and discuss the brief lesson on p. 208 in the Anthology. Answers to the questions will vary considerably.

Questions and Answers

scandals ("Ghosts," p. 173) *family arguments or events*
monster ("Frankenstein," p. 174) *outcast*
piano ("Last Day at the Job," p. 177) *music, pleasure*
constellation ("Of Kings and Things," p. 181) *group, world*
withered ("Medicine," p. 183) *aged, weak*
dreary ("Could Be," p. 185) *empty, lonely, bleak*
smiles ("Thief," p. 193) *happiness, hope*
pruned ("A Work of Artifice," p. 195) *controlled, stunted*
night ("Do Not Go Gentle Into That Good Night," p. 200) *death*

Reading: Figurative Language

Objective: Students will distinguish literal and figurative meanings.

Preparation

Discuss the difference between the literal meaning of a word or expression and its figurative meaning. (The term *figurative language* appears in the Handbook of Terms in Literature.) Have students supply examples of expressions with different literal and figurative meanings.

Then have students read and discuss the lesson on Figurative Language on p. 208 in the Anthology. Have them complete the exercise.

Questions and Answers

1. The young girl blossomed into a beautiful young woman. *Literal: grew, developed, or became; figurative: grew like a flower.*
2. The building decayed during the ebb and flow of time. *Literal: during the passage, or movement, of time; figurative: as time moved like the tide.*

For the second part of this exercise, accept any interpretation of each expression that makes sense. Suggestions follow.

1. road has another hand   *the road branches off; there is a side road*
2. palm out   *stretching out*
3. caresses a forest floor   *goes through a forest*
4. rain sounds are violet voices   *rain sounds are gentle*

Quiz

See p. 7, Administering the Quiz.

Reading Comprehension

1. In "Frankenstein," the monster goes into an old man's house to find safety. What else does he find there? *He finds friendship and companionship as well as safety.*
2. Why has the mother in "Last Day at the Job" decided to retire? *She has decided to retire so that she will have time to do the things she has always wanted to do.*
3. In "Of Kings and Things," what does the poet remember about Joey? What does she wonder about him? *The poet remembers how Joey played stickball, how wonderful he was to watch, and how he looked. She wonders what he is doing now—if he is married and has children, and if he has a good job.*
4. Why is the speaker in "Thief" angry? At whom is he angry? *The speaker in "Thief" is angry because the white men took the land and future hopes from his children.*
5. What is the "half a mile of copper wire" in "Telephone Conversation"? *The "half a mile of copper wire" is the wire between two telephones. It "protects" the people in the poem by allowing them to exchange words without the intimacy of contact.*

Understanding Literature

6. In "Don't Take Your Guns to Town," what do Billy's guns symbolize to his mother? *To his mother they symbolize trouble.*
7. Find one metaphor and one simile in the lyric poems in this section. What is being compared in each one? *Answers will vary.*
8. What technique is used in "Player Piano" to help readers "hear" how a player piano sounds? *The rhythm and rhyme of "Player Piano" help readers "hear" what a player piano sounds like.*
9. In "A Work of Artifice," how is a bonsai tree used to describe the way society treats many women? *A bonsai tree is artificially stunted, pruned, and pinched to assure that it stays small enough to grow in a pot. The poem uses this image to show the way society limits the potential of many women.*
10. What is a "found poem"? How do writers create found poems? *A found poem uses words or phrases that are printed or written elsewhere. The poet finds and presents them poetically.*

Composition

1. Write the words to a song that you know. Decide whether the words make a good poem. Do the words tell a story? Did the songwriter use special images or symbols? Change some of the words or write some of the lines differently to create your own song/poem.

   Suggest that students bring in the words of a song rather than attempt to write one from memory. Students can make their changes in the song as they rewrite it.

2. Choose a story you have read or a movie you have seen. Try to develop its plot and characters into a short narrative poem.

   Some students will find it easier to do this assignment if they list the events of the story plot before trying to put these events into the form of a poem. Suggest that students identify five or six main events rather than focusing on small details.

3. Think of someone you know well and would like to describe in a poem. Write your own lyric poem about the person. You might like to use the letters of the person's name as the first letter of each line in the poem. For example:

   > TONY
   > Taking the time
   > Out of your day
   > Never a frown from
   > You.

   This type of poem is popular among young people, and it's likely that many of your students will be experienced in writing such a poem. Suggest that each student choose the person about whom he or she will write and then write that person's name, one letter on each line, down the margin of a sheet of lined paper. Point out that it is not necessary to compose the lines of the poem in order, as long as it all makes sense when it is done.

4. Think of how a certain musical instrument or machine sounds. Then read the poem "Player Piano" again. Write a short poem and try to use words that sound like the instrument or machine you are writing about.

   If you wish, students can demonstrate how different instruments sound before attempting to write the assignment. Some students may bring in cassettes or records, while others may be able to bring in instruments such as guitars or horns.

5. Find an ad or short article in a newspaper or magazine. Develop some of the words into a found poem that gives readers a new view of the product or the subject of the article.

   Potential found poems are everywhere. This assignment is best done over a period of several days or a week. Have students begin looking about them for material.

Enrichment

1. Students who liked the Dylan Thomas poem might enjoy hearing recordings of the poet reciting his own poetry. Several collections of Dylan Thomas presenting his own works can be found on records and cassettes from Caedmon Records.

2. Country and folk music contain many narrative poems set to music. Invite students to bring in some of their own or the library's records and tapes to share with the class.

Authors

Philip Appleman. Philip Appleman was born in Indiana in 1926. A writer of poems, novels, and a critical anthology on Darwin, his works include *Kites on a Windy Day* (poems) and *In the Twelfth Year of the War* (novel). In his writing he explores social and scientific issues, such as the world population crisis and the theory of evolution. He serves on many national teachers councils and has won awards for his poetry.

Robert Burns. Robert Burns was born January 25, 1759, in Alloway, Scotland. As a boy, he learned countless numbers of his country's traditional songs and ballads by heart. He was a peasant and a peasant poet, and these simple yet profound songs formed the basis for all his best poetry. His attempts to write in polite English failed, and he remains the great poet of Scottish dialect. His best-known single volume is *Poems Chiefly in the Scottish Dialect* (1786). He died in 1796.

Johnny Cash. John R. Cash, part Cherokee Indian, was born on February 26, 1932, in a sharecropper's shack in Kingsland, Arkansas. A singer, guitarist, and songwriter, he began his career in the 1950's recording country and gospel music to his own accompaniment and touring with various groups. His hit songs from that decade include "I Walk the Line," "Folsom Prison Blues" and "Don't Take Your Guns to Town." His music continued to be very popular in the 1960's and 1970's, and he is still one of the best known American country music performers.

Edward Field. Edward Field was born on June 7, 1924, in Brooklyn, New York. He began writing poetry while he was in the Army during World War II. In 1962 he won the Lamont Award from the Academy of American Poets for his collection of poems *Stand Up, Friend, With Me*. This recognition brought him a Guggenheim Fellowship the following year. He has also received the Shelley Memorial Award of the Poetry Society of America. His other books include *Variety Photoplays* and *Eskimo Songs and Stories*.

Langston Hughes. Langston Hughes was born on February 1, 1902, in Joplin, Missouri. He moved to New York City as a young man. A prodigious writer, his works include novels, poems, short stories, biographies, translations, juvenile fiction, and drama; he also wrote songs, articles, and speeches. Hughes is considered by many to be one of America's greatest poets. His poems have been translated into French, Spanish, German, Yiddish, Czech, and Russian, and many have been set to music. Among his collections of poems are *The Dream Keeper, Shakespeare in Harlem, Freedom's Plow,* and *Ask Your Mama*. He died in 1967.

Richard Kostelanetz. Richard Kostelanetz was born on June 12, 1940, in New York. He studied in London and received degrees from Brown and Columbia Universities. A prolific writer, his poems, fiction, and critical essays have been published as books and included in numerous anthologies and periodicals. Among his books are *Visual Language, The Theatre of Mixed Means,* and *Metamorphosis in the Arts.*

Lillian Morrison. Lillian Morrison was born in New Jersey on October 27, 1917. She writes poetry and for many years has maintained a career as a librarian at the New York Public Library. She has written several books of poems and contributed her poems to many major magazines. In addition, she is the editor of a series of books on world poetry. Among her other books are *Sprints and Distances* and *Touch Blue*.

Marge Piercy. Born March 31, 1936, in Detroit, Michigan, Piercy won two writing awards from the University of Michigan before embarking upon a career as a poet and novelist. She is noted as an "activist" writer, strongly involved in the feminist movement. Collections of her poetry include *Hard Loving* (1969) and *Living in the Open* (1976). Her fiction includes *Woman on the Edge of Time* (1976) and *The High Cost of Living* (1978).

Richard Rive. Richard Rive was born on March 1, 1931, in Cape Town, South Africa. His books include *African Songs* (a collection of short stories) and *Emergency* (a novel); he has also compiled a book of African prose. A former South African hurdling champion, he coaches track and teaches English and Latin at the high school level in Cape Town. His other interests include mountain climbing and spearfishing.

Dylan Thomas. Dylan Thomas was born in Carmarthenshire, Wales, on October 27, 1914. His poetry, which first appeared in print in 1938, is most notable for its strength and variety of vocabulary and for its emphasis on the power of feeling. Thomas died in New York City in 1953 while on a speaking tour of the United States. His poetry publications include *Deaths and Entrances* (1946) and *In Country Sleep and Other Poems* (1952). He is perhaps most popularly known for his dramatized poem *Under Milk Wood*, which was completed one month before his death.

John Updike. Born March 18, 1932, in Shillington, Pa., John Updike attended Harvard University and Ruskin School of Drawing and Fine Art in Oxford, England, before achieving success as a short-story writer, poet, critic, essayist, and author of children's books. Updike is noted for his stylistic ability to reconcile details of everyday life and philosophical ideas. He is best known for his "Rabbit" novels, *Rabbit Run* (1960), *Rabbit Redux* (1971), and *Rabbit Is Rich* (1981).

Alice Walker. Born February 9, 1944 in Eatonton, Georgia, Alice Walker has achieved equal success with both poetry and fiction. As a black writer and feminist, she has extended discussion of important social and political issues. Her best-known work includes the novels *The Third Life of Grange Copeland* (1970) and *Meridian* (1976), the volume of short stories *In Love and Trouble: Stories of Black Women* (1973), and the volume of poems *Goodnight Willie Lee, I'll See You in the Morning* (1979).

Section 6
Relationships

Section Focus

The theme of this section is relationships—sharing experiences with others. The stories, letter, account, and poems in this section cover a wide range of human relationships—the family, larger social groups, personal encounters, and loves. The importance of relationships to human existence is portrayed in many different ways.

Have students read and discuss the Introduction on pp. 212–213. Where possible and appropriate, encourage them to relate what they are reading to their personal experience.

This section focuses on helping students use their knowledge of main idea, characterization, and plot to understand the theme in each selection.

Very Special Shoes by Morley Callaghan *(p. 214)*

Synopsis

Mrs. Johnson is ill, and during the winter and spring the family waits for the doctor to tell them what is the matter. Mary, age 11, has been told that her mother has pains in her legs from varicose veins. All winter Mary has been dreaming about having a pair of red shoes she saw in a shop window. She gets paid for doing the housework, and finally she has enough to buy them.

When Mary asks if she can have the shoes, her mother tells her that her father is in debt and the shoes are not a wise purchase. Mary cries, and her mother agrees that she can get the shoes. Mary wears them to show her father, whose anger at the expense has been calmed by his wife. He agrees that they are fine shoes.

Before Mary gets a chance to wear her new red shoes, her mother is hospitalized. She dies during surgery for cancer. Mary's father has the shoes dyed black so that Mary can wear them to the funeral and to school. She wears them every day and takes good care of them. The shoes bring her a secret joy.

Preparation

Ask students if they have ever wanted something very badly that they were unable to afford. Ask them if they ever managed to save up for something and buy it only to have things turn out in an unexpected way. Tell the class that the story they are about to read takes some unusual turns.

Vocabulary

*__varicose__ (*adj.*) — enlarged or swollen
*__anaesthetic__ (*n.*) — drug to deaden sensations or promote sleep
*__console__ (*v.*) — give comfort to
__outraged__ (*adj.*) — extremely upset or angry

*Glossary word

Activities

A. See p. 6, Teaching Vocabulary.
B. Ask students what an *anaesthetic* is used for.
C. Have students give examples of their personal experience of being *outraged*.
D. Have students suggest ways in which a person could be *consoled*.

Quick Quiz

1. varicose: a. stubborn   b. not far away   *c. enlarged*
2. anaesthetic: *a. drug used before an operation*   b. drug used after an operation   c. the study of pain
3. console: a. bring close   *b. comfort*   c. stay with
4. outraged: *a. very upset or angry*   b. completely defeated   c. canceled

113

Setting the Purpose

Direct students to the title "Very Special Shoes," and explain to them that a special pair of shoes are a symbol to Mary, a child in this story. Have them read the story to find out why.

The Selection

This is a very short story that can easily be read by most students in one session. You may wish to break for a brief discussion in the middle.

Have a student volunteer read the headnote aloud. Then have the class read the story silently to find out why the pair of shoes was so special to Mary and why she would never forget them. If you wish, have students stop at the bottom of p. 217 of the Anthology and ask what they think is going to happen next. Then have them go on.

Have students finish the story. Then have them complete Reading Comprehension on p. 219 in the Anthology.

Follow-Up

See p. 7, Teaching Reading Comprehension and For Discussion.

Reading Comprehension

1. Even though Mary was only 11, she did the housework because her mother was *b. too sick* (page 214, col. 1).
2. After her mother said she could not buy the red shoes, Mary   *c. ran into her room and cried* (page 215, col. 2).
3. Mary's family wanted her to change the color of her shoes because   *a. red was not right at a funeral* (page 218).
4. Mary didn't mind changing the color of her new shoes because   *c. they still meant the same to her.* (Page 218, col. 2: "They were no longer the beautiful red shoes. Yet she stared at them and felt a strange kind of secret joy. She felt certain that her mother had gotten her the shoes so she might understand at this time that she still had her special blessing and protection.")

For Discussion

1. Why do you think Mary's father changed his mind about letting her keep the shoes? What do you think her mother had said to him? *Mary's mother knew she was dying and probably told her husband that she wanted Mary to have the shoes (page 217).*
2. Even when the shoes were no longer red, they were special to Mary. Why? What did they represent to her? *The shoes were special because they reminded Mary of her mother. They represented love and protection. The color wasn't important.*

Understanding Literature: Theme

Objective: Students will identify the meaning of symbols and the theme in a short story.

Preparation

Discuss the concept of *theme* with the students. Be sure that they understand theme to be the author's central thought or message. Point out that the theme is often implied.

Explain that an author may use a symbol to help develop the theme in a story. A symbol is something that has a larger meaning than the thing itself.

Then have students read and discuss the lesson on Theme on p. 219 of the Anthology. Have them complete the exercise by writing those things they believe the red shoes symbolize.

Questions and Answers

Possible answers for the first part are: *b. a promise that must not be broken;   c. Mary's mother's love and protection;* and   *d. the death of Mary's mother.*

The best choice of theme is, *"The love between parents and children is developed through understanding and compromise." This best fits the story, although the other idea makes sense. Accept any explanation that students can support.*

Writing

Choose one theme from the pair above. Then outline the plot of a very short story that would convey this new theme. Include some information about the characters and the setting.

This assignment logically follows the discussion of the students' responses to the Understanding Literature exercise above. Have students discuss the choices of theme before starting to write.

Additional Writing

1. Have students pick an object in their lives that has become a symbol of something important. Tell them to briefly describe it and tell what it means to them.

   The object should be an inanimate object: a piece of clothing, a doll, a picture. Students should tell what they associate with the object—a certain time, place, or person—and why that association is so strong.
2. Have students imagine that Mary had had one last chance to speak to her mother before her mother died. What would Mary say? Have students write a brief dialogue for their last meeting.

   Students may wish to write a dialogue in which Mary tells her mother about the shoes, and her mother smiles and tells Mary her reasons for buying the shoes, reasons that Mary could only feel at the end of the selection.

Letter to a Black Boy   by Bob Teague   *(p. 220)*

Synopsis

This selection is a letter by Bob Teague to his infant son Adam. He begins by recounting the experience of caring for his son while mother goes shopping. The boy keeps looking for his mother. Teague says he understands, and goes on to tell about the only mother he knew—his Aunt Letty. When Teague's mother died in childbirth, Aunt Letty raised him as if he were her own. She taught him an important lesson about life—that it is important to dream and to make dreams come true. An incident makes this lesson vivid.

The adults of the entire family were gathered one Thanksgiving at Aunt Letty's invitation. Many of them had not seen each other for years. Aunt Letty inspired them to set up a college fund for the young members of the family. This experience greatly influenced Teague, who now describes it in a letter to his own son.

Preparation

Ask students if they think that it's important for a very young child to be given a sense of family. Tell them that the selection they are preparing to read shows how one father recorded some important family memories for his young son.

Vocabulary

*miffed (adj.) — put into a bad mood
*devised (v.) — planned
 squalling (adj.) — crying loudly
*kinship (n.) — family relationship
 resemblance (n.) — likeness
*reminiscing (v.) — recalling past experiences

*Glossary word

Activities

A. See p. 6, Teaching Vocabulary.
B. See if students can use the words *kinship, resemblance,* and *reminiscing* in the same sentence.
C. Ask students what sort of a selection would contain the words on this list.

Quick Quiz

1. miffed: a. smelled quietly   *b. put into a bad mood*   c. planned a party
2. devised: a. scouted   *b. planned*   c. overturned
3. squalling: a. upsetting   b. camping   *c. crying loudly*
4. kinship: *a. family relationship*   b. small rowboat   c. class for young children
5. resemblance: a. entertainment   b. fight against something   *c. likeness*
6. reminiscing: *a. recalling past experiences*   b. arguing with family members   c. covering all the bases

Setting the Purpose

Ask students what sorts of things they think a father might wish to communicate to his young son. Discuss their responses. Then have students read the headnote to the story on p. 220 in the Anthology.

116

The Selection

This selection is quite short and can be read all at one time. Or, if you prefer, divide it into two sections.

Have students read to the middle of col. 1, p. 222: "... she taught the entire family how to make a common dream come true." Before going on, have students comment briefly on what kind of a person Aunt Letty was. Ask them if they know anyone like that.

Have them complete the selection to find out what dream Aunt Letty helped make come true. When students have finished the selection, have them complete Reading Comprehension on p. 225 in the Anthology.

Follow-Up

See p. 7, Teaching Reading Comprehension and For Discussion.

Reading Comprehension

1. The author told his son about Aunt Letty to illustrate how   *a. mothers hold families together.*
2. Aunt Letty was able to bring the whole family together because   *b. she was the leader of the clan.*
3. The author described his aunts and uncles in such detail because   *b. he wanted his son to know all about the family.*
4. The "common dream" that Aunt Letty helped to come true was   *b. setting up a college fund for the younger members of the family (page 224, col. 2).*

For Discussion

1. The author told his son that mothers are very dependable. How does his story about Aunt Letty illustrate her dependability? *Aunt Letty dropped whatever she was doing in Detroit and came to raise the author from infancy to the age of 17 (pages 220, 222). She helped assure a college education for the young members of the entire family (page 224).*
2. What lessons did the author learn from Aunt Letty? *The most important lesson the author learned from Aunt Letty was to dream beyond his blackness—to look at the larger world outside of the ghetto (page 222, col. 1). He also learned how to make a common dream come true (page 222, col. 1), and probably dependability and patience (page 220, col. 2).*

Understanding Literature: Theme and Main Idea

Objective: Students will locate details to support main ideas related to the theme.

Preparation

Review the concept of a *main idea* supported by details in a paragraph. Tell students that an entire story or article can also have a main idea. This overall main idea or point is often called the *theme*.

Have students read and discuss the lesson on Theme and Main Idea on p. 225 of the Anthology. Then have them complete the exercise.

Questions and Answers

a. You are not owed anything in return for kindness. (Page 220, col. 2: "*Her reasoning, I gathered years later, was that to know might have given me a feeling of guilt. Or of being in her debt.*")

b. You must work hard to get what you want in life. (Page 222, col. 1: "*. . . that it is a world of different pains and pleasures, beauty and ugliness, victories and defeats that all people, everywhere, come to know.*")

c. Families should stick together. (Page 224, col. 2: "*But if we stick together as a family, we can send them all, one or two at a time [to college].*")

d. There are no limits to what you can do or become. (Page 222, col. 1: "*Years later, she taught the entire family how to make a common dream come true.*" Page 224, col. 2: "*I say Raymond ought to have his chance to follow his dream. I say that's what living is all about.*") *Statements of the story's theme will vary.*

Writing

Suppose you have a child of your own. Think about a lesson you learned from someone when you were younger. Write a letter to your child about this lesson, so the child can learn from it.

Encourage students to discuss their response to this assignment before beginning writing. Have each student identify the person he or she remembers and list two or three things to tell about the lesson learned.

Additional Writing

Have students imagine that they are ready to go to college, but that there is no money available to pay for their education. Ask them to write a paragraph telling what they would do and why.

Students may want to write this paragraph in the form of a list. They could relate what they would do first, then second, and so on, until they got the necessary money.

Celebration   by Alonzo Lopez   *(p. 226)*

The Selection

Ask a volunteer to read the poem to the class.

Follow-Up

Discuss the questions that accompany the poem.

Questions and Answers

1. What is the overall feeling of the poem? What words does the speaker use to help

you feel this mood? *The mood is one of excitement and anticipation. The words* dancing, feasting, laughter, talk, *and* games *suggest an exciting celebration.*

2. Why is dancing an important part of the celebration? What kinds of emotions can people show when they dance? *Dancing "with the others" adds to the feeling of being a part of the celebration. People can show a range of emotions when dancing: joy, sorrow, loneliness, excitement, and so on.*

The Troublemaker

from **All Things Wise and Wonderful by James Herriot**   *(p. 228)*

Synopsis

Wesley Binks is a 10-year-old boy who plays tricks and causes trouble. Veterinarian Herriot is one of Wesley's favorite targets. But one day the boy arrives at the animal hospital with Duke, a sick puppy. Dr. Herriot recognizes the problem as distemper, and realizes that there isn't much hope. But the boy is willing to do anything to help his pet. He delivers papers and takes odd jobs to make money for the dog's medical care. Wesley is extremely attached to Duke and the dog seems to take a turn for the better. Dr. Herriot knows, however, that this is only the calm before the storm.

The dog becomes much worse, and Wes asks Dr. Herriot to make a house call. It is necessary to put the dog out of his misery. Dr. Herriot observes that Wesley's home life is dreadful. He realizes that the dog has been the only positive influence on Wesley. After the dog dies, Wesley turns bad again. He doesn't stop at tricks, but turns to real crime and develops a terrible reputation as someone who cares for nothing. Only Dr. Herriot remembers him as someone who once cared greatly for a sick animal.

Preparation

Ask students if they think it's possible for someone who seems to be a troublemaker to care about something deeply enough to change their ways. Tell them that the story they are preparing to read shows that this can happen.

Vocabulary

mongrel (*n.*) — mixed-breed dog
*****distemper** (*n.*) — an often fatal disease of dogs or cats
neglected (*adj.*) — not well cared for
whimpered (*v.*) — cried softly
*****hybrid** (*adj.*) — mixed breed or type
*****vigor** (*n.*) — strength

*****Glossary word

Activities

A. See p. 6, Teaching Vocabulary.
B. Ask students which two words on the list could be used interchangeably. *mongrel and hybrid*
C. Have students give examples of what it might mean to be *neglected*.

Quick Quiz

1. mongrel: a. bit to eat   *b. mixed-breed dog*   c. small monkey
2. distemper: a. expression of anger   b. failure to trust someone   *c. often fatal disease of dogs*
3. neglected: a. interested   b. returned to its owner   *c. not taken care of*
4. whimpered: *a. cried softly*   b. screamed loudly   c. spoke sweetly
5. hybrid: a. expensive   *b. mixed type*   c. married
6. vigor: *a. strength*   b. bitterness   c. animal

Setting the Purpose

Ask students if they think someone labeled a troublemaker can mend his or her ways. Have them read the selection that follows to see what happened to one lad who had received such a label.

The Selection

Have students read to the top of p. 231, col. 1 in the Anthology (the sentence ending ". . . this was the time"). Ask whether they think the dog is going to get better and stay well. Ask them what they think will happen if he doesn't.

Have students finish the story. Ask them if they think Wesley Binks will ever find something or someone to love again. Then have them complete Reading Comprehension on p. 233 in the Anthology.

Follow-Up

See p. 7, Teaching Reading Comprehension and For Discussion.

Reading Comprehension

1. When Wesley was 10, he was already known as a troublemaker because he *a. played mean tricks on people* (page 228).
2. Dr. Herriot knew that Wesley's dog had distemper   *c. as soon as he saw Duke's eyes and nose.* (Page 229, col. 1: The dog's eyes were running and were sensitive to light. His nose was running.)
3. Dr. Herriot understood that Wesley was a   *b. troubled boy.* (Page 230, col. 1: "I saw how neglected he was.")
4. To pay for the doctor's services, Wesley   *c. took odd jobs* (page 231, col. 1).
5. When Duke began to tremble, they knew that he   *b. would die soon* (page 232, col. 1).
6. After Duke was put to sleep, Wesley   *c. began breaking the law.* (Page 233, col. 2: "He never played any more tricks on me. Instead, he started breaking the law.")

120

For Discussion

1. What are some of the feelings Wesley must have had about his home and family life? How do you think they contributed to his becoming a troublemaker? *Answers will vary. Students should realize that Wesley probably felt that no one loved him, and that there was no one for him to love. He may have been treating other people the way he had been treated at home.*
2. What did Wesley find in his relationship with Duke that was missing from the rest of his life? *The dog depended on him, gave him love and affection, and paid attention to him.*
3. How did Wesley prove that he could be a responsible person? Why did he change after Duke died? *He worked to earn money to pay for Duke's medical care. He gave Duke all the things his family didn't give him. When Duke died, no one seemed to need or care for Wesley. His purpose and reward for responsibility was gone. Accept additional explanations that make sense.*
4. This true account showed Dr. Herriot at work. What was he like? Did he seem to be a good doctor and a good person? Why? *Dr. Herriot showed compassion and understanding. Students may infer that he might even have treated Duke without pay. Until there was no hope, he did everything possible to treat the dog.*

Understanding Literature: Theme and Characterization

Objective: Students will make inferences about the theme based on characterization.

Preparation

Explain that the theme of a story may be revealed indirectly through the thoughts and actions of the characters. Then have students read and discuss the lesson on Theme and Characterization on p. 234 in the Anthology. Have them complete the exercise.

Questions and Answers

1. Wesley   *e. tried to change his way of life. Wesley tried to change because he was taking care of his beloved dog, Duke.*
2. Wesley's mother   *b. ignored Wesley's feelings. Wesley had no love from his mother, so he never learned how to love other people.*
3. Wesley's dog   *c. showed real affection for Wesley. Wesley returned his dog's affection.*
4. Dr. Herriot   *a. tried never to show that the situation was hopeless. Herriot realized that the dog was the reason for Wesley's good behavior.*
5. Police sergeant   *d. said the boy was a hopeless case. The sergeant did not know about the one case in which Wesley showed affection—to his dog, who returned the affection.*

Writing

Suppose that instead of returning to his old life as a troublemaker, Wesley became Dr. Herriot's helpful assistant. Write a new ending for the account based upon this change.

Before students complete the writing assignment, they can discuss the proposed alternative ending in class. Refer students to the paragraph in the Anthology at the bottom of p. 233, col. 1, in which Wesley walks away without turning back. Have them rewrite that sentence and then go on to explain what the boy does.

Since You Left by Ch'ang Ch'u Ling *(p. 235)*

The Selection

Have a volunteer read the poem to the class.

Follow-Up

Discuss the questions that accompany the poem.

Questions and Answers

1. A waning moon marks the end of a month or a season. How does the image of the waning moon fit the meaning of this poem? *The image of the waning moon is consistent with the poem's topic—the departure of a lover. A waning moon marks an ending. So does a lover leaving.*
2. What are some other images from nature that could convey the same idea as the waning moon? *Answers will vary. Possibilities include (but are not limited to) falling leaves, the setting sun, and melting snow.*

Road by Larry Libby *(p. 236)*

The Selection

Ask a student volunteer to read the first half of the poem up to the line, "It's a barefoot road. . . ." Have another volunteer read the second half.

Follow-Up

Discuss the questions that accompany the poem.

Questions and Answers

1. Does the speaker of this poem make the place he describes sound like a pleasant place to be? What are some of the descriptions that make it sound inviting? *The speaker does make the place, his world and his life, sound like a pleasant place to be. Inviting descriptions include ". . . the sky is good" and "The wind is gentle there." Accept other inviting descriptions that students can identify.*
2. How does the speaker of this poem sound? Sad? Lonely? Happy? Like someone in

love? Does this poem sound like an invitation for anyone, or for someone special? *Accept any response students can support with details from the poem. The poem suggests that the speaker is content and in love. The invitation is for someone special.*

Long Walk to Forever by Kurt Vonnegut, Jr. *(p. 237)*

Synopsis

Newt and Catharine have grown up next door to each other. Now Newt is in the Army and Catharine is about to get married. Newt arrives one day and asks Catharine to go for a walk. She tells him she is getting married. He says he knows. He also tells her he is absent without leave (A.W.O.L.) from the Army. They go for their walk. Newt tells Catharine that he loves her. She becomes angry and tells him it's a crazy time to be talking like that. She says she is going to marry Henry Stewart Chasens. Newt asks her if she loves Henry. She says "certainly," because she is going to marry him. They rest under an apple tree. Newt falls asleep and Catharine realizes as she watches him that she does love him. Newt gets up to go to town and turn himself in. At the very last moment he turns around and Catharine runs to him and embraces him.

Preparation

Ask students what they think it means to take "a long walk to forever." Where is forever? Is it possible to walk there?

Vocabulary

passion *(n.)* — powerful feeling (of love)
stockade *(n.)* — military prison
adored *(v.)* — felt deep love and respect for

A.W.O.L. — Absent Without Leave; being away without permission

Activities

A. See p. 6, Teaching Vocabulary.
B. See how many of the words students can use in one sentence. Many students will be able to use all four of them in the same sentence.
C. Make sure the students understand what being A.W.O.L. means, and also the consequences involved.

Quick Quiz

1. passion: a. understanding *b. powerful love* c. objective
2. stockade: a. cattle car b. mining field *c. military jail*

3. adored: *a. loved deeply*   b. escaped   c. upset greatly
4. A.W.O.L.: a. absolutely wild over love   b. a week on leave   *c. absent without leave*

Setting the Purpose

Have students read the title of the story and the brief headnote on p. 237 in the Anthology. Ask them what they think is going to happen. Then have them read the story to find out.

The Selection

This is a very short story that can be easily read in one sitting. If you wish, students can read it in two parts and briefly speculate on how they think the story will end.

Have students read to the bottom of p. 239 in the Anthology, which ends " 'You shouldn't have done that,' she said." Ask what they think will happen. Ask what they think *should* happen.

Have students read the rest of the story. Then have them complete Reading Comprehension on p. 242 in the Anthology.

Follow-Up

See p. 7, Teaching Reading Comprehension and For Discussion.

Reading Comprehension

1. Catharine was surprised to see Newt because   *a. he was supposed to be in the Army* (page 237).
2. Newt wanted to go for a walk with Catharine so he could   *b. tell her that he loved her* (page 239).
3. At first, Catharine reacted to Newt's declaration of love with   *c. confusion and anger* (page 239, col. 2).
4. While Newt was asleep, Catharine realized that she   *a. loved him.* (Page 240, col. 2: "While he slept, she adored him with all her heart.")
5. At the end of the story, Catharine thought of Newt as   *b. the man she would marry.* (Page 241: This is implied by the fact that she ran to him when he called. The title "Long Walk to Forever" also suggests this.)

For Discussion

If Catharine really loved Newt, why was she going to marry someone else? *She was probably going to marry Henry Stewart Chasens because he told her that he loved her. Newt never expressed his love for Catharine, so she could not have planned to marry Newt. Accept other explanations that students can justify with details from the story.*

Understanding Literature: Theme and Plot

Objective: Students will make inferences about the theme based on the plot.

124

Preparation

Explain that the *theme* of the story develops along with the *plot*. Each incident is related to the theme in some way.

Have students read and discuss the lesson on Theme and Plot on p. 242 in the Anthology. Then have them complete the exercise.

Questions and Answers

1. Newt convinced Catharine to go for a walk with him. *Newt was able to get Catharine away from her marriage preparations.*
2. Newt studied Catharine's face. *Catharine could not hide her love, and Newt saw it.*
3. Newt kissed Catharine for the first time. *Catharine allowed Newt to kiss her, saying that they should have kissed because they had been so close.*
4. Newt slept under the tree while Catharine watched him. *Catharine's love for Newt grew stronger.*
5. Newt turned and called to Catharine. *Newt gave Catharine one more push to come with him, and she finally allowed her true love to come out.*

Writing

Newt went A.W.O.L. because he wanted to talk to Catharine face to face. Suppose that they had written letters to each other instead. Write two letters. In the first, have Newt reveal his love to Catharine and ask her to change her wedding plans. In the second, present Catharine's response.

Discuss the differences between writing a letter to someone and talking to that person face to face. Ask students which they would prefer in a situation like the one in this story. Students may find it easier to write the letters if they first list the points they are going to make.

If You Hear That a Thousand People Love You
by Guadalupe de Saavedra   *(p. 243)*

The Selection

Help students to pronounce the poet's last name and point out that it appears in the poem several times. Have volunteers read each section.

Follow-Up

Discuss the questions that accompany the poem.

Questions and Answers

1. How would you feel if someone you love sent you this poem? Why? How do

people hear that other people love them? Do you think people count the number of people who love them? *Answers will vary. Students should recognize that the poem is sincere and shows deep love and respect.*

2. Why do you think the poet speaks of himself in the third person *(saavedra)* instead of in the first person *(I)*? What effect does the repetition of the poet's name have on the mood of the poem? *The poet's name adds emphasis and impact to his identity among the "thousand people," "hundred people," "seven people," and "two people" mentioned in the poem. The repetition adds drama and urgency to the message of the poem.*

Section Review

Vocabulary: Word Parts

Objective: Students will write definitions of words and word parts.

Preparation

Make sure that students can define and give examples of *base words*, *prefixes*, and *suffixes*. Discuss what the addition of a prefix or suffix can do to the meaning of a word.

Have students read and discuss the lesson on Word Parts on p. 244 in the Anthology.

Questions and Answers

1. "... she watched her mother's face *eagerly.* ..." *eager—enthusiastic or impatient; eagerly—in an impatient way*
2. "She *gleefully* kept her secret." *glee—delight or happiness; gleefully—happily*
3. "Mothers, on the other hand, are *dependable.*" *depend—count on; dependable—able to be counted on*
4. "The boy *misread* my hesitation." *read—understood; misread—didn't understand*
5. "Wes was *overjoyed.* He almost pranced along with his pet." *joy—happiness; overjoyed—had great happiness.*

Reading: Making Inferences

Objective: Students will make inferences about character motivation.

Preparation

Discuss what it means to make inferences and explain that some things are stated directly but that other things are *not* stated directly. They must be figured out from the facts and details that are provided. Sometimes a reader makes a logical guess based on personal experience or knowledge.

Have students read and discuss the lesson on Making Inferences on p. 244 in the Anthology. Then have them complete the exercise.

Questions and Answers

1. In "Very Special Shoes, " when they went to buy the shoes, Mary's mother was silent because she   *b. knew they couldn't afford them.*
2. The author of "Letter to a Black Boy" wrote to his son in a loving way because he   *b. loved his son.*
3. Wesley's decision not to go back into his house after the dog died in "The Troublemaker" showed that he   *c. didn't feel loved in his house.*

Quiz

See p. 7, Administering the Quiz.

Reading Comprehension

1. In "Very Special Shoes," why did Mary's mother change her mind and let Mary buy the red shoes? *Mary's mother knew that she was dying and would not have another chance to bring Mary happiness. The shoes were something that would help Mary to remember her mother.*
2. What brought the family together in "Letter to a Black Boy"? *Aunt Letty's Thanksgiving dinner brought the family together.*
3. In "Celebration," why does the poet feel so happy? *He is happy because he will share dancing, laughter, and a sense of belonging at a feast that night.*
4. What was the one successful relationship that Wesley Binks had in "The Troublemaker"? How did this relationship change the way he acted? *Wesley's only successful relationship was with his dog. When the dog became sick, Wesley took jobs to earn money to pay the bills. After the dog died, he went back to getting into trouble.*
5. In "Long Walk to Forever," why was Catharine reluctant at first to go for a walk with Newt? *Catharine was about to marry someone else.*

Understanding Literature

6. What did the red leather shoes symbolize for Mary Johnson at the beginning of "Very Special Shoes"? What did they symbolize at the end? *At first the shoes symbolized a goal (page 214, col. 1) and a promise that could not be broken (page 217). At the end they became a symbol of her mother's love and protection (page 218, col. 2).*
7. The theme of "Long Walk to Forever" is that love can conquer all obstacles. In what ways does that theme also apply to "Letter to a Black Boy"? *In "Letter to a Black Boy," love brings the whole family together to agree to finance college education for every child in the family who dreams of going to college (page 224, col. 2).*
8. List several incidents from "The Troublemaker" that illustrate that Wesley Binks's actions were affected by how others treated him. *Answers will vary. Examples include the following: Wesley expected Dr. Herriot to hit him when he first brought Duke to the hospital (page 229, col. 2); Wesley assumed that*

Herriot thought he couldn't pay (page 231, col. 1); *Herriot treated Wesley as a person, and Wesley responded well (he stopped playing tricks on Herriot); Wesley allowed Herriot to comfort him while he cried* (page 233, col. 1); *Wesley left home after Duke died—no one cared for him there* (page 233, col. 1).

9. In the poem "Road," the road represents love. According to the speaker, how long does it take to develop a strong relationship? What must two people do to develop such a relationship? *The speaker suggests that developing a strong relationship takes a long while. The two people must go through life's challenges together* (page 236).

10. What was the conflict that Catharine faced in "Long Walk to Forever"? How did she finally resolve this conflict? *Catharine faced an inner conflict. She was planning to marry Henry, but Newt, whom she loved more deeply, showed up and asked her to marry him. Students can infer that she decided to marry Newt* (page 241, col. 2).

Composition

1. In "Very Special Shoes," "Letter to a Black Boy," and "The Troublemaker," the authors look at the relationship between mothers and children. (Aunt Letty filled the role of mother to Bob Teague.) For each of these selections, write one paragraph in which you explain the mother/child relationship it contains.

   Before students begin this assignment, discuss the mother/child relationship in each of the selections mentioned. Suggest that students list points made during the discussion that they will use in each paragraph. If you wish, an opening sentence for each paragraph can be developed as a group activity.

2. This section included three love poems: "Since You Left," "Road," and "If You Hear That a Thousand People Love You." Imagine that Newt sends one of these poems to Catharine or that Catharine sends one to Newt. Write a letter from the person who receives the poem to the person who sends it. How did the poem make the receiver feel?

   Before beginning this assignment, have students select the character—Newt or Catharine—that they will be. Then have them select and read the poem as if it had just been received. Discuss how receiving the poem would have made them feel. Many students will find it easier to list the points they will make before completing the letter. Students can work on this assignment in pairs if you wish.

3. In almost every selection in this section, love helps characters overcome obstacles. Imagine an obstacle that is difficult to overcome. Then write a short story of your own showing how love helped the characters get past the obstacle.

   Discuss obstacles that love could help people overcome. After each student has supplied an example, he or she can develop it into a story. Have students describe the obstacle in a sentence or two at the top of their paper. Then have them list the specific events in the story. For some students, this will be sufficient. Others will be able to go on and put the material into short story form.

Enrichment

1. Students who enjoyed reading "The Troublemaker" might enjoy other stories by

James Herriot. His bestselling books include *All Things Bright and Beautiful, All Creatures Great and Small, All Things Wise and Wonderful,* and *The Lord God Made Them All.* All are available in paperback, and even in unabridged versions are fairly easy to read.

2. Kurt Vonnegut, Jr. is a popular contemporary author. Have students look for additional examples of his work in the school library.

3. Have students find additional works—short stories or poems—that in some way deal with themes involving human relationships.

Authors

Morley Callaghan.   Born in Toronto, Canada, in 1903, Morley Callaghan began writing short fiction while still a student, and was published in such magazines as Ezra Pound's *Exile.* His fictional concerns are of a strongly psychological nature, and are often given an overtly Christian context. Among his best-known novels are *Strange Fugitive* (1928), *Broken Journey* (1932), and *The Loved and the Lost* (1951).

James Herriot.   James Herriot (whose real name is James Alfred Wight) was born on October 13, 1916. He attended Glasgow Veterinary College in Scotland. A writer of nonfiction and autobiography, he is best known for his accounts of his experiences as a country veterinarian in the farmlands of Yorkshire, England. The simple, honest style in which he writes corresponds to the kind of life portrayed in his books; that is, simple, quiet, and hard-working. His books are very popular—three were best sellers, among them *All Things Wise and Wonderful* and *All Creatures Great and Small.*

Alonzo Lopez.   Alonzo Lopez, a Papago Indian, was born in Pima County, Arizona. He pursued American Indian and anthropology studies at Yale and Wesleyan Universities. His main artistic interest is poetry, although he has been active in dance and drama, and enjoys working in traditional Indian crafts as well. Lopez' poems are included in anthologies of American Indian poetry.

Guadalupe de Saavedra.   A Chicano poet, Guadalupe de Saavedra often expresses in his writing the frustration, pain, and anger felt by the Chicanos in their struggle for equality in the United States.

Kurt Vonnegut, Jr.   Kurt Vonnegut, Jr., was born in Indianapolis, Indiana, in 1922. Between 1940 and 1942 he attended Cornell University before joining the army in 1942. After World War II he attended the University of Chicago, and was later employed by the Chicago City News Bureau as a police reporter. After a time spent in public relations with the General Electric Company in Schenectady, New York, he began his career as a freelance writer. His first novel, *Player Piano,* was published in 1951. His books have been consistently popular, and the early 1970's saw Vonnegut become something of a cult hero, with *Slaughterhouse-Five* being perhaps his best-received novel.

Section 7
Biography

Section Focus

This section contains short biographies of Annie Oakley, Thomas Edison, and Roberto Clemente, and a selection from an autobiography by Nikki Giovanni. The Introduction discusses the characteristics of a biography. It explains that biographies provide new insights and often look back in history to reveal a life and a period in the past. Other biographies are contemporary. An autobiography is written by an individual about his or her own life. Have students read and discuss the Introduction on pp. 248–249 in the Anthology before going on to the selections.

The activities that follow each selection focus on understanding point of view.

The Story of Little Sure-Shot

by Fiona Greenbank *(p. 250)*

Synopsis

Phoebe Ann Moses was one of many children in a very poor family. Her father died when she was very small, leaving only the land and a rifle. The gun fascinated the child, who became an expert shot at the age of nine. Phoebe Ann went to live at a county home and then with a farmer and his wife to take care of their baby. She was brutally mistreated there and finally managed to escape. She returned home and used her skill with a gun to supply restaurants with neatly shot quail.

One day Phoebe Ann competed against the famous marksman Frank Butler, and won the man as well as the match. A year later they were married. She began to perform as "Annie Oakley." Frank became her manager. She joined Buffalo Bill's Wild West Show and performed with it for 17 years. Her fame spread internationally. Then a train crash left her badly hurt and partially paralyzed. Nevertheless, she still shot in exhibitions to raise money for charity. Annie died of a blood disease in November, 1926. Frank died 20 days after she did.

Her life was the subject of a Broadway musical made during the 1940's.

Preparation

Tell students that the selection they are preparing to read is about a very unusual woman who, more than a century ago, succeeded at a man's game better than anyone.

Vocabulary

calico *(adj.)* — spotted; more than one color
*__domestic__ *(adj.)* — devoted to home life
resenting *(v.)* — feeling anger toward
instinct *(n.)* — natural or inborn ability
*__taunts__ *(n.)* — teasing insults
stifling *(v.)* — smothering or covering up
*__bondage__ *(n.)* — slavery
*__vaudeville__ *(n.)* — theatrical entertainment with a number of different acts or attractions
*__matinee__ *(n.)* — afternoon performance
pestered *(v.)* — bothered
writhing *(v.)* — moving about in pain

*Glossary word

Activities

A. See p. 6, Teaching Vocabulary.
B. Have students use the words *taunts* and *resenting* in the same sentence. (They may need to use *resented*.)

C. Have students make a sentence using the words *vaudeville* and *matinee*.
D. Have students give examples of *domestic* life.
E. Ask students to provide examples of human behavior that is based on *instinct*.

Quick Quiz

1. calico: a. type of gray cat b. type of furniture *c. spotted or multicolored*
2. domestic: a. not to be believed *b. devoted to home life* c. person who works for a living
3. resenting: a. giving something to *b. feeling anger toward* c. sending something again
4. instinct: *a. inborn ability* b. example of strength c. learned behavior
5. taunts: a. distant relations b. canvas houses *c. teasing insults*
6. stifling: a. quite enjoyable *b. covering up* c. expressing
7. bondage: *a. slavery* b. covering c. pleasure
8. vaudeville: a. one-person show b. television newscast *c. show with many acts*
9. matinee: a. breakfast treat *b. afternoon performance* c. evening television show
10. pestered: a. entertained *b. bothered* c. boiled over
11. writhing: *a. moving about in pain* b. keeping very still c. singing and dancing

Setting the Purpose

Ask students if they have heard of Annie Oakley. Some may have seen the TV movie or read about her. Tell the class that they are going to read part of her life story.

The Selection

This is a fast-moving selection that can hold the attention of even the most reluctant readers.

Have a student volunteer read the headnote on p. 250 in the Anthology. Then have students read the selection silently to the end of the first paragraph on p. 253, which ends, "She went, smiling, into slavery." Before going on, ask students to predict what they think will happen. Ask if they think that Phoebe Ann made the right choice.

Have students read to the bottom of p. 255, to the sentence that reads, "The card would split in half." Briefly discuss how Annie's life has changed. Have students comment on the relationship between Annie and her husband.

Have students read to the end of p. 257. Ask if they think she will go back to her shooting career. Then have them read the rest of the selection to find out.

When students have finished reading the selection, have them complete Reading Comprehension on p. 258 in the Anthology.

Follow-Up

See p. 7, Teaching Reading Comprehension and For Discussion.

Reading Comprehension

1. Annie first learned to shoot when she was   *b. nine years old.* (Page 251, col. 1: "When she was four, she tried to lift it. . . . when she was nine, a neighbor showed her how to load and aim.")
2. During her childhood, Annie spent two years working for   *c. a cruel farmer and his wife* (page 253).
3. Annie married a man who   *b. was proud of her abilities* (pages 254–255).
4. Annie stopped traveling with the Wild West Show because she   *c. was hurt in a train crash* (page 257, col. 1).
5. In the musical *Annie Get Your Gun*, Annie let Frank win the match because the writers of the musical probably   *a. thought the audience would like it better that way* (page 258, col. 2).

For Discussion

1. In what ways did Annie Oakley seem like a modern woman, even though she was born in 1860? How was her husband different from most other men of his time? *Accept answers students can support with details from the selection. Annie Oakley seemed like a modern woman since she excelled in a career previously reserved for men. Her husband accepted her accomplishments without feeling threatened by her fame.*
2. Why do you think people in the late 1800's liked Wild West shows so much? Why was Annie Oakley's act such an attraction? *People liked Wild West shows because they portrayed American history. They were exciting, and there were probably few types of entertainment like them in the 1800's. Annie Oakley's act was unusual and exciting. People probably couldn't believe that she could perform such amazing feats.*

Understanding Literature: Point of View

Objective: Students will make inferences about the information in a biography.

Preparation

Discuss *point of view* with the class. Make sure that students understand the differences between first-person and third-person point of view. Tell students that biographies are generally written in the third person and that the author can reveal information about the thoughts and feelings of all the characters. An autobiography is a person's own life story and is usually written in the first person.

Have students read and discuss the lesson on Point of View on p. 259 in the Anthology. Then have them complete the exercise.

Questions and Answers

1. "But instead of resenting her, men loved and respected her for her skill."   *third person (This is the type of information normally gotten from people other than*

the subject. However, Annie could have been aware of their respect, and so have said this herself.)

2. "Unhappy at the taunts of the other children, and hungry for a better education, Phoebe Ann offered to go."   *first person (This passage describes why Annie made up her mind, so would probably come from her.)*

3. "Some men of the 1880's would have shouted 'No!' and dragged their wives away. But Frank Butler was secure.   *third person (Annie could have said this, but it is Frank Butler's attitude opposed to other men's attitudes. Therefore, the comment would more likely come from Frank, or other men of that time.)*

4. "Queen Victoria . . . told her, 'You're a clever little girl.'"   *first person (This is what Queen Victoria told Annie, so Annie could have told about it.)*

5. "In the 1940's, Ethel Merman starred in a hit musical. . . . Annie Get Your Gun. . . ."   *third person (This musical was done after Annie's death, so Annie could not have known about it.)*

Writing

Rewrite one incident from the biography as if Annie Oakley were telling it from the first-person point of view.

Before students complete this assignment, make sure that they understand the first-person point of view. All of the events must be those that Annie Oakley experienced herself. Other events must be qualified ("I heard later that. . . ."). Have students pretend that they are Annie, and use the words *I* and *me* as they write.

The Electrical Wizard   by John Dos Passos   *(p. 260)*

Synopsis

Thomas Edison was born in a small Ohio town. His family moved to Michigan when the railroads took away their shipping business. Thomas Edison went to school for only three months because the teacher thought he wasn't very bright. His mother taught him at home, where he tried out experiments in his own laboratory.

He ran a news service on a train, but was fired when he set the car aflame. He got a job as a telegraph operator and got fired when he let a freight train past a switch. He moved from job to job, and wherever he was he tried things out.

He invented a stock ticker and sold it. He invented the mimeograph, the carbon rheostat, and made paraffin paper. He invented a transmitter that helped make telephones possible. He invented the phonograph and the incandescent light bulb, and many other items. He kept at things until he solved them. At 82, he was still working 16 hours a day trying to find a substitute for rubber. Whenever he read about anything, he tried it out.

Preparation

Ask students what they know about Thomas Edison. Most of them will be aware of at least a few of Edison's inventions, but chances are that few will realize the great variety of things Edison accomplished. Explain that the selection they are preparing to read will give them some idea of just how fascinating the man really was.

The author's style is also fascinating. Students should note the almost total lack of emphasis in the narrative, and the humor that is produced because major events receive equal treatment with minor incidents. Also, there is a poetic quality to the selection, which is especially evident on p. 264 in the Anthology.

Vocabulary

incandescent (*adj.*) — glowing brightness caused by heat

speculations (*n.*) — risky business ventures

excursionists (*n.*) — people on trips

laboratory (*n.*) — place to do experiments and work in science

concession (*n.*) — place or permission from an authority to do something

phosphorus (*n.*) — an element that glows in the dark and burns very easily

telegraphy (*n.*) — constructing or operating telegraphs (devices that send messages long distances by transmitting electrical signals over conducting wires)

*__patent__ (*n.*) — right granted by the government to an inventor that protects the inventor and prevents others from using the invention without paying

*__transmitter__ (*n.*) — device that sends messages or signals

mimeograph (*n.*) — machine that makes copies from a typewritten or handwritten original on a stencil

rheostat (*n.*) — an adjustable resistor used to control the current in a circuit (for dimming lights, etc.)

*__paraffin__ (*adj.*) — wax

proposition (*n.*) — plan or scheme for business

generation (*n.*) — production of something, often electricity

*__filament__ (*n.*) — wire in an electric bulb that produces light when current passes through it

fluoroscope (*n.*) — box with a screen used to view objects by X-ray

substitute (*n.*) — something that serves in place of another

*Glossary word

Activities

A. See p. 6, Teaching Vocabulary.
B. This selection contains a number of rather difficult technical terms. It's not necessary to teach them all in advance, but do help students with the pronunciations and definitions as needed.

Quick Quiz

1. incandescent: a. not available at this time *b. bright glow caused by heat* c. place to buy sandwiches

2. speculations: *a. risky business ventures*   b. upsetting diseases   c. interesting experiments
3. excursionists: *a. travelers*   b. scientists   c. commuter trains
4. laboratory: a. bathroom   b. reading room   *c. space for experiments*
5. concession: a. admission of guilt   *b. permission to do something*   c. sugary dessert
6. phosphorus: *a. element that glows in the dark*   b. wealthy   c. element with a strong odor
7. telegraphy: *a. sending messages by wire*   b. reading someone's mind   c. using the telephone
8. patent: a. type of leather shoes   *b. government protection for an invention*   c. laboratory where things are made
9. transmitter: a. small television set   *b. signal-sending device*   c. someone who argues
10. mimeograph: a. to imitate someone   *b. copying machine*   c. scientific chart
11. rheostat: a. poisonous snake   b. steam generator   *c. control for electric current*
12. paraffin: *a. wax*   b. sailboat   c. kite
13. proposition: a. very small word   b. invitation to a party   *c. business scheme*
14. generation: a. nonspecific statement   b. destruction of something   *c. production of something*
15. filament: a. part of a flower   b. electricity that powers a light bulb   *c. wire used in producing light*
16. fluoroscope: a. device used to see around corners   b. device used to see long distances   *c. device used to view objects by X-ray*
17. substitute: a. not as well prepared   b. institute   *c. in place of another*

Setting the Purpose

Tell students that the selection will reveal many interesting things about Edison's life and work. Suggest that they pay careful attention to the tone the author uses to communicate his feelings about the famous inventor.

The Selection

Because this selection contains a number of technical terms, provide careful guidance. Don't require students to read out loud without preparation. You might read the entire selection aloud to the students yourself. In this way you will be able to discuss the technical terms and use expression to help convey the special flavor of this selection.

After students read the headnote (or you read it to them), suggest that they keep Edison's uniqueness in mind as they listen to (or read) the rest of the selection.

Stop for a moment on p. 262 in the Anthology after the sentence "The London *Times* wrote him up." Ask students to comment on what sort of person they think Edison was. Ask if they would hire him to do a job.

Complete the reading of the selection. Discuss Edison's life briefly before having students turn to Reading Comprehension on p. 265 in the Anthology.

Follow-Up

See p. 7, Teaching Reading Comprehension and For Discussion.

Reading Comprehension

1. Thomas Edison went to school for only three months because   *c. the teacher didn't think he was smart* (page 260).
2. Whenever Edison read about something, he   *b. tried out what he had read* (page 260).
3. Edison was such a successful inventor because   *b. he was continually experimenting with new ideas.*

For Discussion

1. What does Edison's work in finding the right filament for his electric lamp show about his technique as an inventor? What does it explain about his success as an inventor? *He tried anything and everything he thought might work, no matter how unusual or silly it seemed. Whenever he got a hunch, he went to the laboratory and tried it out. He was successful because he didn't give up until he had solved the problem.*
2. Edison spent most of his life inventing things that were both practical and commercial. What do *practical* and *commercial* mean? In what ways do his inventions demonstrate both of these qualities? Practical *means useful.* Commercial *means that it can be bought, sold, or used to make money. Accept any examples of these qualities that students can provide from the selection. Most of the inventions mentioned are still in use in one form or another.*

Understanding Literature: Point of View and Character Motivation

Objective: Students will infer the identity of a speaker based on statements of point of view.

Preparation

Discuss how *point of view* in a selection influences what the narrator can say about the *motivation* of the characters. First-person narrators can tell about their own motivation, but they cannot tell for sure what the other characters are thinking. Third-person narrators, on the other hand, can be all-knowing and reveal the thoughts and motivation of all the characters.

Have students read the lesson on Point of View and Character Motivation on p. 265 in the Anthology. Then have them complete the exercise.

Questions and Answers

1. I'll try to teach you all I can, and I'll let you set up a laboratory in the cellar. *Edison's mother*
2. I'm sorry I have to fire you. You're a fine telegraph operator, but you just do too many tricks with the wires.   *Edison's boss*

3. Can you believe it, that guy Edison has applied for a patent on another invention! *A clerk in the patent office*
4. Why am I still working at age 82? There are still lots of things to try out, that's why. *Edison himself*

Writing

Imagine that you are trying to invent something practical and commercial. Write a first-person narrative in which you tell about your invention and the experiments you have performed to try it out.

Suggest that students begin by identifying and briefly describing their invention and its practical and commercial uses. Have them list the steps they followed to try it out.

Clemente—A Bittersweet Story

by Jerry Izenberg   *(p. 266)*

Synopsis

Roberto Clemente's greatness on the baseball field was more than matched by his compassion for his fellow human beings. He died as he had lived, trying to help people who needed him. An earthquake in Nicaragua was a disaster to which he felt he had to respond. He had friends in the stricken city, and he took a personal interest in helping the victims of the earthquake. When he heard that the supplies he had helped to collect were not getting through to those who really needed them, he decided to accompany a mercy mission. On New Year's Eve his plane, loaded with supplies for the earthquake zone, went down. All aboard were killed.

This brief biography of the baseball star who became the National League's Most Valuable Player tells of Clemente's life in the words of several people who were close to him. His friend and teacher, the club owner who started him in professional baseball, and his teammate and close friend Willie Stargell all describe Clemente as a sincere, talented man with a genuine concern for others. Clemente's life and death offer proof that his friends were right.

Preparation

Introduce the title, "Clemente—A Bittersweet Story." Many students will have heard of Roberto Clemente. Ask students if they know what *bittersweet* means. This can be the first vocabulary word discussed.

Vocabulary

bittersweet (*adj.*) — pleasant and painful at the same time
casually (*adv.*) — without serious intention; carelessly

*prominent (*adj.*) — famous or important
*crypt (*n.*) — walled-in burial place, usually of stone
 confidence (*n.*) — belief in one's own ability
*bigotry (*n.*) — prejudice against a race, religion, or belief
*intolerance (*n.*) — unwillingness to understand persons or ideas that are different
     from one's own
 incredible (*adj.*) — unbelievable

*Glossary word

Activities

A. See p. 6, Teaching Vocabulary.
B. Ask students to give examples of events or experiences that might be considered *bittersweet.*
C. Have students find the two words on the list that have nearly the same meaning (*bigotry, intolerance*).
D. Have students provide examples to illustrate the words *prominent* and *incredible.*

Quick Quiz

1. bittersweet: a. easy to remember   *b. both pleasant and painful*   c. scent for a perfume
2. casually: a. as a result of   *b. carelessly*   c. in a nasty way
3. prominent: *a. famous or important*   b. extremely happy   c. larger than most
4. crypt: a. lines for a play   b. baseball field   *c. burial place*
5. confidence: *a. belief in oneself*   b. lack of understanding   c. need to make money
6. bigotry: a. pleasant memories   b. entertainment   *c. prejudice*
7. intolerance: a. understanding   *b. unwillingness to understand*   c. extreme intelligence
8. incredible: a. easy to understand   b. excellent entertainment   *c. difficult to believe*

Setting the Purpose

Have a student volunteer read the title and the headnote aloud. Remind students of what the word *bittersweet* means. Have them read the selection to see if they agree that the story of Clemente's life is bittersweet.

The Selection

Have students read the first page of the selection and the two lines at the top of the second page (pp. 266–267 in the Anthology). Ask if they agree with Roberto Clemente's feelings about friendship. Then have them go on.

Have students read through the first two lines on p. 269, col. 2 in the Anthology, which end ". . . how beautiful a man he was." Discuss briefly Mrs. Casares' memories of her former student.

Have students complete the selection. Ask them to consider whether Clemente was more successful as a professional ballplayer or as a private person. Did he excel at both? Then have them complete Reading Comprehension on p. 271 in the Anthology.

Follow-Up

See p. 7, Teaching Reading Comprehension and For Discussion.

Reading Comprehension

1. Roberto Clemente died while he was flying to Nicaragua to *b. bring supplies after an earthquake* (pages 267, 268, 271).
2. Clemente had been asked to make a speech because *c. people had great respect for him* (page 267, col. 1).
3. Clemente had a special relationship with his *c. teacher.* (Page 268, col. 2: "There would always be a bond between Roberto and his teacher.")
4. The delivery boy didn't blurt out the news that Clemente's plane had gone down because he *a. wanted to break the news gently* (page 269, col. 1).
5. Pedron Zarrilla asked Clemente to join *a. a baseball team in Puerto Rico called the Santurce Crabbers* (page 268, col. 2).
6. During his early years with the Pirates, "even Roberto Clemente couldn't turn them around overnight" because *a. it takes more than one good player to make a winning team* (page 270, col. 1).
7. When Clemente didn't win the Most Valuable Player award in 1960, he was upset because he *b. felt he wasn't being accepted.* (Page 270, col. 2: " 'He felt that he simply wasn't being accepted.' ")
8. Roberto Clemente was the kind of person who *a. cared a lot about his friends.* (Pages 266–267: "He had always said that when people gave you their friendship, you had to be willing to give something in return—no matter what the price.")
9. The author of this biography wants us to remember Clemente as a *b. fine human being.*

For Discussion

1. What does the word *bittersweet* mean? Why do you think the author calls this biography "Clemente—A Bittersweet Story"? *Clemente's life story was a mixture of greatness and tragedy.*
2. What did a sports career do for Clemente? How do you think his life would have been different if he had never played professional baseball? *Answers will vary. His career brought out his finest abilities. It gave him fame and authority to make people do what he asked of them. If he had not played baseball, he might have become an engineer, but he would probably have had the same personality.*
3. The author of this biography quoted people who knew Clemente. Why do you think he used the quotations? *This technique makes the biography authoritative (it is not just the author's thoughts), vivid (these are personal memories), and compelling.*

Understanding Literature: Changing Points of View

Objective: Students will identify whose point of view each statement represents.

Preparation

Explain that the point of view may change during a story. The selection they have just read is an example of this. Have students read and discuss the lesson on Changing Points of View on p. 272 in the Anthology. Then have them complete the exercise.

Questions and Answers

1. "He was not a man who made friends casually." *author*
2. " 'All of us who knew him, and even those who didn't, wept that week.' " *Rudy Hernandez, former teammate*
3. " 'He was a very shy boy, and he went straight to the back of the room and chose the very last seat.' " *Maria Casares, Clemente's teacher*
4. " 'This kid can throw and this kid can run and this kid can hit. We will be patient with him.' " *Pedron Zarrilla, owner of the Santurce baseball club*
5. " 'I think his attitude became one of "Well, I'm going to show them from now on so they will never forget." ' " *Bob Friend, Pirate pitcher*

Writing

Imagine that you are Roberto Clemente. Write about your teacher, your baseball career, or why you help people, from a first-person point of view.

Remind students that they are going to write in the first-person point of view as if they were Roberto Clemente. They should use the words *I* and *me*.

400 Mulvaney Street   by Nikki Giovanni   *(p. 273)*

Synopsis

Nikki Giovanni, an accomplished poet, is returning to Knoxville, Tennessee, the town in which she grew up. She is going to give a speech there. She recalls her childhood and tells of some important memories—people and places that have stuck in her mind. She says, "All that is gone now. Something called 'Progress' changed everything."

Nikki Giovanni describes Mulvaney Street, where she grew up. Her grandparents lived and raised their family there. She tells how sad it was for her grandmother to return to the house alone after her grandfather died. She tells how urban renewal took the house with it and how the family tried to convince Grandmother that the new house on Linden Street was as good or better. When her grandmother died, Nikki believed that it was because "she didn't know where she was and didn't like it." The new house was never the same as 400 Mulvaney Street.

Now, as Nikki Giovanni is traveling home again, she thinks of her family roots and wants her son to know that they came from somewhere, that they belong.

Preparation

Ask students to think about what it would be like to go home after many years of being away. Ask how they think they might feel if they found that the old neighborhood had simply disappeared. Tell them that the selection they are preparing to read is about going home.

Vocabulary

*vanity (*n.*) — too much pride in one's achievements

serials (*n.*) — stories or films shown in installments (soap operas on television, for example)

*dapper (*adj.*) — neat and trim; smartly dressed and groomed

familiarity (*n.*) — closeness

distasteful (*adj.*) — unpleasant

shriveling (*v.*) — drying up and wrinkling; shrinking

exhausted (*adj.*) — extremely tired

*ovation (*n.*) — enthusiastic applause

*Glossary word

Activities

A. See p. 6, Teaching Vocabulary.
B. Ask students if they have ever seen or read *serials.* Have them provide examples, if possible. Point out that television soap operas are a very popular type of serial.
C. Have students give examples of tasks or activities they would consider to be *distasteful.* Then have them identify activities that might make them feel *exhausted.*
D. Have students identify situations that might deserve a standing *ovation.* You might have three or four students demonstrate just what this means.
E. Ask students if they know anyone who could be described as *dapper.*

Quick Quiz

1. vanity: a. excitement   *b. too much pride in oneself*   c. quality of madness
2. serials: *a. stories in installments*   b. breakfast food in boxes   c. first-run movies
3. dapper: *a. smartly dressed*   b. spoon for soup   c. noisy and bothersome
4. familiarity: a. brothers and sisters   b. entertainment   *c. closeness*
5. distasteful: a. not too salty   b. too much to eat   *c. unpleasant*
6. shriveling: *a. drying up and wrinkling*   b. moving snow away   c. complaining and crying
7. exhausted: a. good enough   b. beautifully done   *c. extremely tired*
8. ovation: a. long speech   *b. enthusiastic applause*   c. short holiday

Setting the Purpose

Ask if students have ever read any poems by Nikki Giovanni. Tell them that they will read a poem by this well-known black poet after they complete the selection. Explain that "400 Mulvaney Street" will take them back to Nikki Giovanni's hometown, Knoxville, Tennessee.

The Selection

As you guide students in reading "400 Mulvaney Street," be sure that they understand the flashback technique the author uses to tell her story.

Have a student volunteer read the brief headnote. Comment on the use of the flashbacks and alert students to watch for them in the selection. Have students read to the middle of p. 275, col. 1 in the Anthology: "Something called 'Progress' changed everything." Ask what they think the author means by this line.

Have students continue to p. 276, col. 2 in the Anthology: "There must be a better way." Before going on, discuss the author's feelings at this point. Ask students if they think there is a "better way."

Have students finish the selection. Then have them complete Reading Comprehension on p. 279 in the Anthology.

Follow-Up

See p. 7, Teaching Reading Comprehension and For Discussion.

Reading Comprehension

1. 400 Mulvaney Street was the address of the *a. author's grandparents.* (Page 275, col. 2: "Grandmother and Grandpapa had lived at 400 Mulvaney Street since they'd left Georgia.")
2. Nikki's grandmother did not like her new home because it was *c. not familiar to her.* (Pages 276–277: "There was no familiar smell in that house. . . . Linden Avenue was pretty, but it had no life.")
3. After the author had left Knoxville, the town *a. changed a great deal.* (Page 278, col. 1: "I came back to Knoxville for the funeral and to look for the Gem Theatre and Carter-Roberts Drug Store, but they were all gone.")
4. When the author wrote, "I am buried there with Louvenia," she meant that she *c. would always think of her grandmother and Knoxville together* (page 278, col. 2).

For Discussion

1. What things in Nikki Giovanni's childhood made the strongest impressions on her? *Answers will vary. Mention of her grandmother should be made.*
2. Did the author think the changes in Knoxville were signs of progress? *The word* progress *appears capitalized and in quotation marks on pages 275, col. 1, and 276, col. 2. Students can infer that the author is skeptical.*

Understanding Literature: First-Person Point of View

Objective: Students will make inferences about an author's beliefs based on their reading.

Preparation

Tell students that an autobiography is a person's own life story told from his or her point of view. It is written in the first person. The author uses the words *I* and *me* in telling the story.

Have students read and discuss the lesson on First-Person Point of View on p. 279 in the Anthology. Then have them complete the exercise.

Questions and Answers

1. Progress is always a good thing. *disagree: The progress that changed Knoxville caused it to lose its past.*
2. Your birthplace is always a part of you. *agree: Memories are always with you. You are shaped by what happens early in your life.*
3. Older people deserve respect. *agree: They have a great deal to contribute, and they have lived through many trying times.*
4. You should always follow the rules. *disagree: Sometimes you have to follow your own path, not someone else's rules.*
5. Memories only get in the way of the present. *disagree: Memories can enhance the present by putting it in perspective.*
6. Houses have a life of their own. *agree: Their life is the total of what went on in the houses, and the memories they bring back.*
7. Parents should pass their memories on to their children. *agree: A child needs to know family history to be a complete person.*

Writing

Think of a place you know that has changed. Write a list of words that describe how the place used to look, smell, and feel. Write another list to describe the way the place is now. Use your lists to write a short, *first-person* account about how the place has changed.

Assist students in choosing a place to write about. Make sure that they understand the first-person point of view before they begin to write.

Knoxville, Tennessee   by Nikki Giovanni   *(p. 280)*

Preparation

Tell students that the following poem recounts a fond memory of the author's. As they read the poem, they will recognize a feeling or yearning that is universal.

The Selection

Have students read the poem silently. Then ask a volunteer to read it aloud to the class.

Follow-Up

Discuss the questions that accompany the poem.

Questions and Answers

1. What is so special about summer? How is summer different from the other seasons? *Answers will vary. In the summer you do all sorts of things outdoors without being cold.*
2. What does the poet mean by "and be warm / all the time"? What mood do these lines give the poem? *The poet means an inner warmth that comes from love and security. Accept any interpretation of this that students can explain and support.*

Section Review

Vocabulary: Word Parts

Objective: Students will explain how the meaning of each word is revealed by the meaning of word parts.

Preparation

Write the word *autobiography* on the board and explain that the word parts *auto-*, *bio-*, and *-graphy* reveal the meaning of the whole word. Point out that knowledge of the meaning of word parts can help students figure out the meaning of many unfamiliar words.

Have students read and discuss the lesson on Word Parts on p. 282 in the Anthology. Complete the first two items with the class. Guide students in using a dictionary to write a short explanation of how the meaning of each whole word is related to the meanings of its smaller parts. Then have students complete the exercise.

Questions and Answers

Definitions and explanations will vary.

1. autograph — *auto-*, self; *graph*, written or drawn
2. autohypnosis — *auto-*, self; *hypno-*, sleep; *-osis*, state of
3. automatic pilot — *auto-*, self; *-matic*, moving machine
4. automobile — *auto-*, self; *mobile*, moving
5. biochemistry — *bio-*, life; *chemistry*, study of substances
6. biographer — *bio-*, life; *-graph*, written
7. biopsy — *bi(o)-*, life; *-opsy*, examination, appearance
8. graphics — *graph*, written or drawn
9. graphology — *graph*, written or drawn; *-ology*, study of
10. photography — *photo-*, light; *graph*, written or drawn

Reading: Recognizing Significant Details

Objective: Students will recognize significant details.

Preparation

Discuss significant details and explain that some details support the main idea in a paragraph while other details are less important. Point out that focusing on significant details in a paragraph helps in understanding the whole selection. Then have students read and discuss the lesson on Recognizing Significant Details on p. 282 in the Anthology. Have them complete the exercise.

Questions and Answers

1. "The train pulled out into the cold, fall night, headed for Virginia. Two-and-a-half hours later, there was a crash of iron, and a terrible hissing sound."   *c. The train crashed.*
2. " 'I was born in the Dominican Republic,' Rudy Hernandez said, 'but I've lived on this island for more than 20 years. I've never seen a time or a sadness like that. All of us cried.' "   *a. Everyone cried.*
3. "I was going to Knoxville, Tennessee. I was going other places first. But mostly, to me, I was going home—to Knoxville. I had been asked to speak there."   *c. Knoxville was her hometown.*

Quiz

Reading Comprehension

1. In "The Story of Little Sure-Shot," what work did Annie Oakley do for most of her life? Why did she stop working? *Annie Oakley performed as a sharpshooter for most of her life. She worked in shows and gave exhibitions for charity. She stopped working because she broke her hip in an automobile accident* (page 258, col. 1).
2. Why was Thomas Edison called "the electrical wizard"? What were some of his most important inventions? *Thomas Edison was called "the electrical wizard" because of his many inventions and successful experiments that involved electricity. Among his most important inventions were the incandescent bulb, the phonograph, the rheostat, a transmitter that made telephones possible, a stock ticker, and many other items. (Accept any additional items that students can support.)*
3. How did Roberto Clemente die? What was he doing when he died? *Roberto Clemente died in a plane crash. He was accompanying a load of supplies and food for earthquake victims in Nicaragua.*
4. What is significant about the address "400 Mulvaney Street" to Nikki Giovanni? Why do you think she gave that title to part of her autobiography? *The address was that of Giovanni's grandparents' home, and the author was raised there. She gave that title to part of her autobiography because the place had been so important to her.*
5. What are some of the feelings about Knoxville, Tennessee, that Nikki Giovanni

revealed in her autobiography and her poem? *Answers will vary. Giovanni revealed that she loved Knoxville the way it was in the past, not as it is in the present. She felt comfortable, warm, and loved there. She has good feelings about the people there, even those who still live there.*

Understanding Literature

6. Which of the selections in this section were written in the first person? What are some ways that readers can recognize a first-person narrative? *"Knoxville, Tennessee" and "400 Mulvaney Street," by Nikki Giovanni, were written in the first person. Readers can recognize a first-person narrative by the use of the pronouns* I, we, me, *and* us.

7. In "The Story of Little Sure-Shot," what is one piece of information that Annie Oakley could not have written about herself? Why not? *Annie Oakley could not have written that she was the subject of a Broadway musical, because the musical was produced after her death.*

8. In "The Electrical Wizard," John Dos Passos revealed the qualities that helped Thomas Edison to be a great inventor. What were some of those qualities? *Those qualities included persistence, great curiosity, hard work, and intelligence.*

9. What special technique did the author of "Clemente—A Bittersweet Story" use to tell about the life of Roberto Clemente? *The author used flashbacks, interviews, and the words of people who knew Roberto Clemente.*

10. What are some of the things Nikki Giovanni was thinking about during her speech in Knoxville? *She was thinking about her sense of belonging, life in small towns, and her feelings that life goes on.*

Composition

1. Look in books, magazines, or encyclopedias to find information about someone you want to know more about. Jot down at least 25 facts about the person. Organize the facts into groups. Then develop the facts into a short biography.

   The school librarian could be helpful in getting the material for this assignment. Make sure that each student selects a person about whom there is likely to be enough available information to complete the assignment without extensive research. Historical figures, sports stars, and famous entertainers might be good choices.

2. Imagine that you are the person about whom you have listed the 25 facts. Rewrite part of your biography as a first-person autobiography.

   This assignment shouldn't be too difficult for any student who has satisfactorily completed the first composition. Remind students that a first-person account uses the pronouns *I, we, me,* and *us,* instead of *he/she, they, him/her,* or *them.*

3. Interview several members of your family to find out information about one of your relatives. Develop your interviews into a short biography of the person. Use quotations from the interviews in your biography.

   Before they do the interviewing, have students plan the questions they intend to ask. Have students tape the interviews or take notes. If necessary, review the correct form for writing quotes from people who are interviewed.

4. Find more information about one of the people you read about in this section. Develop your new information into paragraphs to add to that person's biography or autobiography.

   Once again, the school librarian is an important resource. If you wish to have this assignment done in class, collect the needed sources from the library before beginning. This is an excellent assignment for pupil teams or small groups.

Enrichment

1. Students who enjoyed "The Story of Little Sure-Shot" might enjoy the recording of the score of the Broadway show, *Annie Get Your Gun*.
2. Have students do additional research about the life of Thomas A. Edison, and report on his life or his inventions. Have them consider whether the selection by John Dos Passos gives a true flavor of Edison's life and personality.
3. Suggest that students locate and read other biographies or autobiographies of interest to them.

Authors

John Dos Passos. Born in Chicago, Illinois, on January 14, 1886, John Dos Passos interrupted his architectural studies to travel abroad, where he became interested in social issues. In 1926, he helped found the magazine *New Masses* and thus became centrally involved with the working-class literature movement of the 1930's. In 1925, he published *Manhattan Transfer* and is especially remembered for his three novels *The 42nd Parallel* (1930), *1919* (1932), and *The Big Money* (1936). These novels form a trilogy known as *U.S.A.* He died in 1970.

Nikki Giovanni. Nikki Giovanni was born in Knoxville, Tennessee on June 7, 1943. She graduated in 1967 from Fisk University, and for several years taught English and Black Studies at colleges and universities in the New York area. She writes poems for people of all ages and gives frequent poetry readings and lectures. Her poems and essays deal with such topics as childhood, love, the black liberation movement, and the individual's role in the community. Her books include *Black Feeling, Black Talk, Black Judgement; The Women and the Men;* and *My House.* She has made a number of recordings of her poetry and has appeared on television. She is also interested in music, painting, and travel.

Section 8
Nonfiction

Section Focus

Section 8 deals with the genre of nonfiction. The Introduction helps students to distinguish between primary and secondary sources, and discusses the importance of understanding the author's purpose in a work of nonfiction. The elements of style are briefly mentioned and students are invited to explore a range of nonfiction styles and subjects as they read the selections. Have students read and discuss the Introduction on p. 286 in the Anthology. Then as they read each selection, have them consider the author's purpose and style and relate it to what they have learned.

Activities following selections focus on tone; varying tone; tone and changing attitude; serious, formal tone; argumentative tone; and emotional vs. factual tone.

Central Park   by John Updike   *(p. 288)*

Synopsis

In this journal account, John Updike takes his readers with him on a walk through Central Park. It is the first day of spring, and the slushy remains of a recent snowfall still clog the gutters. He tells of different *people* he sees—a policeman, a family with a sled, boys throwing snowballs, men without hats, 12 snowmen, men listening to a spring training baseball game, a girl falling on the ice. Walking through the Central Park Zoo, he passes the cafeteria, a checkers game, and the merry-go-round, which has more music than children. Finally, he describes the *things* he sees—a tire track, footprints around a KEEP OFF sign, a lost red mitten. The last thing mentioned is an airplane.

Preparation

Ask students if they think it is possible to describe a place so that someone who has never been there can know just what it's like. Tell them that the author of the selection they are about to read has made an effort to do just that.

Vocabulary

*resurrected (*adj.*) — brought back to life
 coax (*v.*) — beg or convince to do something
*intact (*adj.*) — in one piece; not broken
 calliope (*n.*) — organ used for circus music
 carousel (*n.*) — merry-go-round
*rivulet (*n.*) — tiny stream of running water
 indignantly (*adv.*) — in a way showing strong displeasure

*Glossary word

Activities

A. See p. 6, Teaching Vocabulary.
B. In addition to the words on the list, this selection contains several animal names that may cause difficulty. When students are reading the paragraph about the Central Park Zoo, make sure they know that a *tahr, aoudad, yak, coati, orangoutan,* and *ocelot* are animals. You may wish to list these animal names on the board and pronounce each one.

Quick Quiz

1. resurrected: a. rebuilt   *b. brought back to life*   c. insulted greatly
2. coax: a. great fake   *b. convince*   c. lake in the park
3. intact: *a. whole, not broken*   b. mean to do something   c. politeness
4. calliope: a. melon for breakfast   b. brass band in a circus   *c. organ run by steam*
5. carousel: a. exciting entertainment   b. wandering around   *c. merry-go-round*

6. rivulet: a. large river   b. nail or tack   *c. tiny stream*
7. indignantly: *a. with displeasure*   b. unfortunately   c. intelligently

Setting the Purpose

Tell students that the selection they are about to read takes place in New York City's Central Park. Ask them to pretend that they are walking with author John Updike, and have them try to see what he sees and hear what he hears.

The Selection

This selection is very short and can be read in one sitting. You may wish to have students read it silently first and then read it aloud, each student reading the description of one sight. If you do this, be sure to aid students by helping them to pronounce the Latin names of animals and any words that cause them problems.

Follow-Up

See p. 7, Teaching Reading Comprehension and For Discussion.

Reading Comprehension

1. In this selection, the author describes sights that were   *a. delightful and interesting.*
2. It was a good day to go to Central Park because spring   *c. brought the park to life.*

For Discussion

What are some ways that the author helps you "see" exactly what he saw? *Accept any response students can support with details from the selection. Among the ways the author helps readers "see" what he saw are his use of vivid colors, which appeal to the readers' senses, and his exact description of the action occurring.*

Understanding Literature: Tone

Objective: Students will choose the correct word to describe the tone in each passage.

Preparation

Explain that *tone* in a piece of literature expresses how the author feels about his or her subject.

Have students read and discuss the lesson on Tone on p. 290 in the Anthology. Have them give examples of different types of tone from other works they have read. Then have them complete the exercise.

Questions and Answers

1. The merry-go-round was nearly empty of children, but overflowing with calliope music. *playful*

2. No one dared come near the merry-go-round, with its dangerously broken-down horses and blaring calliope music.   *angry*
3. The once-beautiful merry-go-round was now nearly empty except for the faint notes of the calliope.   *sad*
4. The merry-go-round was nearly empty, unless you wanted to count the loud calliope music that filled the place.   *sarcastic*

Writing

Close your eyes and think about a place. Write 4 or 5 sentences describing different sights and sounds there.

Encourage students to choose a place they wish to describe and then to form a picture of it in their minds. Have them go directly from mental picture to written words. Tell them that they should try to make their readers see and hear the things that they see and hear.

Steelworker: Mike Lefevre

by Studs Terkel   *(p. 291)*

Synopsis

This is Mike Lefevre's description of his job told in his own words to interviewer Studs Terkel. Lefevre describes himself as "a dying breed"—a "laborer" who does "muscle work." He comments that "you can't take pride anymore." You work hard, but there's nothing "to point to" when you're done. He says that the average laborer isn't stupid—just tired. He remarks that if he had more time he'd use it to get to know his family better. Lefevre describes his workday as boring: "Put it on, take it off, put it on, take it off. . . ." He would personalize the workplace if he were hiring people. And he comments that even someone like da Vinci would be bored if he had to draw the same thing "a hundred times a day."

Preparation

Ask students whether or not they think it's important for a person to enjoy his or her job. Ask them what they think it would be like to work at something that bored them. Tell them that the selection they are preparing to read is about one person's work and what he thinks of it.

Vocabulary

contractor *(n.)* — person who performs work for a certain price
degrading *(adj.)* — lowered in dignity
*__manual__ *(adj.)* — done with the hands

automation *(n.)* — use of automatic machinery to perform jobs so that people are not needed

plaque *(n.)* — sign in honor of something

*__anatomical__ *(adj.)* — having to do with the structure of the body

*Glossary word

Activities

A. See p. 6, Teaching Vocabulary.

B. Have students discuss and give examples of *manual* labor and *automation*. Ask if they know any *contractors*. Compare contracting with working for set wages during a specific period of time.

C. Ask students if they have ever seen a *plaque*. Find an example in your school if possible.

Quick Quiz

1. contractor: a. surveyor   b. worker on a weekly salary   *c. person who does a job for a price*

2. degrading: a. poor marks in school   *b. lowered in dignity*   c. interesting and exciting

3. manual: *a. done with the hands*   b. automatic   c. pleasing to touch

4. automation: a. washing machine and dryer   b. machinery needing people to operate it   *c. use of automatic machinery*

5. plaque: *a. sign in honor of something*   b. book of directions   c. pleasant place to be

6. anatomical: a. automatically finished   *b. dealing with body structure*   c. not to be believed

Setting the Purpose

Tell students that the selection they are about to read is a steelworker's description of his job. Have them think about what it might be like to do the same thing day after day. Have them read the selection to find out what Mike Lefevre thinks about the job.

The Selection

The selection is short and can easily be read in one sitting. If you prefer, it can be divided into two sections, with a brief discussion between them.

Have a student volunteer read the headnote. Then have another student read the first paragraph (in italics), which briefly describes the setting. Have the class read the selection silently to the end of the next-to-last paragraph on p. 292, col. 1 in the Anthology, which ends "Machines can either liberate man or enslave 'im, because they're pretty neutral." Discuss this point briefly before going on.

Have students read the rest of the selection. Then have them complete Reading Comprehension on p. 295 in the Anthology.

Follow-Up

See p. 7, Teaching Reading Comprehension and For Discussion.

Reading Comprehension

1. Mike Lefevre's job required him to do *b. the same thing over and over.* (Page 291, col. 1: "... pick it up, put it down, pick it up, put it down.")
2. When Lefevre said, "I'm a dying breed," he meant that *c. his kind of job would soon be a thing of the past.* (Page 292, col. 1: "Let's face it, a machine can do the work of a man. ...")
3. By *automation,* Lefevre meant *c. machines taking the place of human workers* (page 292, col. 1).
4. Lefevre believed that some working-class people don't fulfill themselves because they *a. are physically exhausted.* (Page 292, col. 2: "It isn't that the average working guy is dumb. He's tired, that's all.")
5. When Lefevre spoke of Michelangelo and da Vinci, he meant *c. famous Italian artists who had lived in the past* (page 295).

For Discussion

1. How did Mike Lefevre feel about his job? What would he change about it if he could? *Lefevre feels that it's difficult to take pride in his work because end results are not obvious, and there is a lack of recognition and stimulation. His job makes him very tired, and he doesn't have much energy for anything else. He would personalize work, shorten hours, and diversify activities.*
2. Mike Lefevre said that with a 20-hour week, people could "really expand." What did he mean by this? How would he expand his life if he didn't have to work so hard? *"Really expand" means doing many other activities besides work. Responses should include reading, playing chess, and spending more time with his family.*
3. Why did Lefevre feel that workers should get more credit for what they do? Do you agree? *He feels that manual labor is underrated compared with intellectual pursuits. Answers to the second question will vary.*

Understanding Literature: Varying Tone

Objective: Students will select the correct word to describe the varying tone in the passages of the selection.

Preparation

Explain that the *tone* in a piece of writing reflects the way the author or speaker feels about the topic. This tone may vary as the author or speaker discusses different subjects. You may wish to distinguish tone from mood, which is the feeling the writer tries to create in the reader.

Have students read and discuss the lesson on Varying Tone on p. 296 in the Anthology.

Questions and Answers

1. "It's hard to take pride in a bridge you're never gonna cross, in a door you're never gonna open. You're mass-producing things and you never see the end result of it." *bitter*
2. "I'll be darned if a computer is gonna eat before I do! I want milk for my kids." *angry*
3. "If I were hiring people to work, I'd try naturally to pay them a decent wage. I'd try to find out their first names, their last names, keep the company as small as possible...." *thoughtful*
4. "Nobody ever checks the pedigree on a mule, do they? But they do on a man. Can you picture walking up to a mule and saying, 'I'd like to know who your granddaddy was?'" *sarcastic*

Writing

Write one more question that Studs Terkel might have asked Mike Lefevre about his job. Then write the steelworker's answer in a tone that seems appropriate.

Before students begin the writing assignment, you might have them role-play an interview between Studs Terkel and Mike Lefevre. Students can then make note of the questions and prepare answers in an appropriate tone.

The Acorn People   by Ron Jones   *(p. 297)*

Synopsis

Ron Jones takes a job as a counselor in a camp for the handicapped. He likes the high pay and the expectation of playing with the kids. Ron quickly learns, however, that the campers are far more seriously handicapped than he had thought. Even the simplest tasks are a struggle. Members of Ron's group make acorn necklaces, which become a symbol of their efforts. They call themselves "the Acorn People."

The camp's director is very organized and gets upset when anything is off schedule. He is upset frequently because the counselors' efforts to meet the needs of the campers often result in changes in the rigid plans. Ron's group decides to climb Lookout Mountain, an excursion Boy Scouts take to earn a merit badge. Despite severe problems, the Acorn People succeed. They set their sights high and overcome their handicaps.

The end of the season is marked by a water show planned by the campers and performed with the help of sympathetic staff, especially Mrs. Nelson, the nurse, who is elected "Queen of Camp Wiggin."

At the end of the summer Ron knows he will always remember the Acorn People. Camp has given them a chance to achieve and dream.

Preparation

Ask students what they think it would be like if the things they take for granted—the everyday things they find so easy—were suddenly to become a struggle. Tell them that the selection they are preparing to read takes place in a camp for handicapped children.

Vocabulary

counselor (*n.*) — someone who supervises activities at a summer camp

handicaps (*n.*) — disabilities; anything that makes life more difficult or stands in the way

career (*n.*) — a person's lifework

schedule (*n.*) — list of things to be done at particular times

***heroine** (*n.*) — girl or woman who is admired for an achievement or for courageous action

lagoon (*n.*) — shallow pondlike body of water

gangplank (*n.*) — flat board used to get people on or off a ship

merit badge (*n.*) — award given to a scout for a special achievement

*Glossary word

Activities

A. See p. 6, Teaching Vocabulary.
B. Make sure that students can distinguish between a *career* (a life's work) and a job. Ask if any of them have thought about a career.
C. Tell students that a *heroine* is a female hero. Ask them to name some heroines, either real or fictional.

Quick Quiz

1. counselor: a. family doctor   *b. camp employee*   c. person who makes laws
2. handicaps: a. extremely warm mittens   b. small cloths   *c. disabilities*
3. career: *a. life's work*   b. part-time job   c. understanding
4. schedule: a. need to be late   *b. list of things to be done*   c. type of employment
5. heroine: a. coward   b. underpaid counselor   *c. female hero*
6. lagoon: a. lovely water bird   *b. shallow pond*   c. restful afternoon
7. gangplank: *a. walkway used to go onto a boat*   b. board used for water games   c. method of cooking steak
8. merit badge: a. book of rules   *b. award for achievement*   c. training kit for scouts

Setting the Purpose

Have students read the brief headnote to "The Acorn People." It says that "Being handicapped doesn't mean you have to give up." Tell them that the selection they are about to read gives several illustrations of this point. Have them read the account to find out how the campers made their summer a big success.

The Selection

This selection is rather long. You may wish to follow this four-part plan.

First, have students read to the end of the paragraph on p. 299, col. 1 in the Anthology, which reads, "So I stayed on." Ask them to discuss Ron's feelings up to that point. Ask if they think he has made the correct decision.

Have students read to the end of the next-to-last paragraph on p. 302, col. 2 in the Anthology, which ends, "We had made it up there—together!" Discuss how they think the campers and their counselors feel at this point. Ask what they think the camp director will think about the activity. Then have them read on.

Have students read to p. 306, col. 1 in the Anthology, which says, "Meanwhile, we practiced our separate parts." Before going on, ask students what they think the show will be like.

Have students read the rest of the selection. Ask how they think the campers feel now that camp is over. Ask how they think Ron Jones feels. Have them complete Reading Comprehension on p. 307 in the Anthology.

Follow-Up

See p. 7, Teaching Reading Comprehension and For Discussion.

Reading Comprehension

1. Ron Jones took the job at Camp Wiggin because he *c. wanted a good-paying job for a few weeks* (page 297, col. 2).
2. The author's first thought, that he wouldn't be playing sports with the campers, turned out to be *b. false.* (Pages 301–302, 307: He swam and hiked with the campers, although their style was a bit unusual.)
3. If Camp Wiggin had been set up for handicapped children, it would not have had *c. cabins with steps.* (Page 297, col. 2: "The camp wasn't set up for handicapped children. . . . Each cabin had three steps, and you can't wheel a chair up a set of stairs.")
4. Each of the campers in Ron Jones's cabin had *b. different physical handicaps* (pages 298–299).
5. The boys decided to climb Lookout Mountain because they wanted to *a. show they were as capable as the Boy Scouts.* (Page 301, col. 1: " 'If Boy Scouts can climb that mountain, can't we?' ")
6. The acorn necklaces became *c. a symbol of the campers' identity.* (Page 300, col. 1: "Spider kept saying, 'We're the Acorn People.' ")
7. No one clapped after the movie about water safety because *a. it showed able-bodied kids doing things the campers could not do* (page 303, col. 2).
8. To Mr. Bradshaw, the most important thing was that the *c. schedule be followed exactly.* (Page 302, col. 2: "Mr. Bradshaw was angry at some of the counselors because they weren't following his schedule. . . .")
9. By the end of the session, most of the children at Camp Wiggin *a. felt better about their ability to succeed.* (Page 307: "We were mountain climbers, pirates, and kings.")

For Discussion

1. Why was climbing the mountain so important to the members of the Acorn Society? What did climbing the mountain represent to them? *The Acorn People wanted to succeed in spite of the obstacles they faced. Climbing the mountain represented an achievement none of them could have accomplished alone.*

2. What did Ron Jones learn from his experiences at the camp? How was he different by the end of camp? *Ron learned that being handicapped didn't mean you had to give up. He discovered a closeness and trust that he would cherish and remember forever. His view of what could be achieved during the summer had changed significantly. At first he had wanted to quit because he thought he might fail.*

3. Why do you think Ron Jones decided to write about what happened with the Acorn People? *Answers will vary. Reasons include a desire to share this experience with others and probably a desire to tell about the successes of the campers.*

4. In what ways could you describe Mr. Bradshaw as being the one who was "handicapped"? *Mr. Bradshaw was inflexible and did not fully understand the needs of his campers.*

Understanding Literature: Tone and Changing Attitude

Objective: Students will choose one passage from the selection that matches the tone and attitude of each statement.

Preparation

Review the definition of *tone* with the students. Make sure they understand that it reflects the author's attitude toward his or her subject. Point out that the tone may change as the author's attitude toward the topic changes.

Have students read and discuss the lesson on Tone and Changing Attitude on p. 308 in the Anthology. Then have them complete the exercise.

Questions and Answers

Accept any choice of passage for each item that makes sense. Answers will vary.

1. At first, Ron's attitude seemed *solemn*. (Page 297, col. 1: "I was a counselor, and like the others I did not know what to say. What do you say to young people who move toward you only because their parents push them? What do you say to young people who seem to have no spirit? What do you say to young people who are covered with blankets to hide their handicaps?")

2. Then, he seemed to have an *angry* attitude. (Page 297, col. 2: "When I saw these kids, I knew I wouldn't be playing sports with them. We'd be lucky, I thought, if we took a few steps together." Page 298, col. 1: "By evening I was tired and angry.")

3. Next, he seemed very *serious*. (Page 297, col. 2: "I wondered what the boys and girls were thinking. What were they feeling? Did they have hopes for the future? But I didn't have time to think about that because there was work to do.")

4. Later, he seemed *excited*. (Page 302, col. 2: "At two o'clock we reached the top of

Lookout Mountain. Spider gave one of his necklaces to the mountain. We had made it up there—together!")

5. Finally, he seemed *sad*. (Page 307: "I didn't make a big deal over their leaving. I think they didn't want to say goodbye. I think they knew I would remember them forever. We were mountain climbers, pirates, and kings. We were the Acorn People.")

Writing

Think about an experience you had in which your attitude changed over time. Make a list of facts about the experience and also list some of your different feelings. Use your lists to describe your experience and your changing attitude. Try to use a different tone in each description to show your changing attitude.

Before students begin the writing assignment, have them each select the experience that they will write about. Encourage students to choose experiences that will easily show their changing attitude.

Some students will find it helpful to list the stages of the experience they are going to write about before putting their ideas into sentences and paragraphs.

Dolphins by Alice Herman Lehrer (p. 309)

Synopsis

This article describes dolphins, which, as mammals, have many characteristics in common with humans. Dolphins use a series of sounds to communicate with each other. Each dolphin has a special whistling sound, or signature, to identify itself. Dolphins can mimic human speech. They use sonar (sound waves) to locate where there are objects in the water. The Navy is presently trying to adapt the dolphin sonar system to lower-pitched sounds that humans can hear so that the system can be used to guide torpedoes.

Dolphins are often taken for porpoises, which look alike in some ways but are really quite different. Porpoises are not as intelligent, and they have differently shaped teeth and fins.

Fishermen used to think dolphins were good luck. Now, some consider dolphins a nuisance because they get tangled in the nets, thereby allowing tuna to escape. Dolphins are protected by law, but many are illegally killed.

Preparation

Ask students if they know which animal is most like humans in characteristics such as intelligence and ability to communicate. Discuss their responses. Then tell them that the dolphin may be more like humans than previously thought. The selection they are preparing to read will tell them more about this.

Vocabulary

*__mammal__ (*n.*) — warm-blooded animal that feeds milk to its young
__lever__ (*n.*) — bar or handle used to lift or turn something
__signature__ (*n.*) — identifying sound
__mimic__ (*v.*) — copy or imitate
*__dorsal__ (*adj.*) — on the back
*__sonar__ (*n.*) — device that uses sound waves to locate objects underwater
__oceanariums__ (*n.*) — large aquariums with seawater
__precisely__ (*adv.*) — exactly
__bionic__ (*adj.*) — applying human or animal problem-solving strategies to fields
    such as computer sciences
*__harass__ (*v.*) — bother

*Glossary word

Activities

A. See p. 6, Teaching Vocabulary.
B. Although students might not be able to locate the word *oceanariums* in a dictionary, most of them will be able to figure out its meaning. Ask which two words could be combined to make the new word *oceanarium (ocean and aquarium)*.
C. Review the definition of *mammal*. Have students give other examples of mammals.
D. Have students explain what a *signature* is for a human being. See if they can relate this meaning later to the use of the word in the article on dolphins.
E. Ask students what it means to *mimic* something or someone. Have a student provide an example.

Quick Quiz

1. mammal: a. fish that lives in the ocean   *b. warm-blooded animal that feeds its young milk*   c. animal that communicates with language
2. lever: a. place for speedy exit   b. round doorknob   *c. handle for lifting*
3. signature: *a. identifying sound*   b. typewritten name   c. underwater camera
4. mimic: a. entertain   *b. copy or imitate*   c. run around
5. dorsal: a. universal   b. under the belly   *c. on the back*
6. sonar: a. having to do with the sun   *b. device that locates objects with sound waves*   c. device that locates objects with light waves
7. oceanariums: *a. large aquarium with seawater*   b. public beaches and lakes   c. European waters
8. precisely: a. not nicely   *b. exactly*   c. undervalued
9. bionic: *a. applying human or animal problem-solving strategies*   b. designed by an underwater computer   c. energy food fed to dolphins and other mammals
10. harass: a. underwater   *b. bother*   c. build up

160

Setting the Purpose

The article students are about to read is an informative essay about beings that are close to humans in many ways—dolphins. Tell students that the article will challenge some of their ideas about human superiority.

The Selection

The selection is not too long, but it does contain some technical language and concepts. You may wish to break the reading as follows.

First, have students read the headnote and the article up to the middle of p. 311, col. 2 in the Anthology. Have them consider what it might be like if humans had the dolphins' sonar system. What would humans be able to do?

Then have students finish the article. Ask students what they think the future of the dolphin will be—existence or destruction? What might happen if humans and dolphins learn to communicate with each other?

When the discussion is over, have students complete Reading Comprehension on pp. 312–313 in the Anthology.

Follow-Up

See p. 7, Teaching Reading Comprehension and For Discussion.

Reading Comprehension

1. An experiment showed that dolphins are able to communicate with each other because *a. one dolphin told another how to get a reward of fish* (page 309, col. 1).
2. Dolphins have shown that they can imitate the way *c. people talk.* (Pages 309–310: "Dolphins who have come in contact with human beings can imitate words, laughter, and even the tones of different voices.")
3. Without echo-location, dolphins would probably *b. bump into objects in the water* (page 311, col. 1).
4. Humans cannot hear dolphin sonar because the sounds are too *b. high in pitch* (page 311, col. 1).
5. Dolphins in water shows use sonar to *a. do tricks at the same time* (page 311).
6. Dolphins are like cows inside because they have *c. several stomachs* (page 311, col. 2).
7. The dolphin is an enemy in some parts of the world because it *b. gets in the way of fishermen.* (Page 312, col. 1: "Thousands of dolphins have been killed by fishermen who feel they must protect their business.")
8. The author of this article believes dolphins are very *c. intelligent.*

For Discussion

1. How do dolphins communicate with one another? In what ways are their methods of communicating well suited to their environment? *Dolphins communicate by using sounds such as squeaks, whistles, chirps, clicks, and creaking. These sounds*

are suited for use in an underwater environment because the way the sounds travel enables dolphins to know distances. Other creatures can't hear the sounds, which makes using them safe.

2. Why are many scientists very interested in the way dolphins act? *Dolphins can mimic human speech. They can communicate and pass detailed information to each other. Their use of sonar has important scientific and military application.*

3. Should humans capture dolphins to study how they act? Or should dolphins be left alone in their natural environment? *Answers will vary. Accept any response students can explain and support.*

4. Do you think all the information the author has presented about dolphins is true? What techniques does the author use to help you trust the information that she presents? *Accept any responses students can support. Among the techniques the author uses to gain the reader's trust are the use of statistics (numbers) and the mention of specific authorities by name. Technical terms (including some in Latin) add to the legitimacy.*

Understanding Literature: Serious, Formal Tone

Objective: Students will identify the tone of a passage, and will briefly explain which of two passages is more effective.

Preparation

Discuss the concept of *tone*. Make sure that students understand that the tone reflects the author's approach toward his or her subject (as contrasted with mood—the feeling the author intends to create in the reader.)

Have students read and discuss the lesson on Serious, Formal Tone on p. 313 in the Anthology. Then have them complete the exercise, which asks them to evaluate two passages on the same material—one using a serious tone; the other, a flippant one.

Questions and Answers

1. "It's done by 'echo-location.' Scientists conducting the tests usually hear no sounds. But the dolphin is sending them out, too high for human ears. The sound waves bounce off objects and create sonar—a sort of echo in the water—so the dolphin knows exactly what is there."

2. Dolphins use a really wild technique called "echo-location." They make sounds too high for humans to listen in on. The sound waves bump into things and then come back in an echo, letting the dolphins in on the big secret of what is there.

   The tone of the second passage is casual, flippant, perhaps even a bit humorous. (Accept any reasonable response. One person's humor is another one's rudeness.) The serious presentation is intended to get the ideas across more effectively. Be prepared, however, for the student who successfully defends the notion that the second passage is more effective because it talks to the reader in his or her own language.

Writing

According to this article, dolphins are similar to porpoises. Look up *porpoise* in an encyclopedia. In a serious, formal tone, write 2 paragraphs about porpoises.

Dolphins and porpoises are often confused with one another. Encourage students to become "experts" on the differences between dolphins and porpoises by doing research. Bring an encyclopedia to the classroom or refer students to other reference books in the library. Have them outline the important facts before writing.

Emotion Twists Issues— Stick to the Facts

by Kevin E. Steele   *(p. 314)*

Synopsis

This article by Kevin Steele begins with two vignettes—one circulated by anti-handgun activists, the other by the NRA through its magazine *American Rifleman*. The first, in the words of a "lonesome grandmother," tells how her grandson was shot by an unknown assailant. The second tells how a storekeeper defended himself during a robbery. Steele claims that the first is designed to influence the noncommitted citizens on the issue of gun control. He says the second is an unemotional presentation of the facts. Steele then goes on to point out that automobile accidents kill far more people than guns. He says that banning guns will disarm the law-abiding citizens and not end violent crime. The author suggests that people who are in favor of gun control do research on how many lives are saved each year because of the handgun.

Preparation

Tell students that people sometimes use facts to support an emotionally charged issue. Tell them that other people may use the same facts and come to different conclusions. This and the next article show how the same facts can support different arguments.

Vocabulary

vignettes (*n.*) — small, graceful literary sketches
* **virulently** (*adv.*) — bitterly; spitefully
noncommitted (*adj.*) — not holding a definite point of view on an issue
* **elicit** (*v.*) — to bring out
* **appalling** (*adj.*) — causing great horror
anguish (*n.*) — suffering or distress
* **deterrent** (*n.*) — something that prevents (using fear or doubt) something from happening
* **dissect** (*v.*) — to cut apart
insidious (*adj.*) — sneaky and dangerous
travesty (*n.*) — ridiculous or shameful imitation
naive (*adj.*) — lacking in experience or judgment
* **assumptions** (*n.*) — things taken for granted

*Glossary word

163

Activities

A. See page 6, Teaching Vocabulary.
B. This selection contains a number of difficult words. Ask students to give examples from their personal experience to illustrate words on the list, such as *appalling, anguish, deterrent, travesty,* and *naive.*

Quick Quiz

1. vignettes: a. tasty vegetables   *b. literary sketches*   c. unbelievable tales
2. virulently: a. in a meaningful way   b. in an excellent mood   *c. bitterly or spitefully*
3. noncommitted: a. on one's own   *b. without a definite opinion*   c. under the weather
4. elicit: *a. to bring out*   b. not honest   c. turn on the light
5. appalling: a. very attractive   *b. causing great horror*   c. covering for a floor
6. anguish: a. sandwich   b. close relative   *c. suffering*
7. deterrent: a. strong soap powder   *b. prevention*   c. unpredicted problem
8. dissect: a. after-dinner sweet   *b. to cut apart*   c. make extremely dry
9. insidious: *a. dangerously sneaky*   b. extremely pleasant   c. in the center of
10. travesty: a. heavy cloth decoration   b. entertaining sideshow   *c. shameful imitation*
11. naive: *a. lacking in experience*   b. very intelligent   c. nasty to others
12. assumptions: a. religious medals   *b. things taken for granted*   c. extra payments

Setting the Purpose

Tell students that they are about to read an article that discusses gun control. It presents one side of this issue. Tell them to read carefully and to try to distinguish facts from emotional statements.

The Selection

This selection is very short and can easily be read in one session.

Begin by having students read the brief headnote and the two vignettes that begin the article. Discuss them briefly before going on. Remind students to keep the facts separate from the opinions as they read.

Have students read the rest of the article. When they have finished, have them complete Reading Comprehension on p. 317 in the Anthology.

Follow-Up

See p. 7, Teaching Reading Comprehension and For Discussion.

Reading Comprehension

1. Steele said that *American Rifleman* presents   *a. facts, not emotional appeals* (page 315, col. 1).

2. Handgun Control, Inc., would like to have laws passed to *b. ban the sale of handguns.* (Page 315, col. 2: "They hope to rival the membership of the NRA, and with that membership it is hoped that legislation banning the handgun will eventually come from Capitol Hill.")
3. In the year 1979, fewer people were killed with guns than *c. in automobile accidents* (page 316, col. 1).
4. According to the article, of all the guns produced in the U.S. each year, the number used in violent crimes is *c. less than 1%* (page 316, col. 1).
5. Steele felt that banning handguns would *b. restrict an individual's right to self-defense.* (Page 317: "We cannot allow our right of self-defense to be taken from us. . . .")

For Discussion

1. What are some facts that Kevin Steele presented in his article? Did he always stick to the facts or did he sometimes appeal to readers' emotions? *Accept any facts that students can support from the article. For example, the author cited the fact that in 1979, 51,900 Americans were killed in automobile accidents; this figure "represents a number that is almost 500% over the number of Americans who are fatally injured with a handgun during a violent crime" (page 316, col. 1). Call students' attention to the places in the article in which the author appears to make an emotional appeal.* (For example, page 316, col. 2: "Let all those who expound the virtues of Handgun Control, Inc., post signs on their front doors advertising that 'no handguns are in this house.' Let *them* rely solely on police protection and we will see just how long it takes them to realize their error.")
2. According to the author, why are cars more dangerous than guns? Do you agree? Why or why not? *The author feels that cars are more dangerous because so many more Americans have been killed in car accidents than in handgun-related incidents (page 316, col. 1). Answers will vary to the second and third parts of this question.*
3. What reasons did the author give to explain his support for the sale of legal handguns? With which reasons do you agree? With which reasons do you disagree? *His reasons included the following: violent crime will not be eradicated by the banning of handguns (page 316, col. 1; page 317); the handgun "is a strong deterrent to crime" (page 316, col. 2); the sale of handguns constitutes the "right of self-defense" (page 317). Answers to the second and third parts of this question will vary.*

Understanding Literature: Argumentative Tone

Objective: Students will recognize arguments for or against an issue.

Preparation

Define *argumentative tone* for students. Point out that writers often use it when they want to make a strong stand for or against an issue.

Have students read and discuss the lesson on Argumentative Tone on p. 318 in the

Anthology. Then have them complete the exercise, which requires them to differentiate between arguments *for* the writer's side and arguments *against* the other side.

Questions and Answers

1. "But has Handgun Control, Inc., done all its homework?"   *against*
2. "Alcoholics, unfortunately, are not [licensed, recorded, and restricted]."   *for*
3. "Yet victims of auto-related accidents are not clamoring and organizing for legislation to 'ban the car.' "   *for*
4. "The handgun in the hands of a licensed, law-abiding citizen is a strong deterrent to crime."   *for*
5. "Shields makes his mistake in blaming the loss of life on the weapon used, instead of on the criminal using it."   *against*
6. "We cannot allow our right of self-defense to be taken from us. . . ."   *for*

Writing

The gun-control problem is just one of the many controversial issues that are often in the news. Choose another topic (such as nuclear energy, the draft, equal rights for women, etc.). Take one side of the issue, and make a list of statements arguing for your side and against the other side.

Explain that a sound argument is based on facts. Encourage students to support statements of opinion with facts based upon research. After each student has selected an issue, allow time for exploring the facts. Then suggest that students limit their list of statements to 5 or 6 important points.

Guns: A Serious Problem   by Ann Landers   *(p. 319)*

Synopsis

This article begins with a letter to Ann Landers, telling of a senseless and unprovoked murder of a young man. The letter is followed by Landers' comments on the issue of gun control. She points out that in 1976, twice as many Americans were killed by guns at home as were killed in Vietnam during a 10-year period. Crimes committed with guns represent a significant cost to the taxpayer each year. Americans kill each other at a far greater rate than citizens of any other country. Landers points out that guns are available to anyone who wants them and that the easy availability of guns leads to accidental deaths—nearly 4,000 in one year—as well as to crime. She suggests that her readers tell their Representatives and Senators exactly how they feel about the issue of gun control.

Preparation

Tell students that the selection deals with the other side of the gun-control issue.

Vocabulary

irresponsible (*adj.*) — not responsible; unwilling (or unable) to answer to a higher
  authority or code of rules
lobbies (*n.*) — groups of people who seek to influence the votes of lawmakers
recuperation (*n.*) — recovery from illness or injury
*__compensation__ (*n.*) — payment
minors (*n.*) — young people not of legal age
idiots (*n.*) — completely foolish or senseless persons
*__brandishing__ (*v.*) — shaking or waving something
*__adept__ (*adj.*) — skilled
grudges (*n.*) — feelings of ill will
infinitely (*adv.*) — without limits; exceedingly great
intentionally (*adv.*) — on purpose
*__excruciating__ (*adj.*) — extremely painful; unbearabale

*Glossary word

Activities

A. See p. 6, Teaching Vocabulary.
B. Have students see how many words on the list they can use in one sentence.
C. Be sure that students understand the meaning of the word *lobbies* that will be
   used in this article.

Quick Quiz

1. irresponsible: a. easy to get along with   *b. not responsible*   c. under the
   weather
2. lobbies: a. inexpensive hotel rooms   b. things to do in your spare time   *c.
   groups of people seeking to influence lawmakers*
3. recuperation: a. preparation of dinner   b. method of learning   *c. recovery
   from injury*
4. compensation: a. excitement   *b. payment*   c. deep thought
5. minors: *a. young people*   b. baseball fields   c. steelworkers
6. idiots: a. animals   *b. foolish people*   c. good friends
7. brandishing: a. making marks on   b. entertaining   *c. waving about*
8. adept: a. owing money   *b. skilled*   c. interested
9. grudges: *a. feelings of ill will*   b. slices of sweet cake   c. people of few words
10. infinitely: a. soon to end   *b. without limits*   c. not too large
11. intentionally: a. by accident   b. extended efforts   *c. on purpose*
12. excruciating: *a. extremely painful*   b. too expensive to buy   c. mildly un-
    pleasant

Setting the Purpose

Remind students that the article "Emotion Twists Issues—Stick to the Facts" presented only one side of the gun-control issue. As they read the other side, encourage
them to keep in mind the facts and arguments presented by Kevin Steele.

The Selection

This selection is very short and can be read in one session.

Have a student volunteer read the letter to Ann Landers. Then have students discuss possible responses before reading Landers' answer.

Have students read Landers' answer. Ask them to discuss it briefly. Then have them complete Reading Comprehension on p. 323 in the Anthology.

Follow-Up

See p. 7, Teaching Reading Comprehension and For Discussion.

Reading Comprehension

1. Ann Landers knows that most Americans want gun control because   *a. polls show this idea to be true* (page 319, col. 2; page 322, col. 2).
2. If 98 percent of all burglaries are committed when no one is at home, it would seem that   *a. a gun isn't much protection against burglary.*
3. According to Landers, most people who are killed by guns are shot by   *c. relatives or people they know* (page 322, col. 1).
4. Landers believes that banning guns would   *b. save lives.* She agrees that "people kill people" but points out that guns make it much easier to do so (page 321, col. 1).

For Discussion

What are some of the facts that Ann Landers presented? How do her facts compare with those presented by Kevin Steele in "Emotion Twists Issues—Stick to the Facts"? *The facts included the following: approximately 25,000 Americans were killed by guns in 1976 (page 319, col. 2); twice as many Americans were killed by guns at home in 1976 as were killed in the Vietnam War (page 319, col. 2); fatalities and wounds inflicted by guns cost United States taxpayers approximately $4 billion a year (page 320). In comparison to Steele, Landers relies heavily on statistics. Answers to the second question will vary. Students may state that Landers has more statistics, and from more authoritative sources. Steele also uses his statistics to support an emotional appeal, much more emotional than Landers'.*

Understanding Literature: Emotional vs. Factual Tone

Objective: Students will identify emotional and factual statements.

Preparation

Discuss the use of tone in presenting an argument. Point out that a *factual tone* is designed to appeal to a reader's mind. An *emotional tone* is intended to appeal to a reader's feelings.

Have students read and discuss the lesson on Emotional and Factual Tone on p. 323 in the Anthology. Then have them complete the exercise.

Questions and Answers

1. "It makes me sick to know that whoever did this awful thing is out there some-where—walking around with that gun." *emotional tone*
2. "There are at least 90 million guns out there and many are in the hands of crazy, irresponsible people." *factual tone*
3. "Are the gun manufacturers and lobbies in Washington stronger than the voice of the people?" *emotional tone*
4. "Gun killings and wounds cost the United States taxpayer at least $4 billion a year, according to the U.S. Department of Justice." *factual tone*

Writing

Choose one side of a controversial issue. Write one paragraph in which you make an emotional appeal for your side. Write another paragraph in which you make a factual appeal for your side.

Before students begin this assignment, encourage them to discuss possible topics. On the board, develop two lists of words—one of words that will appeal to emotion, another of words that will help present facts. Then have students complete the assignment.

Section Review

Vocabulary: Technical Terms

Objective: Students will identify technical terms from the selections.

Preparation

Define *technical term* for students. Explain that words used in a special way in a particular subject area or job are called technical terms.

Have students read and discuss the lesson on Technical Terms on p. 324 in the Anthology. Then have them complete the exercise.

Questions and Answers

Hemitragus jemlaicus ("Central Park," p. 288)—tahr (an animal)
bonderizer ("Steelworker: Mike Lefevre," p. 292)—a machine that bonds two pieces of metal together
muscular dystrophy ("The Acorn People," p. 298)—a disease in which the muscles waste away
echo-location ("Dolphins," p. 311)—use of sound waves and echoes to find position
sonar ("Dolphins," p. 311)—sound waves under water used to locate objects
oceanariums ("Dolphins," p. 311)—large aquariums filled with seawater
workmen's compensation ("Guns: A Serious Problem," p. 320)—money paid to workers that compensates (or makes up for) some loss

Reading: Separating Facts and Opinions

Objective: Students will indicate whether statements express a fact or an opinion.

Preparation

Tell students that a *fact* is a statement about something that exists or has happened. An *opinion* is a statement that tells how someone feels about something. It is important to be able to tell the difference between a fact and an opinion.

Have students read and discuss the lesson on Separating Facts and Opinions on p. 324 in the Anthology. Point out that writers may try to use opinions as if they were facts in an effort to persuade readers. Tell students to pay close attention to this. Then have them complete the exercise by indicating whether each statement is a fact or an opinion.

Questions and Answers

1. "If I had a 20-hour workweek, I'd get to know my kids better, my wife better." *opinion*
2. "I think the poet owes something to the guy who builds the cabin for him." *opinion*
3. "He was very small, and his legs were crippled by polio." *fact*
4. "An adult bottle-nosed dolphin can keep 20 pounds of fish inside his body. . . ." *fact*
5. "Criminals who resort to the use of lethal weapons . . . are animals, pure and simple." *opinion*
6. ". . . 98 percent of burglaries are committed when no one is at home." *fact*

Quiz

See p. 7, Administering the Quiz.

Reading Comprehension

1. The walk in "Central Park" takes place in the spring. Name two signs of spring that John Updike wrote about in his journal account. *The signs include the half-frozen pond, the condition of the ground under foot (slushy snow melting), the way people are dressed, and the activities.*
2. Why did Mike Lefevre want workers to have a 20-hour workweek? *A 20-hour workweek would allow workers to spend more time with their families and expand personally* (page 292).
3. Why did the boys in "The Acorn People" decide to climb Lookout Mountain? *They decided to climb Lookout Mountain because Boy Scouts could do it and it was worth a try* (page 301, col. 1).
4. What is one way in which dolphins are more advanced than humans? *Dolphins are far superior to humans in the use of sonar* (page 310).
5. What is one major reason Kevin Steele gives for not banning handguns? What is one major reason Ann Landers gives for banning handguns? *One major reason*

Kevin Steele thinks handguns should not be banned is that he believes people should be able to defend themselves. One major reason that Ann Landers thinks handguns should be banned is to save lives. Accept any other answers that students can support with reference to the selections.

Understanding Literature

6. What are some different forms of nonfiction? What are some of the major purposes of nonfiction? *Forms of nonfiction include biographies, books, columns, debates, editorials, essays, feature and news stories, histories, interviews, journal accounts, diaries, letters, and magazine or newspaper articles. Nonfiction may be written to narrate, describe, analyze, inform, entertain, or persuade* (pages 286–287).

7. What tone did John Updike use in "Central Park"? *John Updike used a playful, amused tone* (page 290, col. 2).

8. How did Ron Jones's attitude toward his job change in "The Acorn People"? *At first Ron thought that he would never get close to the campers and he wanted to quit* (page 298, col. 1). *By the end of the season he knew that he would cherish the experience forever* (page 307).

9. Why did the author of "Dolphins" use a serious, formal tone? *This tone encourages readers to trust the accuracy of the author's information* (page 313, col. 2).

10. What methods do Kevin Steele and Ann Landers use to convince readers that handguns should or should not be banned? *They use persuasion based upon research. They present facts and statistics. And both authors present arguments and appeals in favor of their respective points of view.*

Composition

1. Keep an "observation journal." Take a walk through a familiar place. Carry a notebook with you and jot down everything you see or hear. Later, write a description of what you observed. Make sure your tone fits the feeling you had on your walk.

   Refer students to the selection about Central Park if you wish. Suggest that each student select a place to observe. It need not be on the scale of a large park but could be a room, for example. To help students select an appropriate tone for the place being described, have them ask themselves the question, "How does this place make me feel?" Tone is the underlying expression of those feelings that an author wishes to communicate to the reader.

2. Look for a persuasive article in the editorial section of a newspaper or magazine. List some of the writer's arguments in the article and some of the methods used to try to get readers on his or her side. Write 2 or 3 paragraphs about the writer's stand on the issue and his or her persuasive techniques.

   Have students bring the persuasive articles they have found to class. More than one article on the same topic will enhance discussion. Then have each student list the points made in the article he or she will use for the assignment. Have them think about the strategies of persuasion these arguments represent. Then have them write the composition. For most students, one paragraph about the arguments and a second paragraph about the techniques will be sufficient.

3. Choose one of the topics below to research for a report, or discuss a different topic with your teacher. Then go to a library and search through the card catalog and the *Readers' Guide to Periodical Literature* to find sources for your research. Read several sources and make a list of facts about your subjects. Develop the list into a written report.
   a. The first airplanes
   b. Fast-food restaurants
   c. New trends in music
   d. The value of jogging

   This assignment is an excellent opportunity to review (or teach) the use of the card catalog and the *Readers' Guide to Periodical Literature*. The topics are likely to interest students while being easy enough to research. You may, of course, wish to add a topic that would be of special interest to your students.

Enrichment

1. Students who found the account of Mike Lefevre, the steelworker, to be of interest might like to read additional selections from *Working* by Studs Terkel.
2. Have students locate and read additional examples of nonfiction in newspapers and magazines. Have them pay particular attention to examples of persuasive writing.
3. Have students compare written newspaper accounts of a news event to the reporting of the same event on television or radio.

Authors

Ann Landers. Ann Landers (whose real name is Esther Pauline Lederer) was born on July 4, 1918, in Sioux City, Iowa. She is best known for her syndicated advice column that appears daily in nearly one thousand newspapers in the United States. She has been responding to readers' problems since she was hired for the job by the Chicago Sun Times in 1955. In her column and books, Landers deals with topics such as marriage, drugs, sex, and parent-teenager relationships, although these are only a few of the seemingly limitless subjects she addresses in her snappy, common-sense style. Her identical twin sister, Pauline Esther Friedman Phillips writes another highly popular advice column—"Dear Abby."

Studs Terkel. Born in New York City on May 16, 1912, Terkel worked at many jobs before becoming a radio and television broadcaster in 1945. He is best known for his personal interest in the history of ordinary people, and his ability to put a sincere voice into the writing of it. His publications include *Hard Times: An Oral History of the Great Depression* (1970) and *Working: People Talk About What They Do All Day and How They Feel About What They Do* (1974).

Section 9
Humor

Section Focus

The focus of Section 9 is humor. The section begins with a humorous satire on air pollution and ends with a hilarious story about a teenage girl's quest for beauty.

The Introduction on p. 328 in the Anthology begins with an example of humor and goes on to discuss the different techniques of humorous writing, including the use of incongruity, satire, puns, and exaggeration.

Have students read and discuss the Introduction in class. If you wish, some students might like to volunteer additional examples of humor in the spirit of the penguin story.

The activities that follow the selection focus on understanding satire and irony, exaggeration, puns, and ironic situations.

Fresh Air Will Kill You   by Art Buchwald   (p. 330)

Synopsis

In this satire, Art Buchwald tells of going to Flagstaff, Arizona, for a speaking engagement. He notices right away that there is something peculiar about the place. It is the fresh air that is bothering him. He isn't used to it. His host assures him that it's safe to breathe fresh air. Buchwald says that no one who lives in a major city can tolerate fresh air for very long.

Buchwald says he misses sneezing, and the fresh air is making him dizzy. He finds a truck, pays the driver five dollars to let him breathe the exhaust fumes for a half hour, and then feels revived enough to give his speech. He finally goes to Los Angeles and is happy to breathe the smog-filled air and sneeze again.

Preparation

Tell students that this short article by humorist Art Buchwald is a satire that deals with the problems of air pollution. By joking, Buchwald shows how people have come to accept a dangerous condition.

Vocabulary

†**satire** (*n.*) — literature that uses irony or sarcasm
***polluted** (*adj.*) — foul or unclean
 lecturing (*v.*) — giving speeches
 advantage (*n.*) — benefit or gain
***tolerance** (n.) — ability to stand something
 industry (*n.*) — manufacturing business

*Glossary word
†Handbook of Terms in Literature

Activities

A. See p. 6, Teaching Vocabulary.
B. Have students use the words *polluted, tolerance,* and *industry* in the same sentence. Or, you may wish to let them write two sentences, using one pair of the words in one sentence and another pair in the other sentence.
C. Have students think of examples to illustrate the word *advantage.*

Quick Quiz

1. satire: *a. ironic or sarcastic writing*   b. a jewel   c. factual essay
2. polluted: a. impossible to breathe   b. painted a strange color   *c. foul or unclean*
3. lecturing: a. stretching   *b. giving speeches*   c. yelling at
4. advantage: a. place to look   *b. benefit*   c. exciting event
5. tolerance: a. prejudice   b. communication device   *c. ability to stand something*
6. industry: *a. manufacturing*   b. experiences   c. air pollution

Setting the Purpose

Ask students if they think it is possible to make a point by saying just the opposite of what you mean. Tell them that this is what Art Buchwald does in the article they are about to read. Have them read "Fresh Air Will Kill You" to see how Buchwald uses this technique.

The Selection

This article is very short and can be read all at once. Have students read it through silently. Then two or more student volunteers can read it aloud, each taking the part of one of the speakers.

After reading the article, have students complete Reading Comprehension on p. 332 in the Anthology.

Follow-Up

See p. 7, Teaching Reading Comprehension and For Discussion.

Reading Comprehension

1. In this article, Art Buchwald made fun of   *b. the problem of air pollution.*
2. The author first suspected that something was wrong in Flagstaff because   *a. the air smelled funny.* (Page 331: "What's that smell?")
3. To solve his fresh air "problem," the author   *c. breathed truck exhaust fumes* (page 332).
4. The article suggests that a major cause of air pollution is   *c. both of the above* [*truck exhaust fumes and industry*].
5. In this article, Art Buchwald   *a. showed how people get used to bad conditions.* (Page 331: " . . . people are getting so used to polluted air that it's very difficult for them to breathe anything else.")

For Discussion

1. Does Buchwald really believe that fresh air will kill people? What point is he trying to make? *No, he does not believe that fresh air will kill people. He is trying to make exactly the opposite point—that polluted air causes discomfort.*
2. Which parts of the article seem funny or crazy? Why do you think the author decided to use humor to make his point? *The whole article seems crazy because the normal situation is reversed. Students may cite the end of the story, when Buchwald breathes exhaust fumes and can't wait to get to Los Angeles. Answers to the second question will vary.*
3. Can you think of any other problems and bad conditions that people have accepted as normal? *Answers will vary. Some answers might be poor public transportation, shoddy merchandise, and poor treatment by sales clerks.*

Understanding Literature: Satire and Irony

Objective: Students will explain the irony in ironic statements.

Preparation

Discuss satire and irony with students. Tell them that *satire* is writing that makes fun of a situation or a character for the purpose of making a particular point. Ask students how the article they have just read is an example of satire.

Define *irony* as a contrast of ideas in which one thing would seem to be true, but a very different thing actually occurs. Ask students for examples of ironic situations.

Then have students read and discuss the lesson on Satire and Irony on p. 333 in the Anthology. Have them complete the exercise, which asks them to explain the point the author of the article is trying to make with each of five ironic statements.

Questions and Answers

1. " 'Tests have proved that you can breathe fresh air day and night without its doing any harm to the body.' " *It is ironic that the statement is about fresh air. Polluted air is what requires testing for harmful effects.*
2. " 'Nobody who has lived in a major city can stand fresh air for a very long time.' " *The reverse is true. People who have lived in a major city often miss fresh air.*
3. " 'If I'd known I was coming to a place that had nothing but fresh air, I would have brought a surgical mask.' " *A surgical mask might be a defense against polluted air, not fresh air.*
4. " 'Flagstaff can't seem to attract industry. I guess we're really behind the times.' " *Lack of industry is often an asset today, as is fresh air.*
5. " . . . when I got off the plane, I took one big deep breath of the smog-filled air, my eyes started to water, I began to sneeze, and I felt like a new man again." *Most people respond to smog, watering eyes, and sneezing with complaints. They don't feel good about such discomfort.*

Writing

Clip an editorial cartoon from a newspaper. Then, in one or two paragraphs, explain the point of the cartoon. How has the cartoonist used satire or irony to make the point?

For this assignment, be sure that each student selects a cartoon that is easily understood. Discuss the points to be made before students begin to write.

And They Lived Happily Ever After for a While
by John Ciardi   *(p. 334)*

The Selection

Before having students read this poem, tell them that it deals in part with the same subject as Art Buchwald's article. Have them keep this in mind as they read. After students have read the poem silently, ask a volunteer to read it aloud.

Follow-Up

Discuss the questions that accompany the poem.

Questions and Answers

1. How would you describe the mood of this poem? How do the people in it feel? *The mood is satirical. The people seem to be resigned to their situation.*
2. Why is this poem in the "Humor" section of this book? *The poem cannot be taken seriously. You may wish to introduce the term "tongue in cheek" to describe the ironic humor in this selection.*
3. What will happen when the "needles quiver shut on the zero mark"? *The oxygen will be completely gone and the people will die.*
4. In what ways is this poem like "Fresh Air Will Kill You"? *It deals in a humorous way with the serious problem of air pollution. It shows that people seem to be able to get used to anything for a while.*

The Cow Who Liked to Kick

by Ambrose Bierce   *(p. 336)*

Synopsis

Aunt Patience owns a cow named Phoebe. Instead of producing milk, Phoebe spends her days and nights kicking everyone and everything in sight. Nevertheless, Aunt Patience loves Phoebe and demands that each new farmhand brush the cow every morning. This invariably results in the farmhand leaving the farm. No farmhand is willing to come to work for Aunt Phoebe, so she decides it's time to get married again. No one wants to marry her, but somehow she catches the last eligible male around, a man named Jeremiah Huggins. She orders him to care for Phoebe, but the crafty Huggins dresses up a cast-iron pump to look like himself. When Phoebe kicks the pump, she is injured and stops kicking. Weeks later, Aunt Patience lets her guard down and approaches the cow. Phoebe gives her a kick that leaves the woman neatly plastered onto a stone wall. A mason couldn't have done a better job with a trowel.

Preparation

Ask students if they know what the word *exaggeration* means. Have them provide examples. Then tell them that the story they are about to read uses exaggeration as a technique to make its point.

Vocabulary

*exaggerating (*v.*) — overstating an idea beyond truth
profitable (*adj.*) — worthwhile
meteor (*n.*) — shooting star

demanding (*adj.*) — insisting; difficult to please
employees (*n.*) — hired hands
gossiped (*v.*) — talked about someone
eligible (*adj.*) — available and fit or able
mischief (*n.*) — trouble
familiar (*adj.*) — well known
observer (*n.*) — someone who watches
trowel (*n.*) — spreader for cement; hand shovel

*Glossary word

Activities

A. See p. 6, Teaching Vocabulary.
B. See if students can use the words *profitable, demanding,* and *employees* all in one sentence.
C. Ask if someone who *gossiped* all the time might get into *mischief.* How might this occur?
D. Ask what sights might be *familiar* to an *observer* of nature.

Quick Quiz

 1. exaggerating: a. making smaller   b. telling the truth   *c. overstating an idea*
 2. profitable: a. the right size   *b. worthwhile*   c. predictable
 3. meteor: *a. shooting star*   b. short distance   c. argument
 4. demanding: a. easy to please   *b. insisting*   c. adding up to
 5. employees: *a. hired people*   b. users   c. bosses
 6. gossiped: a. used slowly   *b. talked about someone*   c. liked animals
 7. eligible: *a. available and fit*   b. easy to read   c. unworkable
 8. mischief: a. head of something   b. woman farmer   *c. trouble*
 9. familiar: a. mother and father   *b. well known*   c. always in trouble
10. observer: a. waiter   b. stubborn one   *c. one who watches*
11. trowel: a. cloth for drying   *b. spreader for cement*   c. small rooster

Setting the Purpose

Tell students that "The Cow Who Liked to Kick" is a satire that uses exaggeration to make its point. Tell them that the author, Ambrose Bierce, was well known for his short stories. As students read, have them look for things in this story that could be facts, and for items that are obviously fantasy.

The Selection

This story is short and easy to read and can be handled by most groups at one sitting.

Have students read up to the point where Aunt Patience marries Jeremiah Huggins (p. 338, col. 1). Before continuing, ask them to predict what they think will happen. Ask what they would do in similar circumstances.

When students have completed the story, ask them if they think Aunt Patience got what she deserved. Then have them complete Reading Comprehension on p. 340 in the Anthology.

Follow-Up

See p. 7, Teaching Reading Comprehension and For Discussion.

Reading Comprehension

1. Phoebe helped Aunt Patience by *a. driving off farmhands before they were paid.* (Page 337, col. 1: "All the farmhands left before their first paychecks.")
2. Aunt Patience married Jeremiah because *b. she wanted someone to do the farmwork for her.* (Page 337, col. 2: "But there was no one to plant her crops. And even if there had been, who would harvest them?")
3. Jeremiah tricked Phoebe by *b. putting his own clothes on a cast-iron pump* (page 338, col. 2).
4. By the end of the story, *a. Phoebe had changed completely.*

For Discussion

1. How did the story end? In what way does the ending show that justice was finally achieved? *Phoebe gave Aunt Patience a kick that plastered her onto a wall. Justice was done because Aunt Patience, who had subjected countless others to Phoebe's kicks, finally got kicked herself.*
2. What sort of people are Aunt Patience and Jeremiah? How are they alike or different? *The author presents both as exaggerated, or even cartoon, characters. Both use clever schemes to get their way. However, Aunt Patience only wants to use people for what service they can give her. Jeremiah seems to be less of a manipulator.*

Understanding Literature: Exaggeration

Objective: Students will identify examples of exaggeration.

Preparation

Discuss *exaggeration* and have students give as many examples of it from their personal experience as they can.

Have them read and discuss the lesson on Exaggeration on p. 340 in the Anthology. Then have them complete the exercise.

Questions and Answers

1. "This creature was not a good cow or a profitable one." *no exaggeration*
2. "On good days, Phoebe would have many animals in the air all at once." *exaggeration—funny*
3. "Men married their cooks, their enemies' sisters—whomever they could find." *exaggeration—unkind*
4. "Whenever he went into a cornfield, the crows would fight to sit on his shoulders." *exaggeration—funny*
5. "My aunt had never dared get this close to her beloved cow before." *no exaggeration*

Writing

Go back to the story and find at least eight examples of exaggeration. Then rewrite each one to make it realistic. Is it still funny? Why or why not?

If you wish, the exaggerations in the story can be identified as a group activity before individual students take on the task of rewriting them to be realistic. This is a writing activity that can be done by pupil teams as well as independently. Students should realize that the examples, which would ordinarily be commonplace occurrences or descriptions, are humorous because of the exaggeration.

Who's on First?   by Bud Abbott & Lou Costello   *(p. 341)*

Synopsis

"Who's on First?" is a comedy routine made famous by Abbott and Costello. Each of the ballplayers on the St. Louis team has a name that also means something else. For example, "Who" is the name of the first baseman, so that when Costello asks "Who's on first?" Abbott, of course, answers "Yes." The entire piece contains this type of play on words. The only way students will get the full impact of this humor is to read the routine aloud, and we suggest that they do.

Preparation

Ask students if they know what a *pun* is. Tell them that the selection they are about to read is made up of puns and plays on words. Explain that Abbott and Costello performed a famous comedy routine during the 1940's. Many people laughed at their humorous act, and the students will also enjoy reading the lines.

Vocabulary

peculiar (*adj.*) — odd or strange
absolutely (*adv.*) — certainly; without a doubt
naturally (*adv.*) — of course

comedy routine (*n.*) — humorous act or show

Activities

A. See p. 6, Teaching Vocabulary.
B. Have students think up funny questions that can be answered by using the words *absolutely* or *naturally*.
C. See how many examples students can dream up to illustrate the word *peculiar*.

Quick Quiz

1. peculiar: a. not truthful   b. expensive   *c. odd or strange*

2. absolutely: a. too large to count   *b. certainly*   c. not so close
3. naturally: *a. of course*   b. still alive   c. one too many
4. comedy routine: a. funny but plain   *b. a humorous act*   c. a bit of tragedy

Setting the Purpose

Remind students that the selection they are about to read is made up of many plays on words. Tell them that people used to go to theaters to see comedy routines such as this one. Have them read the selection aloud to see why.

The Selection

This selection is best done as Abbott and Costello did it—as an act. Have students read it silently to prepare. Then have two volunteers assume the parts and read it aloud. Many Abbott and Costello movies are shown on television, so some students will know the sort of expression and actions Abbott and Costello would have used.

Follow-Up

See p. 7, Teaching Reading Comprehension and For Discussion.

Reading Comprehension

1. When Abbott said, "On the St. Louis team, Who's on first," he meant that   *c. the player's name was Who* (page 341, col. 1).
2. When Costello asked, "Then, who's playin' first?" and Abbott said, "Yes," Abbott meant that   *a. Costello had named the first baseman correctly* (page 341, col. 1).
3. When Costello said, "I don't care," he was   *b. saying what he meant* (page 344, col. 2).
4. Costello got confused because   *a. all the players' names had other meanings.*

For Discussion

1. What was Abbott's role in this comedy routine? What did Costello do? How do their two roles fit together? *Abbott's role was to tell Costello the names of the players on the St. Louis team. He set up the puns and acted as if there was no reason for Costello to be confused. Costello's role was to find out the names of the players. Their roles fit together since both played it straight and persisted in spite of the hilarious confusion.*
2. Do you think someone who didn't understand English well would understand this routine? Why or why not? *Answers will vary. Students can infer that the humor depends on an understanding of the play on words. Of course, the important words are simple words. Much of the humor in this routine results from confusion, and even people who do not know English well would understand it, as long as they realize that the two characters are speaking on different levels.*

Understanding Literature: Puns

Objective: Students will select the pun that completes each joke.

Preparation

This lesson is about *puns* as a form of humor. Ask students if they know what a pun is. If you can stand it, encourage them to provide examples. Be sure the students understand that a pun is a play on words—a way of using words that sound the same but have different meanings and make something funny.

Have students read and discuss the lesson on Puns on p. 345 in the Anthology.

Questions and Answers

1. "Why did the window call the doctor?" "Because it had a *pane.*"
2. "Everything in my uncle's store costs a penny." "That makes a lot of *cents.*"
3. "Which building has the most *stories?*" "The public library."
4. "If you put six ducks in a crate what do you have?" "A box of *quackers.*"
5. "What was the most popular ride in the king of Egypt's amusement park?" "The *Pharaoh's* wheel."

Writing

Write a short dialogue of your own in which you introduce 4 or 5 puns. One character should set up the jokes while the other one presents the puns.

If you wish, students can work in pairs on this assignment. Some students will find it easier to try the puns out loud before writing them.

How Beautiful With Mud

by Hildegarde Dolson   *(p. 346)*

Synopsis

In Hildegarde's first year of high school she becomes conscious of the ads for beauty products. She spends her allowance and much of her time trying to become beautiful. Her family frequently asks, "What is Hildegarde doing in the bathroom?"

She is tempted by an ad for Beauty Clay, a miraculous product that costs $4.98, but wonders how she can get the money. Then her father offers to give her five dollars if she makes the honor roll. Hildegarde struggles to do so and succeeds. Finally, she talks the druggist into ordering the product.

At last it comes. Hildegarde applies the product and lets it harden. The directions suggest 20 minutes, but Hildegarde figures if she leaves it on for 40 minutes, she will become twice as beautiful. When she tries to remove the mask, she can't. The concrete-like clay is stuck to her face. She goes downstairs for a knife, encounters her brother, and swears him to secrecy.

When Hildegarde finally manages to remove the Beauty Clay, bits of her skin come off, too. Her face is not beautiful as promised, but red and raw. At her brother's suggestion she tells her parents that she has been frostbitten. They don't believe her, but let it go. Hildegarde plans her ultimate revenge and decides that some day she, too, is going to write advertisements.

Preparation

Tell students that "How Beautiful With Mud" is an account of a young girl who fell for the overstated claims of an advertisement and got something other than what she bargained for. Ask students if they have ever been persuaded to purchase something and then been disappointed. Discuss their responses.

Vocabulary

*tactful (*adj.*) — doing and saying the right thing
*appalled (*adj.*) — filled with horror
inquiries (*n.*) — questions
rigid (*adj.*) — hard and stiff
visage (*n.*) — face
*illusions (*n.*) — false ideas
revenge (*n.*) — paying back for a wrong

prevailed upon (*v.*) — persuaded

*Glossary word

Activities

A. See p. 6, Teaching Vocabulary.
B. Ask students which words on the list could describe the way a person acted or felt (*tactful, appalled*).
C. Ask students to suggest examples to illustrate *illusion* and *inquiries*.

Quick Quiz

1. tactful: a. sticky or difficult   b. secure and safe   *c. saying the right thing*
2. appalled: a. wrapped in a sheet   b. showed up suddenly   *c. filled with horror*
3. inquiries: *a. questions*   b. replies   c. rudeness
4. rigid: *a. stiff*   b. right   c. wrong
5. visage: a. viewpoint   *b. face*   c. small town
6. illusions: a. campaigns   b. refusals   *c. false ideas*
7. revenge: *a. paying back for a wrong*   b. attempt to turn around   c. try to do over again
8. prevailed upon: a. went ahead of   *b. persuaded*   c. stuck up for

Setting the Purpose

Ask if students would buy a product that an ad said would make a miraculous change in their appearance. Tell them that Hildegarde did just that, with surprising results. Have them read "How Beautiful With Mud" to find out what she bought and what happened.

The Selection

Have students read the account in three parts, and discuss each part as they go along.

Begin by having a student volunteer read the headnote aloud. Then have the class read silently up to p. 348, col. 2: "My only problem was how to lay my hands on $4.98." Before continuing, ask students if any of them have had an experience in which their family reacted the way Hildegarde's did when she used the Nipso. Then ask how they think Hildegarde will manage to get the money she needs for Beauty Clay.

Have students read to the bottom of p. 349, col. 2: "I needed a face—any old face." Ask what they think Hildegarde is going to do now.

Have students finish the story to find out if or how Hildegarde saved her face. Then have them complete Reading Comprehension on p. 352 in the Anthology.

Follow-Up

See p. 7, Teaching Reading Comprehension and For Discussion.

Reading Comprehension

1. When Hildegarde became a teenager, she   *c. wanted to become beautiful.* (Page 346, col. 1: "I, too, would be beautiful.")
2. The problem with Nipso was that it   *b. smelled terrible* (page 346, col. 2).
3. Hildegarde thought Beauty Clay was worth $4.98 because   *a. the woman in the ad looked beautiful.* (Page 348, col. 2: "Boy, was she beautiful.")
4. The story of Beauty Clay's discovery in Europe was probably   *a. an invention of the person who wrote the advertisement.*
5. When Hildegarde left the clay on her face too long, it   *c. became very hard to remove.* (Page 349, col. 2: "It was like splashing at the Rock of Gibraltar.")
6. Hildegarde decided to become an ad writer in order to   *b. trick other people the way she had been tricked* (page 352).

For Discussion

1. Why did Hildegarde become interested in beauty products? *Hildegarde became interested in beauty products when she reached adolescence. She saw pictures in magazines of beautiful women who used beauty products. She determined to have them and be beautiful, so she would be attractive to men.*
2. When she saw the results of the Beauty Clay, the author said, "My illusion had been cracked wide open—and not by a silver knife." What did she mean by this statement? *Her false ideas about Beauty Clay were abruptly corrected.*
3. What did Hildegarde learn from her experience with Beauty Clay? Do you think this changed her thinking about becoming beautiful? Why or why not? *She learned that, in some cases, advertising claims may be exaggerated. Her plan to get revenge shows that her thinking changed.*
4. Can you think of any ads like the one for Beauty Clay? How do they sell the product? Why do people respond to this kind of advertising? *Answers to the first*

184

question will vary. The ads sell products by playing on people's desires. Although the products may not be effective for all, people buy them because they want to be beautiful, or popular, or whatever the ad implies.

Understanding Literature: Ironic Situations

Objective: Students will describe the expectations and results in ironic situations.

Preparation

Explain that humor writers sometimes use irony to make a point or to make readers laugh. The story students have just read contains a number of *ironic situations.* Something is expected, but the opposite results.

Have students read and discuss the lesson on Ironic Situations on p. 353 in the Anthology. Then have them complete the exercise in which they are required to contrast what Hildegarde expects to happen with what actually does happen.

Questions and Answers

1. She spent hours in the bathroom every night. *She hoped the hours in the bathroom would make her beautiful. Instead, they just made her family curious.*
2. She tried Nipso on her legs. *She thought Nipso would make her legs flawless. Instead, her family told her how bad it smelled.*
3. She went to the drugstore with $5. *She expected the druggist to give her a jar of Beauty Clay for her $5. Instead, he said he had never heard of Beauty Clay.*
4. She left the Beauty Clay on twice as long as suggested. *She thought that leaving the Beauty Clay on for twice as long would make her twice as beautiful. Leaving it on that long made it almost impossible to remove.*
5. She finally removed the Beauty Clay. *She expected to be beautifully transformed. Her skin was red, raw, and damaged.*

Writing

Make up two products and write an advertisement for each. Promise people anything, as long as you persuade them to buy the product. (This is probably what Hildegarde had in mind when she planned to become an ad writer.)

Before having students write their own ads, you might have them locate and evaluate ads in magazines. Discuss whether or not the advertisements are believable.

Section Review

Vocabulary: Idioms

Objective: Students will write the meaning of idiomatic expressions.

Preparation

Tell students that an *idiom* is an expression with a special meaning that differs from the meaning of the individual words. For example, the person who says "I could eat a house" is not threatening to consume a real house, but is simply telling how hungry he or she is. Ask students to volunteer as many idioms as they can.

Have them read and discuss the lesson on Idioms on p. 354 in the Anthology. Then have them complete the exercise.

Questions and Answers

1. "... I *felt like a new man* again." *felt better, completely recovered*
2. "I *gave my heart* to my Bonnie ..." *fell in love with*
3. "*Her heart belonged* to Phoebe ..." *cared most for*
4. "And get things *shipshape*." *in order*
5. "With the *speed of lightning*, Phoebe gave a terrible kick." *very quickly*
6. "Phoebe herself began *spinning like a top*." *turning around rapidly*
7. "It took three trips to convince him he must order it immediately, money *on the line*." *right there*
8. "In fact, it was *dirt cheap* at the price." *very cheap, as cheap as dirt*
9. "I got home to the empty house at 20 minutes of four, and *made a beeline for* the Beauty Clay." *direct line*

Reading: Author's Purpose

Objective: Students will match titles with statements of the author's purpose.

Preparation

Discuss the concept of *author's purpose* for writing something. Ask students why they think certain things are written. Ask them what different reasons an author might have.

Have students read and discuss the lesson on Author's Purpose on p. 354 in the Anthology. Then have them complete the exercise.

Questions and Answers

1. to show how advertisements sometimes trick people *"How Beautiful With Mud"*
2. to make people aware of the problems of air pollution *Fresh Air Will Kill You"*
3. to use words in a funny way *"Who's on First?"*
4. to make fun of life on a farm *"The Cow Who Liked to Kick"*
5. to show how people learn to live with problems rather than try to correct them *"Fresh Air Will Kill You"*
6. to convince people to change their way of life *"And They Lived Happily Ever After for a While"*
7. to show that people usually get what they deserve in the long run *"The Cow Who Liked to Kick"*
8. to create confusion *"Who's on First?"*

Quiz

See p. 7, Administering the Quiz.

Reading Comprehension

1. What did Art Buchwald notice about the air in Flagstaff, Arizona? How did he deal with this? *He thought the air smelled funny because it was fresh. He breathed truck exhaust.*
2. In the poem "And They Lived Happily Ever After for a While," what happened to the air the couple breathed? *The air became so polluted that the couple built an oxygen tent.*
3. How did Phoebe the cow treat Jeremiah differently from everyone else in "The Cow Who Liked to Kick"? Why? *She allowed Jeremiah to brush and comb her because he had outsmarted her and broken her spirit.*
4. What were the names of some of the players and their positions in "Who's on First?" *The players and their positions: Tomorrow, pitcher; Today, catcher; Who, first base; What, second base; I Don't Know, third base; I Don't Care, shortstop; Why, left field; Because, center field.*
5. How did Hildegarde explain the way she looked to her parents after she had used Beauty Clay? *She told them she had been frostbitten and had rubbed her face with snow.*

Understanding Literature

6. What problem did Art Buchwald satirize in "Fresh Air Will Kill You"? What point did he make? *Art Buchwald satirized the problem of air pollution. He made the point that people can live with a problem for so long that they start to think that the problem is not a problem, and don't do anything to solve it.*
7. How is the title of the poem, "And They Lived Happily Ever After for a While" ironic? *The title of John Ciardi's poem is ironic because "ever after" and "for a while" are opposites.*
8. What technique did Ambrose Bierce use in "The Cow Who Liked to Kick"? *Ambrose Bierce used exaggeration.*
9. What is a pun? How do puns cause confusion in "Who's on First?" *A pun is a play on words. Puns cause confusion in "Who's on First" because each player's name means something else.*
10. In what way is Hildegarde's experience with Beauty Clay an example of irony? *Hildegarde's experience with Beauty Clay is an example of irony because it did not make her look beautiful. It made her look awful.*

Composition

1. Choose one of the following situations and turn it into a short comedy story. Try to point out something that is funny or ridiculous about life.
   a. people leave a fortune to their cats or dogs
   b. people spend all their time watching television rather than getting out and doing things.

c. people never throw anything away no matter how old or broken it is

  Discuss the situations presented in this assignment before having students write. Some students will find it easier to list the points they are going to make before writing sentences and paragraphs.

2. A limerick is a kind of poem that is usually funny. Read the limerick below. Then try to write a few limericks of your own. Your limericks should follow the same rhyming pattern as the example.

> There once was a girl from St. Lou
> Who wouldn't do what other people do;
> She went everywhere
> With a bow in her hair
> And an arrow attached to her shoe.

  You may wish to provide a few other examples of limericks and discuss their rhyme scheme and the meter before having students write their own limericks.

3. Describe a situation in which everything seemed to go wrong. It might involve cooking, shopping, getting dressed, traveling somewhere—anything. Try to make your description funny. You might use exaggeration or irony to add to the humor.

  Students might enjoy telling about these situations before they write. Have them give examples of exaggeration and briefly discuss what makes them humorous. Most students will find it easier to list the points they are going to include before writing a complete description.

Enrichment

1. Art Buchwald's columns are syndicated nationally and are available in many newspapers. Have students find and read some of them.
2. Students who enjoyed "The Cow Who Liked to Kick" might like to read additional stories by Ambrose Bierce. Two collections of his stories are listed in the short biography at the end of this section.
3. Have your school librarian or media consultant help you obtain some of the old Abbott and Costello routines on video cassette or record.

Authors

Bud Abbott and Lou Costello.　William (Bud) Abbott was born on October 2, 1895, to a family of circus performers. Lou Costello was born in Paterson, New Jersey, on March 6, 1908. The two met in 1929 in a Brooklyn theater, where Costello was doing a vaudeville show and Abbott worked in the theater box-office. They formed a partnership, with Abbott serving as Costello's straight man. Their act consisted of short skits in a slapstick style that they performed on radio. The team—Costello as the bumbling fat man and Abbott as the sarcastic skinny man—soon had a regular spot on the Kate Smith Hour, where they first performed the now immortal baseball routine, "Who's on First?" Their popularity continued to grow, bringing them their own radio program, which lasted for eight years, and a contract with Universal Pictures. They made over 30 films together. Costello died in 1959; Abbott in 1974.

Ambrose Bierce. Born June 24, 1842, of a poor farming family in Ohio, Bierce began his artistic career as a cartoonist in San Francisco. He then became a newspaper columnist and short-story writer. His stories, marking an important development in American short-story writing, are brief, closely organized, and often cynical, even bitter, in tone. Bierce disappeared in Mexico in 1914 and his fate remains unknown. Amoung his best-known works are *Can Such Things Be?* (1893) and *Fantastic Fables* (1899).

Art Buchwald. Arthur Buchwald was born in Mount Vernon, New York, on October 20, 1925. One of the best-known humor columnists in America, Buchwald began his career writing for newspapers in Paris in the late 1940's. After fourteen years of writing in Paris and other European cities, he moved to Washington, D.C., and continued to write columns, which were syndicated in over 350 newspapers. Among his books are *The Buchwald Stops Here, Down the Seine and Up the Potomac With Art Buchwald,* and *How Much Is That in Dollars?* Buchwald's interests were not limited to journalism; he collaborated on two pieces for theater and a book for a musical. He died in 1982.

John Ciardi. John Ciardi, a poet and poetry critic, was born in Boston on June 24, 1916. He taught English for a number of years, but eventually abandoned it to devote his time to writing. Among his many collections of poetry are *Other Skies, I Marry You: A Sheaf of Love Poems,* and *Person to Person.* Ciardi also writes for children; his most popular collection of children's poems is *I Met a Man.* His fascination with words and language led him to write the multi-volume *A Browser's Dictionary and Native's Guide to the Unknown American Language.* He hopes to expose poetry to a larger audience, for he feels that poetry is neglected and frequently misunderstood by the average reader. The recipient of many awards, Ciardi lectures and gives readings often. His English translation of Dante's *The Divine Comedy* is regarded by some authorities as a classic.

Hildegarde Dolson. Hildegarde Dolson was born in Franklin, Pennsylvania, on August 31, 1908. She worked as an advertising copywriter for leading department stores in New York City and as a freelance writer, the latter until her death in 1981. She and her husband, Richard Lockridge, both wrote mystery stories. Among her mysteries is *A Dying Fall.* Dolson wrote a number of books for children, one of which—*We Shook the Family Tree*—she illustrated herself. She contributed articles to many popular magazines, such as *The New Yorker* and *Harper's.* Of her fourteen books, two others are *The Husband Who Ran Away* and *The Great Oildorado.*

Section 10
Identity

Section Focus

The theme of this section is identity—how we discover who we are and how we present ourselves to other people. The section contains three stories of personal growth, at different stages of life, and one poem.

Before students begin the first selection, have them read and discuss the Introduction on pp. 358–359 in the Anthology. Discuss the concept of identity and ask students what they think the word means. Then discuss briefly how a person grows in self-understanding.

The Introduction helps set the purpose for the entire section. As students read each selection, ask them to think about what each of the characters is learning about identity. Section 10 focuses on helping students understand the motivation of the characters in each selection.

By Any Other Name   by Santha Rama Rau   *(p. 360)*

Synopsis

Santha Rama Rau tells the story of how she and her sister Premila were sent to an Anglo-Indian school when she was five and Premila was eight. On the first day, the headmistress, who doesn't like Indian names, gives the children "pretty English names"—Cynthia and Pamela. The story contains several examples of prejudice against Indian children in the British-run school. The Indian children sit in the back of the classroom. All the children eat sandwiches for lunch. Not even the Indian children have Indian food for lunch.

Santha, now "Cynthia," does not really feel responsible for what Cynthia is doing. She has, for the time, become someone else. She finds the work easy because her mother has taught her so well at home. She has trouble playing tag because at home she has been allowed to win. She lets other children win and then wonders why they do not do the same for her.

On the day of Premila's first test, things change. Premila leaves her classroom and takes Santha home. When they get home, Premila tells her mother that, for the test, the teacher made the Indian children sit in the back with a desk between them because, according to the teacher, "Indians cheat." Premila tells her mother, ". . . I don't think we should go back to that school." Her mother agrees.

Preparation

Ask students what they think it would be like to be a small child in a new school that had completely different customs from those at home. Add a dose of prejudice to these differences and discuss how the child might feel. Tell students that the story they are preparing to read relates the experiences of two young Indian children in a British school.

Vocabulary

headmistress (*n.*) — woman who runs a school
personality (*n.*) — what a person is like
longing (*n.*) — desire or wish
compete (*v.*) — play to win
nursemaid (*n.*) — woman employed in the home to care for children
*****curry** (*n.*) — a spicy food common in India

*Glossary word

Activities

A.   See p. 6, Teaching Vocabulary.
B.   Ask students what *personality* is. Have them give examples of qualities that make up someone's personality.
C.   Ask students if they have ever eaten *curry*. Some students may be able to describe its taste: slightly sweet and very spicy.

D. Have students identify the two words on the list that refer to positions of employment (*headmistress, nursemaid*). Could a man do either of these jobs? If so, what would he be called (*headmaster*)?

Quick Quiz

1. headmistress: a. leader of a team   b. person who makes hats   *c. woman who runs a school*
2. personality: *a. what someone is like*   b. need for privacy   c. serious conversation
3. longing: a. stretching   b. waste   *c. desire*
4. compete: a. finish   b. play fairly   *c. play to win*
5. nursemaid: a. hospital employee   *b. woman who cares for children*   c. teacher of young children
6. curry: a. large mixing bowl   b. chicken and onions   *c. spicy Indian food*

Setting the Purpose

Ask students if they think that changing a child's name would change that child's personality. Ask what they would do if they had an unhappy experience in school because of prejudice. Tell them that the story they are about to read focuses on two little girls who go to a new school. Have them read the story to find out how Premila and Santha cope with the problems they encounter.

The Selection

This story can be read in two parts, with a brief discussion between them.

Have a volunteer read the headnote. Then have the class read the story silently to p. 363, col 2: "She told me on the way home never to do that again in front of the other children." Before going on, have students discuss what the day at school has been like for Premila and Santha. See how many specific examples of prejudice they can find.

Ask students what they think is going to happen when Premila and Santha go back to school. Have them read the rest of the story to find out. Then have them complete Reading Comprehension on p. 366 in the Anthology.

Follow-Up

See p. 7, Teaching Reading Comprehension and For Discussion.

Reading Comprehension

1. The headmistress said she changed the girls' names because   *b. she didn't like Indian names.* (Page 360, col. 1: " 'Oh, my dears,' she said. 'Those names are much too hard for me. Suppose we give you pretty English names.' ")
2. The real reason Premila wanted to take sandwiches to school was that   *b. she wanted to eat what the British children ate.* (Page 364, col. 1: "She also told Mother that we should take sandwiches from now on. It wasn't that *she* cared, she said. But sandwiches would be easier for me to handle.")

3. When the teacher gave a test, she   *b. separated the Indian students.* (Page 364, col. 2: " 'We had our test today. The teacher made me and the other Indians sit at the back of the room, with a desk between each of us. . . . She said it was because Indians cheat.' "

4. Santha wasn't bothered by the school incident because   *c. it hadn't happened to the "real" her.* (Page 364, col. 2: "I understood what had happened. I remember it all very clearly. But I put it aside, because it all happened to a girl called Cynthia. And I was never very interested in her.")

For Discussion

How do you think all the Indian children were changed by going to a British school? *The Indian children had to give up their Indian habits, at least while they were in school. This might have affected how they acted at home, too, because at school they were taught that Indians and everything Indian were bad.*

Understanding Literature: Character Motivation

Objective: Students will explain the motivation of characters' actions and will indicate whether the motivation is stated or implied in the selection.

Preparation

Tell students that *character motivation* is the reason that a character acts in a particular way. If a character is believable, the reader will be able to discern that character's motivation.

Sometimes a character's motivation is presented directly. A character may explain why he or she is doing something, or may comment upon another character's behavior. Sometimes a narrator explains a character's motivation.

A character's motivation is sometimes not explained directly, but is implied. Explain that a character may behave in a particular way because of that character's personality, or because of events that have already occurred.

Have the students read and discuss the lesson on Character Motivation on p. 366 in the Anthology. Then have them complete the exercise.

Questions and Answers

1. Premila's mother taught her at home.   *Implied—she suspected prejudice in the Anglo-Indian school* (page 360, col. 2).

2. Santha did not compete well in games.   *Stated—"I had never really learned how to compete in games"* (page 363, col. 1)

3. Premila told Santha not to call out to the nursemaid.   *Implied—Premila didn't want to attract attention or be different from the other children* (page 363, col. 2).

4. Santha asked what *apple* meant.   *Stated—"I had never seen an apple before. I didn't know what it meant"* (page 362, col. 2).

5. Premila took Santha home from school.   *Stated—the teacher had said that Indians cheat, and had made the Indians sit in the back of the room* (page 364, col. 2).

6. The girls' mother sounded both unhappy and angry when Premila told her about the test. *Implied—she resented the prejudice of the British teacher* (page 364, col. 2).

Writing

Pretend you are the mother of Premila and Santha. Write a letter to the headmistress of the Anglo-Indian school. Explain to her why your children will not be returning to the school.

Before students begin to write, discuss the issues posed in the selection. Then have each student list the reasons that explain why the children will not be returning to the school. This will make it easier for the students to put the material into the form of a letter.

The Rocking Horse   a teleplay by Doris Halman   *(p. 367)*

Synopsis

The teleplay takes place in a storage warehouse in which McElroy, the boss, tells employee Corcoran that he will be needed for "a rush job." A woman named Mrs. Grayson is coming to make final disposal of things she has stored for 25 years. Corky tells his boss that "people who dump their belongings make . . . [him] sick."

Corky goes home that night and promises his two-year old son that he will not put the boy's crib in storage. He also promises his son a rocking horse. Corky tells his wife that a rocking horse named Wag was his own most prized possession before his mother left him and he was adopted by the Corcorans. The next day, while getting the stored things ready for Mrs. Grayson to inspect, Corky finds an old rocking horse with the initials *W.A.G.* He realizes that Mrs. Grayson must be his mother, but does not reveal this to her. As she is looking at the things, she begins to explain why she left them in storage for so many years. Her husband had been killed when her son was four. She put her son into an orphanage so she could travel on business in an effort to support him. She became ill and was told she had little time left to live. Thinking it best, she gave him up for adoption.

Corky shows Mrs. Grayson the picture of his own son. She then realizes that she is Corky's mother. Corky invites her to go home with him.

Preparation

Tell students that the teleplay they are preparing to read focuses upon the feelings an adopted child has for the mother whom he believes abandoned him years before. Ask if they think it is possible for a child to hold onto happy memories when things go wrong.

194

Vocabulary

*authoritative (*adj.*) — in command; able to give orders
orphanage (*n.*) — home for children without parents
*indiscriminately (*adv.*) — in a thrown-together or jumbled manner
dispose of (*v.*) — get rid of
*efficient (*adj.*) — able to get a job done fully and quickly
impulsively (*adv.*) — quickly; without much thought
predicament (*n.*) — difficult situation

*Glossary word

Activities

A. See p. 6, Teaching Vocabulary.
B. Ask students if they think it is possible to do something *impulsively* and *indiscriminately* at the same time.
C. Ask students if they think doing something *impulsively* would be likely to get them into a *predicament*.

Quick Quiz

1. authoritative: a. understanding   *b. in command*   c. personally eager
2. orphanage: a. school for children   b. children's hospital   *c. home for parentless children*
3. indiscriminately: *a. in a jumbled way*   b. without any friends   c. neatly in line
4. dispose of: *a. get rid of* b. make light of   c. pay mind to
5. efficient: a. beautiful and friendly   b. unpleasantly rude   *c. able to do something well*
6. impulsively: a. to the beat of music   b. weakened by illness   *c. without much thought*
7. predicament: a. mayor or governor   *b. difficult situation*   c. need for great hurry

Setting the Purpose

Ask students to think about why a person might leave household goods in storage for more than 25 years. Would these possessions still be important to that person after such a long time?

Ask students if any of them had a favorite toy as a young child. Ask them how they think they might react if they came upon this toy years later. Explain that the teleplay they are about to read involves an adult who encounters some childhood memories in a most unexpected way. Have them read the play to find out how his memories affect him.

The Selection

The reading of this play can be divided into three parts. Each part will provide an excellent opportunity for discussion.

Have students read to p. 370, col. 1: "A little white one, eh?" Ask students to comment on Corky's attitude toward the person who left her things in storage for so long. Ask them why they think he reacted so strongly when Mac talked to him about it. Then ask them about Corky's relationship with his wife and child. Have them continue reading to find out what he does when Mrs. Grayson comes to the warehouse.

Have students read to p. 373, col. 1, where Mrs. Grayson says "Thank you." Ask them to discuss how Mrs. Grayson and Corky are getting along at this point. Have them predict what they think is going to happen.

Have students read to the end of the play. Ask them at what point they think Mrs. Grayson realized Corky was her son. Then have them complete Reading Comprehension on p. 378 in the Anthology.

Follow-Up

See p. 7, Teaching Reading Comprehension and For Discussion.

Reading Comprehension

1. When Mac told Corky about Mrs. Grayson, Corky acted   *c. angry.* (Page 368, col. 1: " . . . people who dump their belongings make me sick!")
2. Corky wanted to give his son a rocking horse because   *b. he remembered his own rocking horse.* (Page 369, col. 1: "I want Tommy to have a rockin' horse because I had one and I loved it better'n anything in the world. . . .")
3. Corky had often dreamed that Wag would   *a. come and take him back to his mother* (page 369, col. 1).
4. Corky refused Mac's offer to go home from work early because   *b. he wanted to confront his mother* (pages 370–371).
5. When Corky said, "Folks always dump out their relatives first thing," he really meant   *b. his mother had deserted him.*
6. Mrs. Grayson began to cry when she saw Wag because she   *c. was remembering her son.*
7. When Corky showed her the photograph of his son, Mrs. Grayson   *b. realized that Corky was her son.* Page 378: "Why he. . . . [*Sternly disciplines the giveaway voice.*] He looks very much like you, Mr. Corcoran.")
8. When Corky said, "C'mon, let's go home," he meant   *a. his home was her home, too.*

For Discussion

1. What different opinions did Corky and his boss have about why someone would leave things in storage for 25 years? Why were their opinions different? *Corky was sickened by the fact that someone would store her belongings for 25 years, and felt that poverty and death were the only excuses for nonretrieval. McElroy felt there could be other reasons for someone to store her things for such a long time. Corky's opinions were influenced by his childhood experience. His boss's opinions were influenced by his experiences in the storage business.*

196

2. How did Corky's childhood experience affect the way he brought up his son? *Corky made a special effort to spend time with his child. He wanted to make sure he gave the boy something (the rocking horse) he had had as a child, as well as those things of which he had been deprived.*

3. How did Corky treat Mrs. Grayson at first? How did his attitude toward her change? Why did it change? *At first, before he met Mrs. Grayson, he reacted in a hostile way. He didn't think much of anyone who would leave her belongings in storage for 25 years. Then, when he found the rocking horse among her things, he realized that she was his mother. When he first met her he was businesslike and cold. His attitude changed when he learned that she had never intended to leave him.*

4. Why had Corky dreamt about the rocking horse when he was a little boy? Why did he still think about it? *He had dreamt about it because he thought Wag might take him to his mother. Students can infer that he still thought about it because it had been so important to him. Answers will vary.*

5. What was the importance of Corky's photograph of his son? *Corky's son looked like Corky, and the picture made Mrs. Grayson realize that Corky was her own son.*

Understanding Literature: Character Motivation

Objective: Students will match each present action with the past event that motivated that action.

Preparation

Tell students that a character's behavior is sometimes motivated by events that occurred much earlier in that character's life. Discuss some of the examples of this from the play they have just read. Have students read and discuss the lesson on Character Motivation on p. 379 in the Anthology. Then have them complete the exercise.

Questions and Answers

1. Corky becomes angry when Mac tells him about "the Grayson woman." *a. Corky was given up by his mother when he was four.*

2. Corky makes two promises to his son. *a. Corky was given up by his mother when he was four.*

3. Corky becomes very pale after he sees the rocking horse in storage. *b. As a child, Corky often rode his favorite toy, a rocking horse.*

4. Mrs. Grayson becomes emotional when she sees the vase and trunk. *c. Mrs. Grayson's husband was killed in an auto accident.*

5. Mrs. Grayson begins to cry when she sees the picture of Corky's son. *a. Corky was given up by his mother when he was four.*

Writing

Add another scene to the play to show what happens when Corky brings his mother to his home.

Have students discuss the possible elements of the scene in which Corky brings his mother to his home. Have them talk about how Corky's wife and little boy might react. Some students will find it helpful to take notes during the discussion. Then have the students write the scene.

A Trip for Mrs. Taylor   by Hugh Garner   *(p. 380)*

Synopsis

Mrs. Taylor gets up at five o'clock, an hour earlier than usual. She dresses, has her tea, and gets ready for her day very quietly so that she won't disturb her landlady. She thinks about her late husband, and about her grown son who lives in Montreal. Life on a pension is hard and lonely.

This day is going to be different. Mrs. Taylor takes a heavy cardboard suitcase that she has packed carefully and makes her way to the railroad station. She buys a ticket and waits for the train to Montreal. She meets a young woman with a baby in her arms and a small boy who is acting difficult. She takes command of the situation and helps the mother, Mrs. Rawlinson, with the baby and the boy. She thinks back to when her children were young. She once again feels useful. They board the train. Mrs. Taylor is not, however, going all the way to Montreal. She bids her new friends farewell and gets off at the next stop. That's as far as she can afford to go. She gets on a bus and goes home with memories of her happy morning.

Preparation

Ask students where they would like to go if they could take a train trip. Ask what they would pack and take with them. Tell them that the story they are preparing to read is about a trip that Mrs. Taylor takes. Tell them that it's probably different from any trip they would have imagined.

Vocabulary

*pension (*n.*) — payments to a retired or disabled person
envied (*v.*) — were jealous of
*arthritis (*n.*) — painful disease causing stiff joints
embarrassment (*n.*) — uncomfortable feelings of self-consciousness
hand-crocheted (*adj.*) — made by hand with a small hooked needle and yarn

*Glossary word

Activities

A. See p. 6, Teaching Vocabulary.
B. Ask students if they think that a person with arthritis could hand-crochet things easily. Ask why or why not.
C. See if students can use the words *pension*, *envied*, and *embarrassment* all in the same sentence.

Quick Quiz

1. pension: a. thoughts while being retired *b. money paid to a retired person*
   c. strong feelings of worry
2. envied: a. loved very much *b. was jealous of* c. looked carefully
3. arthritis: a. type of rash *b. disease of the joints* c. great unhappiness
4. embarrassment: *a. self-conscious, uncomfortable feelings* b. excellent way to
   find some entertainment c. something to use quickly
5. hand-crocheted: a. knitted by machine b. fashion gloves *c. made with a
   hooked needle*

Setting the Purpose

Tell students that Mrs. Taylor is an elderly woman who doesn't have a lot of money.
Her children live far away. Tell them that she plans a trip. Ask where they think she
might go. Then have them read the story to find out.

The Selection

This is a fairly short selection that can easily be read in two parts.

Have students read the headnote and then begin the story. Have them read to the
paragraph on p. 384, col. 2 that ends with Mrs. Taylor rocking the baby. Ask what
they think Mrs. Taylor is thinking about. Then have them go on.

Have students finish the story. Ask if they were surprised at the ending. Then have
them complete Reading Comprehension on p. 386 in the Anthology.

Follow-Up

See p. 7, Teaching Reading Comprehension and For Discussion.

Reading Comprehension

1. You could tell that Mrs. Taylor was excited about her planned trip because she
   b. was ready two hours early (page 380, col. 2).
2. Life was sometimes hard for Mrs. Taylor because *c. she was lonely and very
   poor* (page 381).
3. The woman and children Mrs. Taylor met at the train station *a. made her feel
   needed once again.* (Page 386: "It was nice being able to help. You'll never know
   how much I enjoyed it.")
4. Mrs. Taylor felt good after her trip because *c. she had been a part of life again.*
   (Page 386: Mrs. Taylor remembered "only the excitement and thrill of going
   away, and the new friends she had made.")

For Discussion

1. What does the story reveal about the problems older people sometimes face in our
   society? How did Mrs. Taylor cope with these problems? *Answers include finan-
   cial problems, loneliness, and feelings that one is no longer needed. Mrs. Taylor
   managed her money as well as possible, skimping on some things to have others.*

She dealt with her loneliness and feelings of uselessness by doing things for her son and daughter-in-law, and taking her "trips."

2. How did the trip remind Mrs. Taylor of happy times in her past? *Being with small children reminded her of the time when her own family was young.*

Understanding Literature: Character Motivation

Objective: Students will state whether the motivation is indicated by a character's words or by the narrator.

Preparation

Be sure that students understand that a character's own words may reveal motivation. At other times, a narrator reveals the thoughts and feelings of a character.

Have students read and discuss the lesson on Character Motivation on p. 387 in the Anthology. Then have them complete the exercise.

Questions and Answers

1. Mrs. Taylor had decided to go on a train trip. *Narrator—Mrs. Taylor saw holiday crowds hurrying off to the station and wanted to be part of them.*
2. Mrs. Taylor was ready two hours ahead of time. *Narrator—Mrs. Taylor was excited about going on her trip, and she didn't want to be late.*
3. Garry acted up in the train station. *Mrs. Rawlinson—Garry knew that his mother couldn't manage him while she was carrying the baby.*
4. Garry behaved when Mrs. Taylor told him to. *Mrs. Rawlinson—Garry always obeyed his grandmother, and Mrs. Taylor may have reminded him of his grandmother.*
5. Mrs. Taylor made friends with the young mother. *Narrator—Mrs. Taylor realized that she had been starved for conversation.*
6. Mrs. Taylor cried when she held the baby. *Narrator—The baby reminded Mrs. Taylor of her own children when they were small, and she would have loved to have those moments back again.*
7. Mrs. Taylor went on a short trip and not all the way to Montreal. *Mrs. Taylor—She couldn't afford to go to Montreal, and said that she didn't really want to go that far.*
8. Mrs. Taylor smiled as she boarded the bus to return home. *Mrs. Taylor—She smiled because she had had a wonderful trip.*

Writing

Imagine that you are Mrs. Taylor and that you keep a diary. Write a diary entry about your trip. Tell about some of the events of the day. In each case, try to explain your motivation and some of your thoughts and feelings.

Ask volunteers to suggest a list of events that took place on the day of the trip. Write the events in sequence on the board. Then ask students to try to imagine Mrs. Taylor's thoughts or feelings about each event. Remind them to write the diary entry from the first-person point of view.

Dirge Without Music by Edna St. Vincent Millay *(p. 389)*

The Selection

Explain that a *dirge* is a funeral song or a song of grief or death. Tell students that in this famous work the poet presents a specific point of view. Read the poem aloud to the class and ask if they can tell what the words "I am not resigned" mean in the context of the poem. Then ask volunteers to read each stanza.

Follow-Up

Discuss the questions that accompany the poem.

Questions and Answers

1. A *dirge* is a funeral song or a song about grief or death. What do you think the poet means when she says, "I do not approve. I am not resigned"? In the phrase "but the best is lost," what is "best"? *The poem presents the view that death is unacceptable. "So it is, and so it will be, for so it has been, time out of mind" (line 2) recognizes the fact that people always have and always will die. But whether they are crowned with lilies, or with laurel, and even if elegant, curled, fragrant rose blossoms will grow, death remains unacceptable because the best is lost. In this sense, the "best" refers to "The answers quick and keen, the honest look, the laughter, the love" (line 9). It may also be interpreted as the unity and presence of an individual as opposed to a fragment, a formula, or a phrase.*

2. The "indiscriminate dust" is the dust of the grave. It doesn't single out anyone. What does the speaker say are the things in life that make someone special or precious and not like everyone else? *The most directly stated answer is line 12: "More precious was the light in your eyes than all the roses in the world." Other qualities mentioned include loving hearts, wisdom, loveliness, the capacity to love and think, beauty, tenderness, kindness, intelligence, wit, and bravery. The honest look, the laughter, and the love may be considered the most special.*

Section Review

Vocabulary: Shades of Meaning

Objective: Students will recognize shades of meaning and choose the synonym that best fits the context.

Preparation

Explain that very slight differences in meaning may make the choice of one synonym preferable over another. For example, *swindle* and *trick* are synonyms, but in the sentence, "He played a trick on me," the word *swindle* does not fit the context.

Have students read and discuss the lesson on Shades of Meaning on p. 390 in the Anthology. Then have them complete the exercise that follows.

Questions and Answers

1. "The little Indian girl . . . looked at my food with *longing*."
2. "I had never really learned how to *compete* in games."
3. "**Corky:** Okay. Then decide what you want *destroyed,* and what you want put up for sale. . . ."
4. "She *warned* him to be a good boy and do what his mother told him."

Reading: Critical Reading

Objective: Students will develop their ability to read critically, and to understand characters and the values of the author.

Preparation

Explain to students that developing an understanding of the values of an author and the characters in a work of literature is called *critical reading*. When a person reads critically, he or she evaluates and makes judgments about what is being read.

Suggest to students that they will be able to tell how critically they are reading if they use what they have learned about the characters to predict what the characters might do or say outside of what you are reading.

Have students read and discuss the lesson on Critical Reading on p. 390 in the Anthology. Then have them complete the exercise.

Questions and Answers

1. People who are young don't realize how lucky they are. *Mrs. Taylor: She longed to be like the younger, more active people who could take trips and were not lonely.*
2. The most important thing you can do for a child is to be there when he or she needs you. *Corky: His father was killed and his mother had to give him up for adoption.*
3. People want to be alike, not different. *headmistress: She had trouble dealing with people who were different from her.*
4. Stand up for your rights, and don't let other people push you around. *Premila: She was a proud person who had been pushed too often.*
5. Even a little joy can make a person genuinely happy. *Mrs. Taylor: The short trip gave her lasting pleasure.*
6. Learning to forgive is a difficult but valuable lesson. *Corky: He forgave his mother, and gained her presence for the rest of her life.*
7. Without her child, a mother's life has less meaning. *Mrs. Grayson or Mrs. Taylor: Both women "lost" their children and became lonely and felt useless.*

Quiz

See p. 7, Administering the Quiz.

Reading Comprehension

1. How did the headmistress feel about Indian children in "By Any Other Name?" How do you know? *The headmistress didn't understand or accept Indian children. She changed their names to English names.*
2. What two promises did Corky make to his son in "The Rocking Horse"? *Corky promised that he wouldn't put the boy's crib in storage, and that he would get his son a rocking horse.*
3. What were some of the problems faced by Mrs. Taylor in "A Trip for Mrs. Taylor"? *Mrs. Taylor was lonely and no longer felt needed. She also had trouble making ends meet on her pension.*
4. Why was Mrs. Taylor's trip so enjoyable for her? *Meeting a young mother with an infant and a small boy helped make Mrs. Taylor's trip enjoyable. She enjoyed the conversation and felt needed.*
5. What is the "best" that the poet felt was lost in "Dirge Without Music"? *The "best" was the full, complete presence of an individual.*

Understanding Literature

6. Which of Premila's actions were motivated by her desire to fit in with the British school children? *Premila told her sister to go sit with her class as the other children were doing. She asked her mother to give them sandwiches for lunch. She told Santha not to call out to the nursemaid. She used the expression "donkey's years" that she had learned in school.*
7. What drove Mrs. Grayson to put her son up for adoption? *Mrs. Grayson decided to put her son up for adoption because she had been very ill and the doctors had told her she did not have long to live. She did what she thought would be best for him.*
8. Why was Corky so unpleasant to Mrs. Grayson when he first saw her? *Corky was unpleasant to Mrs. Grayson because he felt that she had abandoned him. He was angry at her.*
9. What are some of the factors that motivated Mrs. Taylor to take her trip? *Mrs. Taylor had seen holiday crowds hurrying into the train station about a week before her decision. She wanted to be part of the crowds and the excitement again. She was also motivated by loneliness.*
10. What do you think motivated Edna St. Vincent Millay to write "Dirge Without Music"? *Answers will vary. She may have lost people who were close to her, and she doesn't wish to let them go that easily.*

Composition

1. Imagine that you are an Indian official who has been appointed to investigate discrimination in the school in "By Any Other Name." Write a short report to your boss explaining what problems exist in the school, and make some suggestions for changes.

   Discuss this topic in class before having students write. Ask each student to fold a sheet of paper in half lengthwise. In the left column each should list any problems. In the right column, suggestions for solving each problem can be listed. Students may stop when they have gone this far or they may work the material into a written report as the assignment directs.

2. Suppose Premila had kept a diary. Write out the entries she might have put into her diary on her first day in the Anglo-Indian school and on her last day there.

Remind students that a diary is written in the first person. Have them try to imagine themselves in Premila's shoes in order to understand how she felt.

3. Take the part of Mrs. Grayson before she met Corky in the warehouse. Write a letter to your son, wherever he is, explaining why you had to give him up for adoption.

Have students refer to the selection for the specific facts about Mrs. Grayson giving up her son for adoption. Students can list the facts they will include before writing the letter.

4. What do you think a community should do for its elderly citizens so that they won't be as lonely as Mrs. Taylor? Make a list of steps the community might take. Then develop your steps into a short description of a community senior-citizen program.

This is an excellent assignment for pupil teams or small groups. Have the class discuss the possible steps a community might take. Then have students list these steps. Some students may stop after completing the list. Others may go on to develop the list into a program description.

5. Think about some of the characters you have read about in this book. Choose one character that you think is a lot like you. Make a list of ways you and the character are alike. Then develop your list into a short comparison.

For this assignment, have each student fold a sheet of paper in half lengthwise. In the left column, students can list words that describe the chosen character. In the right column, students can tell how that character is like him or herself. Then the most important of these comparisons can be written in sentences and finally in a paragraph.

6. Choose one character in the book who seems very different from you. Make a list of differences. Then develop your list into a brief paragraph about the contrast.

For this assignment, have students follow the same procedure suggested for the preceding composition.

Enrichment

1. Some students might like to do research to learn more about their own family history or name. A personal time line, family tree, scrapbook, or drawing can be constructed to illustrate aspects of identity.

2. Students may be interested in reading nonfiction about the challenges presented at different stages in life. Have them consult the librarian for appropriate titles.

3. For further reading about the theme of identity, some students might enjoy *Roots*, by Alex Haley. Or have the school librarian or media consultant assist you in locating a tape or a videotape of the television show based on Haley's book.

Authors

Hugh Garner. Born on February 22, 1913, in Yorkshire, England, Hugh Garner was raised in Toronto, Canada. He wrote stories, novels, and plays, some under the pseudonym Jarvis Warwick. His works include *The Silence on the Shore; Author, Author;* and *Present Reckoning.* His writing is represented in over 70 anthologies. Garner was a frequent contributor of stories and articles to magazines, and his television dramas were broadcast in Canada, England, and Australia. In 1963 he received the Canadian Governor General's Award for English Fiction for his book *Best Stories.* He died in 1979.

Doris Halman.   Doris Halman was born in Ellsworth, Maine, on October 28, 1895. She went to school in Boston and graduated from Radcliffe College in 1916. Her plays include *Will O' the Wisp* and *The Land Where Lost Things Go.* Her works have been performed in Boston, New York City, Chicago, and Detroit.

Santha Rama Rau.   Born on January 24, 1923, in Madras, India, Santha Rama Rau was educated in England and traveled widely while still a child. On returning to India from South Africa in 1939, she rediscovered her attachment to her native land. After attending Wellesley College, she wrote her first book, *Home to India* (1945), and India continued to influence her writing. Her works include *East of Home* (1950), *This Is India* (1954), and the novel *Remember the House* (1956).

Edna St. Vincent Millay.   Born in Rockland, Maine, on February 22, 1892, Edna St. Vincent Millay is a famous American poet who has been called "the female Byron." Her early work includes love sonnets that earned her considerable admiration. She was most successful in the 1920's and '30's, during which time she was active in the artistic and literary circles of Greenwich Village in New York City. She won a Pulitzer Prize in 1923 for *The Ballad of the Harp-Weaver.* She wrote plays (including *The Lamp and the Bell*), and, under the pseudonym Nancy Boyd, a collection of essays entitled *Distressing Dialogues.* Later in her career she turned to political and social problems for the subjects of her writing. An avid traveler, she made a voyage to the Orient and moved with her husband to a house near Austerlitz, New York, in the Berkshire Mountains. She died there in 1950. Her other well-known works include *Renascence and Other Poems* and *Conversation at Midnight.*

Section 11
The Novel

Section Focus

This section presents a complete, short novel: *The Pearl* by John Steinbeck. Students are encouraged to apply the many skills they have learned in previous sections to reading a novel. The section introduction on p. 394 in the Anthology calls attention to the novelist's use of plot and subplot, special techniques of characterization, development of theme, and the use of symbols. A short biography of John Steinbeck precedes the novel.

Have students read and discuss the Introduction and the biography before they begin *The Pearl*. Both have direct application to reading the novel. You may wish to point out that *The Pearl* reflects Steinbeck's interest in both nature and the oppressed.

The Pearl is presented in the Anthology in three parts: chapters 1 and 2; chapters 3 and 4; and chapters 5 and 6. Each part is followed by Reading Comprehension and Discussion questions, and activities in Understanding Literature and Writing. The Teaching Guide follows this three-part plan. (As an alternative, you may prefer to have some students read the complete novel without interruption. If so, present the vocabulary for each of the three parts before students begin chapter 1.)

Activities in this section focus on characterization, plot and subplots, and theme in a novel.

Biography: John Steinbeck   *(page 396)*

Synopsis

John Steinbeck was born in California in 1902. Many of his books and stories have California settings, including *Torilla Flat* and *Of Mice and Men,* his first two successful works. His works often featured poor or oppressed people, for whom Steinbeck had great compassion and understanding.

Steinbeck received the Pulitzer Prize for *The Grapes of Wrath* (1939), and soon became one of the most famous writers of the twentieth century. He published many books, always focusing on the actions, words, and thoughts of people. He was awarded the Nobel Prize for literature in 1962. He died in 1968.

Preparation

Ask students if they have seen play or movie versions of *East of Eden, Of Mice and Men,* or *The Grapes of Wrath.* Have volunteers describe (or explain yourself) the powerful, emotional appeal of these works—stories of ordinary people facing tremendous challenges, challenges that come from sources much more powerful than the people. Then tell students that the biography they are about to read is of the author who wrote these works.

Setting the Purpose

Explain to students that John Steinbeck was one of the great American writers of the twentieth century. What made his writing so popular? Students will discover general reasons for Steinbeck's popularity in the biography, and will experience his powerful writing when they read *The Pearl.*

The Selection

The biography should be read in one sitting, possibly in conjunction with the Introduction on p. 394 in the Anthology. When students have finished reading, lead a short discussion on Steinbeck, using the For Discussion questions that follow.

Follow-Up

The questions below, which do not appear in the Anthology, may be used as a follow-up in the selection.

For Discussion

1. How old was Steinbeck when he published his first financially successful book? What book brought Steinbeck widespread fame? How did he deal with that fame? *Steinbeck was 33 years old when his first financially successful book,* Tortilla Flat, *was published in 1935.* The Grapes of Wrath *brought Steinbeck fame. However, he was really a shy person and the fame made him retreat from the public. He even went to the Galapagos Islands to escape from public view.*

2. What are some of the characteristics of Steinbeck's writing? *Steinbeck had great sympathy and understanding for the underdog, for people who struggled to have better lives. His careful study of nature shows in his works, as in* The Pearl, *where the main characters are almost a part of nature. But he always focused on people— how they act, talk, and think in their environment.*

The Pearl   Chapters 1 & 2

by John Steinbeck   *(page 398)*

Synopsis

In his small house, Kino wakens at dawn and sees his wife Juana and their infant son Coyotito. He feels content as he hears in his mind the Song of the Family. But the song becomes the Song of Evil as a scorpion moves slowly down the rope of the baby's cradle, a hanging box. Juana mumbles an ancient magic against the evil, and a Hail Mary, too, but Coyotito shakes the rope and the scorpion falls into the box and bites him. Kino demolishes the scorpion, but it's too late. Juana sucks the poison from the baby's wound. They then take the infant to the doctor, who is busy indulging himself in a sumptuous meal. He will not see poor Indians who can't afford to pay. The doctor's servant tells Kino that the doctor is busy with a serious case. Kino is furious and smashes his knuckles as he hits the doctor's gate in frustration.

Kino and his wife take the baby and go to their canoe, a prized possession, on the beach. Juana makes a poultice from seaweed for the child's scorpion bite. Kino and Juana then take the boat out into the sea, where Kino dives and searches for pearls. He sees an enormous oyster and thinks he sees the gleam of a large pearl in it before the oyster closes tightly. Then he returns with his basket to the boat and begins to open the smaller oysters. Juana tells Kino to open the big one, and he does. In it is a perfect pearl as large as a seagull's egg—"The Pearl of the World." Juana removes the poultice from the baby's shoulder and sees that the swelling has gone down. Kino holds the pearl and shrieks with joy.

Preparation

Tell students that the work they are about to read is a short novel sometimes called a *novella*. Explain that it is a *parable*—a story in which one purpose is to teach a lesson.

Vocabulary

Chapter 1

*parable (n.) — short story for the purpose of teaching a moral lesson or telling a truth about life

wavering (adj.) — flickering; moving about

*crevices (n.) — cracks; slitlike openings

scorpion (n.) — an insect like a spider that looks like a tiny lobster; it has a poisonous stinger at the end of its tail

plaintively (adv.) — sadly; expressing sorrow

puncture (n.) — hole made by a sharp object (such as a scorpion's stinger)

fatigue (n.) — extreme tiredness

determination (n.) — firm intention to do something

*consolation (n.) — comfort

*indigent (adj.) — extremely poor

Chapter 2

*estuary (n.) — place where a river meets the sea

clarities (n.) — clear views

*bulwark (n.) — source of support or protection

poultice (n.) — soft wet material or bandage used to soothe aches or a wound

*undulating (adj.) — wavy

deliberately (adv.) — very carefully

speculatively (adv.) — hoping for good luck or profit

*incandescence (n.) — glow

*receding (v.) — going back; withdrawing

rigid (adj.) — stiff

*Glossary word

Activities

A. See p. 6, Teaching Vocabulary.
B. Ask students to give examples of *determination* from their own experience. Ask how they would provide *consolation* to someone if it were necessary.
C. Have students define and give examples to illustrate *indigent*.
D. For what would a *poultice* be used? How could you make one?

Quick Quiz

1. parable: a. equality among many   b. two of a kind   *c. story to teach a lesson*
2. wavering: a. saying goodbye   *b. flickering*   c. steady
3. crevices: a. wide openings   b. solid walls   *c. cracks*

4. scorpion: a. deep understanding *b. spiderlike insect that stings* c. elderly fortuneteller
5. plaintively: a. simply *b. sorrowfully* c. happily
6. puncture: *a. hole made by a sharp object* b. tool used for making holes c. hole made by a blunt object
7. fatigue: a. good health b. alertness *c. weariness*
8. determination: *a. firm intention to do something* b. upsetting event c. final ending of something
9. consolation: a. group of stars *b. comfort* c. entertainment
10. indigent: a. very angry b. courteous *c. extremely poor*
11. estuary: a. meeting of lake and stream b. meeting of stream and river *c. meeting of river and sea*
12. clarities: a. hazy scenes *b. objects seen clearly* c. groups that help people in distress
13. bulwark: a. rifle b. moat *c. source of protection*
14. poultice: a. chickens and ducks b. dry powdery medicine *c. wet bandage*
15. undulating *a. wavy* b. smooth c. moving straight ahead
16. deliberately: *a. very carefully* b. not truthfully c. with great freedom
17. speculatively: a. expecting something bad *b. hoping for something good* c. eagerly
18. incandescence: a. darkness *b. glow* c. twinkling
19. receding: *a. withdrawing* b. going ahead of c. doing it over
20. rigid: *a. stiff* b. brand new c. soft

Setting the Purpose

Tell students thay they will be reading *The Pearl* in sections, the beginning, middle, and end. Discuss what they should be looking for in the first two chapters: setting, characterization, conflict, and any theme that may appear. Then have them read the first two chapters of the novel.

The Selection

Have students read and discuss the opening to chapter 1 on p. 398 in the Anthology. Then have them begin the novel.

Have students read up to p. 401, col 2, just before Kino and Juana see the scorpion. Here, Steinbeck describes the setting and main characters in great detail. Call attention to the many vivid images. Encourage students to visualize just what the scene must have been like.

Have students read the rest of chapter 1 (up to p. 406 in the Anthology). Briefly discuss the doctor as a symbol of evil. Then ask students what they think will happen next.

Have students read chapter 2, beginning on p. 407 in the Anthology. Ask them what difference, if any, they think the pearl will make in Kino's life. Have them predict what they think will happen next. Comment on the last paragraph (p. 412) and call attention to the fact that the child seems to be recovering from the scorpion bite. Discuss the symbolism. When students have finished chapter 2, have them complete Reading Comprehension on p. 413 in the Anthology.

Follow-Up

See p. 7, Teaching Reading Comprehension and For Discussion.

Reading Comprehension

1. The first time Kino sensed the Song of Evil was when he *a. saw a scorpion above the baby's bed.* (Pages 401–402: "In his mind a new song had come, the Song of Evil, the music of the enemy. . . . The scorpion moved delicately down the rope toward the box. . . . ")
2. The baby did not receive medical attention because *b. the doctor refused to treat a poor Indian* (pages 404–406).
3. Kino's family went out on the boat *b. to find a pearl so they could afford to pay the doctor* (page 409, col. 2).

For Discussion

1. What were the different songs that Kino heard? How did the songs influence his life? *Kino heard many songs, including the Song of the Family, the Song of Evil, the Song of the Enemy, the Song of the Pearl That Might Be, and the Song of The Undersea. Accept any response to the second question that students can explain and support with details from the novel.*
2. How would you describe the way of life of Kino and Juana? In what ways were they content with their life? In what ways were they discontent with their life? *Answers will vary. Kino and Juana lived a simple, poor life. However, as long as they had food, shelter, their boat, and their health they were happy, because they could stay alive. They were discontented with their treatment by the rich doctor, and those who looked down upon them.*

Understanding Literature: Characterization

Objective: Students will identify characters and techniques of characterization.

Preparation

Make sure students understand that there are several ways in which an author can reveal characters to the reader. By now most of the students will be able to suggest some of these techniques if asked. You may wish to list these techniques of *characterization* on the chalkboard in preparation for the exercise on p. 413:

a. how character looks
b. how character acts
c. what character says
d. what character thinks
e. what other characters say or think about character

Have students read and discuss the lesson on Characterization on p. 413 before completing the exercise.

Questions and Answers

1. "His eyes were warm and fierce and bright and his mustache was thin and coarse." *Kino—how the character looks: Kino was a coarse person with alert senses.*
2. "Kino sighed with satisfaction—and that was conversation." *Kino—how the character acts: Kino did not use many words. He expressed his feelings through body language or actions.*
3. "Kino had wondered often at the iron in his patient, fragile wife." *Juana—what other characters think: Juana appears to be meek, but is actually a very strong person.*
4. " 'Have I nothing better to do than cure insect bites for "little Indians"? I am a doctor, not a veterinary.' " *Doctor—what a character says: The Doctor is pompous, and thinks he is too good for the Indians.*
5. "And he shut the gate quickly out of shame." *Doctor's servant—how the character acts: The servant is ashamed to shut the door on his own people.*
6. "In the surface of the great pearl he could see dreams form." *Kino—how the character thinks: Kino had dreams for a better life.*

Writing

Write two paragraphs about Kino. In the first, describe how Kino looks. In the second, describe his feelings. Find details in chapters 1 and 2 of *The Pearl* to help you.

For this activity, you may prefer to have students work in small groups to locate details that describe Kino's looks or feelings. Suggest that students list adjectives or phrases in two separate columns before they write each paragraph.

The Pearl   Chapters 3 & 4

by John Steinbeck   *(page 414)*

Synopsis

The news of the discovery of the pearl spreads through the town almost instantly. Everyone becomes interested in Kino and his pearl—the priest, the doctor (who now claims he is treating Coyotito), the pearl buyers—everyone. Kino and Juana naively believe that everyone shares their joy. Kino fantasizes about what new riches will do for him. He will be married in the church; he will educate his son. The doctor arrives, gives the child a capsule, and says he will return. But the capsule sickens the child, and the doctor comes back just in time to "cure" him. When the doctor asks when Kino can pay, Kino promises he will pay when he sells the pearl. As the doctor asks about the pearl, Kino's eyes involuntarily glance toward the spot in the earth floor where the gem is buried for safekeeping. That night, Kino drives off a potential thief who comes to the house. Juana says the pearl will destroy them and that they should get rid of it, but Kino refuses. A new day dawns, and with it Kino's hopes are renewed.

Kino and Juana dress in their finest and go to sell the pearl. Although the townspeople believe that the buyers are in competition, in fact they are all working together and they cheat the pearl divers. The first dealer looks at the pearl and says it is like fool's gold—just a curiosity with no value. He offers 1,000 pesos. Kino replies that it is worth 50,000 and that he will not be cheated. The offer is raised to 1,500 pesos. The other dealers say that the pearl is too large to be worth anything. Kino says he will take it to the capital. The dealers realize they have overplayed their hand, but it is too late and Kino leaves with his pearl.

Some of Kino's neighbors think he is a fool to have passed up 1,500 pesos, which to a poor man is a lot of money. Others think Kino is right to have resisted being cheated. The Song of Evil becomes stronger. That night, another effort is made to steal the pearl. Kino is injured in a fight with the thief, but the pearl is safe. Again Juana begs her husband to get rid of the pearl, which she now believes will destroy them. Kino becomes even more determined to go on.

Preparation

Ask students what they think will happen now that Kino has the "Pearl of the World." Ask what they think the reaction of others in the town will be.

Vocabulary

Chapter 3

colonial *(adj.)* — living among one's own kind in a colony or group
*****judicious** *(adj.)* — sensible or wise
semblance *(n.)* — appearance
*****essence** *(n.)* — basic quality or nature of something
residue *(n.)* — what is left after part has been taken away
precipitated *(v.)* — caused
*****prophecy** *(n.)* — prediction of future events
transfigured *(adj.)* — changed in appearance
benediction *(n.)* — a blessing
subjugation *(n.)* — under the control of another
dissembling *(v.)* — hiding one's true thoughts or motives
involuntarily *(adv.)* — automatically; unwillingly
*****furtive** *(adj.)* — sneaky
lucence *(n.)* — light
consecrated *(adj.)* — holy

Chapter 4

*****tithe** *(n.)* — small part or portion
extravagant *(adj.)* — wasteful or extreme
countenanced *(adj.)* — permitted
insubstantial *(adj.)* — unreal
aggressiveness *(n.)* — forcefulness; boldness
*****spurned** *(v.)* — rejected
legerdemain *(n.)* — trickery or deception

213

contemptuous *(adj.)* — scornful
curiosity *(n.)* — strange thing; oddity
appraiser *(n.)* — one who assigns a value or price to something
*__collusion__ *(n.)* — secret agreement for purposes of fraud
coagulating *(v.)* — changing from liquid to a solid
monstrosity *(n.)* — enormous, ugly, or abnormal thing
*__lethargy__ *(n.)* — lack of energy
entranced *(adj.)* — filled with wonder

*Glossary word

Activities

A. See p. 6, Teaching Vocabulary.
B. Ask students the difference between a *curiosity* and a *monstrosity*. Ask if something could be both.
C. Have students give an example of a *prophecy*. Have them give an example of *collusion*.
D. See if students can list several things that they do *involuntarily*.

Quick Quiz

1. colonial: a. living at home   *b. living among one's own people in a colony*   c. living alone
2. judicious: *a. wise*   b. nervous   c. funny
3. semblance: *a. appearance*   b. existence   c. example
4. essence: a. ending   b. appearance   *c. basic quality*
5. residue: a. whole object   *b. remainder*   c. in habit
6. precipitated: *a. caused*   b. resulted from   c. thought about
7. prophecy: a. experience   b. excess profits   *c. prediction of the future*
8. transfigured: a. went on a diet   *b. changed in appearance*   c. visited the next town
9. benediction: a. reference book   b. insult   *c. blessing*
10. subjugation: *a. controlled by another*   b. underwater ship   c. equal to another
11. dissembling: a. taking apart   b. being honest   *c. hiding true thoughts*
12. involuntarily: *a. automatically or unwillingly*   b. in a most expensive way   c. in great distress
13. furtive: a. moving quickly   *b. sneaky*   c. animal skin
14. lucence: a. darkness   b. fragrance   *c. light*
15. consecrated: *a. holy*   b. unholy   c. built
16. tithe: a. rope   *b. small portion*   c. large portion
17. extravagant: a. poor   b. economical   *c. wasteful or extreme*
18. countenanced: a. totaled figures   *b. allowed*   c. denied
19. insubstantial: a. real   *b. not real*   c. blind
20. aggressiveness: *a. forcefulness*   b. meekness   c. restless
21. legerdemain: a. laughter   b. honesty   *c. trickery*
22. contemptuous: *a. scornful*   b. respectful   c. painful
23. spurned: a. urged on   *b. rejected*   c. accepted

214

24. curiosity: a. untruthfulness *b. oddity* c. clarity
25. appraiser: a. one who complements *b. one who assigns a price* c. one who rewards
26. collusion: a. crash between two things *b. secret agreement* c. deep understanding
27. coagulating: *a. becoming solid* b. becoming liquid c. becoming a gas
28. monstrosity: *a. enormous or ugly thing* b. pleasant sight c. something bigger than life
29. lethargy: a. relaxation b. activity *c. lack of energy*
30. entranced: a. trapped *b. filled with wonder* c. uncaring

Setting the Purpose

Discuss with students the elements of the novel they should look for in the next two chapters. These include rising action, increasing conflict, greater characterization, plot complications, and further explication of the theme. When you have finished the discussion, have students read chapters 3 and 4 of the novel.

The Selection

Begin by reading the first sentence of chapter 3 (p. 414 in the Anthology) to the students: "A town is a thing like a colonial animal." Discuss the meaning of that sentence and the first paragraph. Then have students read on to find out what the town did when the news of Kino's pearl spread. Have them stop at the point where the doctor comes in to see the child, and lies about why he refused to see him earlier (p. 420, col 2). Ask students what they think the doctor is going to do, and why.

Have students finish chapter 3. Ask who they think tried to steal the pearl. Ask them to support their speculation. *(It probably was someone sent by the doctor, because he had a clue from Kino about where the pearl was buried.)*

Ask students what they think is going to happen when Kino takes his pearl to the dealers. Have them read chapter 4 to find out. When students have finished chapter 4, have them complete Reading Comprehension on p. 441 in the Anthology.

Follow-Up

See p. 7, Teaching Reading Comprehension and For Discussion.

Reading Comprehension

1. Kino looked at the pearl and imagined *c. great things in the future* (pages 416–417).
2. The doctor came to see Coyotito because *b. the family was now rich* (page 414).
3. The first person who tried to steal the pearl was probably sent by the *a. doctor.*
4. When Kino said, "I am a man," he meant he *b. expected to be treated fairly* (page 440, col. 2).

For Discussion

1. What different reactions did the townspeople have to the finding of the pearl?

Why did they react as they did? *Some were excited. Some were jealous. Some, like the doctor, saw something in it for them. Their reactions were based on their personalities. If they were fearful, they said that Kino should take the pearl buyers' price. If they were strong, they said that Kino was right.*

2. Why did the pearl buyers treat Kino as they did? Do you think he was right to refuse to sell the pearl? *The pearl buyers had been cheating poor Indians for years. They worked together to take advantage of Kino. Accept any opinion on whether Kino should have refused to sell his pearl as long as students can explain and support it.*

Understanding Literature: Plot and Subplots

Objective: Students will arrange events in the correct order and identify each as part of the main plot, subplot, or both.

Preparation

Explain that in a long work such as a novel, the *plot* often has one or more subplots. A *subplot* is a story inside the main story. Events in the subplot are often connected to events in the main plot.

Have students read and discuss the lesson on Plot and Subplots on p. 441 in the Anthology. Make sure that they understand that the main plot of *The Pearl* deals with finding the pearl and trying to sell it. Have them identify the story of the baby's scorpion bite and its treatment as a subplot. Then have them complete the exercise.

Questions and Answers

The answers are arranged in their proper order.
1. Juana said, "Go to get the doctor."   *subplot*
2. The doctor refused to treat the baby.   *subplot*
3. Kino and Juana searched for pearls.   *both*
4. Kino dreamed of the great things the future would hold for his son.   *main plot*
5. The doctor came to Kino's house.   *subplot*
6. Someone broke into Kino's house and tried to steal the pearl.   *both*
7. Kino was told his pearl was valueless.   *main plot*
8. Kino decided to travel to the capital.   *main plot*

Writing

Write a paragraph in which you predict several plot events you think will occur in the last part of *The Pearl*. How do you think the main plot will end? Why?

Discuss what students think will happen next in *The Pearl*. Have them predict the events that might follow what they have already read. Have them guess how the novel will end.

Before having students write what they think will happen, have them list their predictions. Then they can put the items on their list in paragraph form and explain their predictions.

The Pearl   Chapters 5 & 6

by John Steinbeck   *(page 442)*

Synopsis

Juana gets up during the night and goes to the water's edge to throw the pearl away. She feels it has brought nothing but evil. Kino, in a rage, stops her. On the way back to the house he is attacked by thieves who want the pearl. He kills one man, but is knocked unconscious. The pearl rolls away. Juana finds the pearl, and tells Kino that the man is dead and that they must leave. They try to leave before daylight, but their canoe has been destroyed. They turn, only to see their house up in flames. Kino's brother, Juan Tomás, hides the family for one day until they can make their escape. Juan Tomás asks Kino if he will give up the pearl, and Kino refuses because he says it has become his soul.

Kino and Juana leave town, carrying Coyotito. They soon discover that they are being followed. They work hard to elude the trackers, but it is very difficult. Kino hides Juana and Coyotito in a cave and tells her to keep the baby quiet. He then sneaks down to the trackers. Before he reaches them Coyotito cries. As Kino attacks, the men shoot at the sound, thinking it is a coyote. Kino manages to kill the trackers, but Coyotito is killed. Kino and Juana return to the town with the lifeless body of their son. They throw the pearl back into the sea, and the music of the pearl is gone forever.

Preparation

Ask students to comment on the way the pearl has changed Kino's life so far. Ask them to think about how Kino and Juana differ on their feelings about what is happening. Tell them that the next chapter they are going to read begins with a major disagreement between the two.

Vocabulary

Chapter 5

retrieving *(v.)* — getting back
abandoned *(v.)* — left behind; went away from
searing *(adj.)* — burning
conscious *(adj.)* — aware
*__conceived__ *(v.)* — thought of
authority *(n.)* — power to act or direct others
leprosy *(n.)* — dreaded disease once thought to be so contagious that a person with leprosy was avoided at all costs
fondled *(v.)* — touched lovingly
misfortune *(n.)* — bad luck

Chapter 6

*exhilaration *(n.)* — excitement

monotonously *(adv.)* — in a dull or boring way

*illusion *(n.)* — false impression; something unreal

guttural *(adj.)* — harsh; sound made in the throat

sentinel *(n.)* — guard

goading *(n.)* — urging on

monolithic *(adj.)* — giving the appearance of being cut from one large block of
stone

irresolution *(n.)* — weakness of purpose

petulant *(adj.)* — fretful; showing annoyance

*amulet *(n.)* — charm worn to keep away evil

*germane *(adj.)* — closely related; having to do with

apprehensively *(adv.)* — fearfully

illumined *(v.)* — lit up

hysterical *(adj.)* — overcome by grief; crying madly

*remote *(adj.)* — removed from; at a distance

immune *(adj.)* — not affected by

*Glossary word

Activities

A. See p. 6, Teaching Vocabulary.
B. Have students provide examples of a misfortune. Ask which they would rather have, *misfortune* or *illusion*. Have them explain and support their responses.
C. Have a student volunteer act out something (any familiar task or action) *apprehensively*, and then with *irresolution*. Is there similarity between the two?

Quick Quiz

1. retrieving: a. sending away   *b. getting back*   c. forgiving
2. abandoned: *a. left behind*   b. took along   c. remembered
3. searing: a. extremely wet   b. extremely cold   *c. extremely hot*
4. conscious: a. unaware   *b. aware*   c. asleep
5. conceived: a. heard of   *b. thought of*   c. saw
6. authority: a. writer   b. commission   *c. power to do something*
7. leprosy: a. authority   *b. dreaded disease*   c. poverty
8. fondled: a. discovered   b. bounced about   *c. touched lovingly*
9. misfortune: a. entertainment   b. excellent luck   *c. bad luck*
10. exhilaration: *a. excitement*   b. breathing out   c. sadness
11. monotonously: a. single-mindedly   *b. in a dull way*   c. in an exciting way
12. illusion: a. cooperation   *b. something unreal*   c. strong belief
13. guttural: *a. harsh*   b. soft   c. loud
14. sentinel: a. leader   b. airplane   *c. guard*
15. goading: a. laying back   *b. driving on*   c. standing still

16. monolithic: a. several pieces   *b. one large block*   c. single-track train
17. irresolution: a. revolution   b. intention   *c. weakness of purpose*
18. petulant: a. part of a flower   b. happy   *c. showing annoyance*
19. amulet: *a. charm that wards off evil*   b. drinking cup   c. magic spell
20. germane: a. distantly connected   *b. closely related*   c. totally unrelated
21. apprehensively: a. very carefully   *b. fearfully*   c. intentionally
22. illumined: *a. lit up*   b. blotted out   c. illegal
23. hysterical: a. unbelievable   b. under control   *c. crying madly*
24. remote: *a. removed from*   b. extremely quiet   c. not understanding
25. immune: a. upset   *b. not affected by*   c. irritated

Setting the Purpose

Discuss with students what they should expect at the end of a novel. The plot will reach a *crisis,* or moment of greatest conflict, and will then be resolved. The theme will be fully expressed when the plot has run its course. Have students read chapters 5 and 6 to see how the story turns out.

The Selection

Have students read chapter 5 up to p. 444, col. 1: "... she went creeping up the beach after Kino." Ask whether they think Juana is right to try to get rid of the pearl.

Have students finish the chapter. Ask what they think Kino is going to do now that he has murdered a man. Then discuss Kino's reason for refusing to give up the pearl. Ask if students think he is being wise or foolish.

Have students read chapter 6. Although the chapter is long, it is fast paced. Encourage students to read it without breaking for discussion.

When students have finished the novel, have them discuss what has happened. Ask if they think that Kino did the right thing in throwing the pearl back to the sea. Ask if they think he deserved what happened.

Have students complete Reading Comprehension on p. 465 in the Anthology.

Follow-Up

See p. 7, Teaching Reading Comprehension and For Discussion.

Reading Comprehension

1. Juana took the pearl and   *c. tried to throw it in the water* (page 442, col. 1).
2. Juana knew for sure that the old life was gone forever when   *b. she saw the man Kino had killed* (page 444, col. 1).
3. When Kino said, "This pearl has become my soul," he meant   *b. it meant everything to him* (page 448, col. 2).
4. The trackers hunting Kino and the pearl   *b. murdered the baby in their efforts* (page 462, col. 2).
5. Kino and Juana threw the pearl away because   *c. it had brought them only trouble* (page 464, col. 2).

For Discussion

1. Why did Kino act as he did when Juana attempted to throw away the pearl? *Kino had dreams for the future that he knew only the pearl could give him. He did not want anyone to steal his dreams.*
2. What do you think would have happened to the family if Juana had succeeded? Would it have been a fitting ending for the story? *Answers will vary. The family would probably have continued their existence, just as their ancestors had done for generations before them. Kino would have been bitterly disappointed. It would not be a fitting ending, because throwing away the pearl would have been the easy, safe way out. Kino was too strong to remain in his poverty without fighting to get out.*

Extra Topic

What finally happened to the pearl? Was that a fitting ending? *Kino threw the pearl back into the sea. Together Kino and Juana watched it sink. A crab stirred up the sand at the bottom of the sea and the pearl was buried (page 464, col. 2). Accept any opinions about the appropriateness of the ending that students can explain and support. It seems to be appropriate. Kino's struggle against evil began when he took the pearl from the sea. The evil eventually defeated him, so he had to put the pearl back, and go back to his former existence.*

Understanding Literature: Theme

Objective: Students will make inferences about the theme in a short novel.

Preparation

Discuss with students what *theme* is in a work of literature. Be sure that they understand that it is the author's comment on some aspect of life. The theme may be considered the author's message to readers. Sometimes the theme presents a moral—a lesson on how people should live.

The Pearl presents a moral lesson with its theme. Steinbeck tells readers that right away. He calls his work a parable, which means that it is a story intended to teach a lesson.

Have students read and discuss the lesson on Theme on p. 465 in the Anthology. Then have them complete the exercise, which will help them understand the theme of *The Pearl*.

Questions and Answers

1. According to Steinbeck's introduction, the retold story has become a tale   *b. of good and evil and nothing in between* (page 398).
2. Kino's Song of the Family and Song of Evil suggest that   *c. life has conflicting forces.*
3. Kino's experience with the pearl suggests that   *a. wealth doesn't guarantee happiness.*

Writing

Pretend you are either Kino or Juana. Write a paragraph describing your feelings as you watched the pearl hit the water. Write another paragraph about your hopes for the future.

Some students will find it easier to complete the writing assignment if they discuss their responses first. After the discussion, suggest that students list the feelings they intend to describe before writing sentences and paragraphs.

Section Review

Vocabulary: Using Context Clues

Objective: Students will use context clues to define unfamiliar words.

Preparation

Explain that the sentence or paragraph in which a word appears is its *context*. Remind students that the context often provides a clue to the meaning of an unfamiliar word.

Have students read and discuss the lesson on Using Context Clues on p. 466 in the Anthology. Then have them complete the exercise, which asks them to check the contextual meaning they derive from the sentences with a dictionary definition. *Accept definitions that fit the context. Dictionary definitions will vary.*

Questions and Answers

1. "Behind him Juana's fire leaped into flame and threw spears of light through the *chinks* in the brush-house wall. . . ." *cracks*
2. "He was growing very *stout*, and his voice was hoarse with the fat that pressed on his throat." *fat*
3. "The town lay on a broad *estuary*, its old yellow plastered buildings hugging the beach." *inlet of the sea*
4. "Spotted *botete*, the poison fish, lay on the bottom in the eel-grass beds. . . ." *poison fish*
5. " 'As a *curiosity* it has interest; some museum might perhaps take it. . . .' " *rare or unusual thing*
6. "Kino lay as *rigid* as the tree limb. He barely breathed. . . ." *stiff*

Reading: Cloze Exercise

Objective: Students will practice completing a modified cloze exercise.

Preparation

Explain to students that a *cloze exercise* is a passage that has some words omitted.

The reader's job is to supply the words that belong in the context. Point out that a number of reading tests use cloze exercises to test reading comprehension. Suggest that students use this exercise to practice their test-taking skill. (Note: These items are modified cloze exercises. Students may encounter different forms on different tests.)

Have students read and discuss the Cloze Exercise on p. 466 in the Anthology. Then have them complete the exercise.

Questions and Answers

1. "A town is a thing separate from all other towns, so that there are no two towns _____ ." *alike*
2. "His face was fatherly . . . and his eyes twinkled with _____ ." *friendship*
3. "In his mind a new song had come, the Song of Evil, the music of the _____ ." *enemy*

In the following passage, *accept any reasonable synonym students offer to fill in the blanks.*

"Hush," said Kino. "Do not speak any more. In the morning we will sell the pearl, and then the evil will be gone, and only the good remain. Now hush, my wife." His dark eyes scowled into the little fire, and for the first time he knew that his knife was still in his hands, and he raised the blade and looked at it and saw a little line of blood on the steel.

Quiz

See p. 7, Administering the Quiz.

Reading Comprehension

1. How did the doctor treat Kino and Juana when they first came to see him? Why did the doctor act that way? *The doctor acted superior and refused to see them because they were too poor to pay* (page 406).
2. Why was Kino reluctant at first to open the large oyster shell that contained the great pearl? *Kino was afraid that there wouldn't be a pearl in the oyster. Perhaps the gleam he had seen was a reflection, a piece of flat shell, or simply an illusion. Students can infer that he didn't want to be disappointed* (page 412, col. 1).
3. What were some of the things Kino hoped to do with the money he would receive from selling the pearl? *He hoped to get married in the church, to have Coyotito baptized, and to provide the child with an education. He also dreamed of a number of specific material things, including a new harpoon and a rifle* (pages 416–417).
4. What happened when Kino tried to sell the pearl to the dealers? What did he decide to do with the pearl? *The dealers tried to cheat him. They told him the pearl was too large to have any value. They called it a curiosity and a monstrosity. They offered 1,000 pesos and finally 1,500 pesos. Kino told them he would take the pearl to the capital and sell it there* (pages 434–437).

5. When the trackers shot at the "coyote," what happened? What did Kino and Juana do next? *The trackers killed the baby. Kino and Juana returned to their town with the body of the child. They threw the pearl back into the sea* (pages 462–464).

Understanding Literature

6. How did Kino and Juana react after the baby was bitten by the scorpion? What do their actions reveal about their individual characters? *Kino destroyed the scorpion with great violence. He smashed it, beat it, and ground it into the dirt. Juana immediately tended to the child. She sucked the poison from the wound, and then called for the doctor. When the doctor wouldn't come, Juana said they would go to him* (pages 402–403). *Kino reacted to the source of the problem; Juana sought the cure.*

7. What kind of person was the doctor? How do you know what he was like? *The doctor was selfish and evil. He was fat, and he lived an idle and luxurious life.* (The doctor is described on pages 404 and 406.) *Some students will go on to add the details of how the doctor suddenly became interested in the child when Kino found the pearl and was no longer a poor man.*

8. When did Kino first hear the Song of Evil? At what other times did the song come to his mind? *Kino first heard the Song of Evil when he saw the scorpion moving down the rope of the baby's hanging box* (page 401, col. 2). *Accept any additional examples that students can locate. These include when the doctor is there, when thieves are lurking outside to try to get the pearl, when the dealers were trying to cheat him, when the house was burned down and the canoe was stolen, and when they were being followed by the trackers.*

9. What is the main plot of *The Pearl*? What is its subplot? What is one event that is part of both the main plot and the subplot? *The main plot of* The Pearl *involves the finding of the pearl, the troubles that result, and the ultimate disposal of the pearl when Kino throws it back into the sea. The subplot involves the baby's fight for survival, beginning with the scorpion bite, the symptoms and "cure" caused by the evil doctor, and ending ultimately in the child being shot by the trackers. The event that is part of both the main plot and and the subplot is the shooting of the baby.*

10. How do the events in the novel convey the theme that wealth doesn't always bring happiness? *Answers will vary. The pearl is a symbol of wealth and opportunity for Kino and his family. But in the context of the oppressive, evil forces around him, the "maybe pearl," the wealth, brings nothing but grief and misfortune.*

Composition

1. Chapter 1 of *The Pearl* contains a detailed description of morning in Kino's family. Write a description of some of the sights, sounds, smells, and actions of the morning in your own household. Make your description 2 paragraphs.

   Suggest that this assignment, or at least the notes for it, be written at home, on the spot. This should result in more vivid descriptions than if students are asked to recall the sights, sounds, smells, and actions of the day's beginning. When students bring in their notes, they can develop this material into sentences and paragraphs in class.

2. The doctor is used by Steinbeck as a symbol of evil. Create a character of your own to symbolize evil. Describe this character's actions.

   Have students begin to create their evil character by describing what he or she looks like. Then have them tell what the character does. They should give their character an appropriate name.

3. Suppose Kino had sold the pearl to the highest bidder among the pearl dealers, even though his price was low. Write 2 or 3 paragraphs telling how Kino's life might have been different if he had sold the pearl.

   Discuss what Kino's life might have been like if he had sold the pearl. Then have students list the events they plan to include before writing each paragraph.

4. Suppose that Kino had not awakened in time to stop Juana from throwing the pearl away. Write a conversation that they might have had when Kino discovered the pearl was gone.

   Discuss what reaction would have been likely if Kino had discovered that Juana had thrown away the pearl. Ask how Kino would probably have felt and what he might have said and done. Remind students to precede each line of dialogue with the name of the character who is speaking.

5. The story of the pearl illustrates that money doesn't always bring happiness. Try to think of a situation of your own to convey that theme. Jot down a series of plot events first. Develop your events into a short story.

   For this assignment, suggest that students work in small groups or pupil teams. Each group can list the events they will include in the plot. Then the items on the list can be written in sentences. This will be a good stopping point for some students. Other students can go on and develop the list into a story that has a beginning, a middle, and an end.

Enrichment

1. Students who wish to read additional work by John Steinbeck may be directed to his collections of stories, and to *The Red Pony,* a short novel that is quite easy to read. Students who are able to handle Steinbeck's longer works should, of course, be encouraged to do so

2. *Travels With Charley* is a journal kept by Steinbeck as he traveled around the United States with his dog as a companion. The book is entertaining and may be read in segments.

3. Much of Steinbeck's work has found its way on to film. Your school librarian or media consultant may be able to help you locate some films for showing in school.